The Information-Literate Historian

The Information-Literate Historian

A Guide to Research for History Students

Jenny L. Presnell

New York   Oxford
OXFORD UNIVERSITY PRESS
2007

Oxford University Press

Oxford University Press, Inc., publishes works that further Oxford University's objective of
excellence in research, scholarship, and education.

Oxford New York
Auckland   Cape Town   Dar es Salaam   Hong Kong   Karachi
Kuala Lumpur   Madrid   Melbourne   Mexico City   Nairobi
New Delhi   Shanghai   Taipei   Toronto

With offices in
Argentina   Austria   Brazil   Chile   Czech Republic   France   Greece
Guatemala   Hungary   Italy   Japan   Poland   Portugal   Singapore
South Korea   Switzerland   Thailand   Turkey   Ukraine   Vietnam

Published by Oxford University Press, Inc.
198 Madison Avenue, New York, New York 10016
www.oup.com

Oxford is a registered trademark of Oxford University Press

Library of Congress Cataloging-in-Publication Data
Presnell, Jenny L.
The information-literate historian : a guide to research for history students / Jenny L. Presnell.
    p.cm.
  ISBN-13: 978-0-19-517652-0 (alk. paper)
  ISBN-13: 978-0-19-517651-3 (pbk. : alk. paper)
  ISBN-10: 0-19-517652-9 (alk. paper)
  ISBN-10: 0-19-517651-0 (pbk. : alk. paper)
    1. History—Research. 2. History—Sources—Study and teaching. 3. History—Research—
Methodology. 4. History—Study and teaching (Higher) —United States. 5. Research. I. Title.

D16.2.P71 2006
907.2—dc22   2006040129

9 8 7 6 5 4 3 2 1

Printed in the United States of America
on acid-free paper

For my parents,

Joseph (1921–1994) and Carmen (1930–1998) Presnell,

and, of course, Ellie the Labrador

Contents

Preface

The creation of this book grew out of my experience teaching a course on historical research in the History Department of Miami University (Ohio). The purpose of the class was to prepare students in basic research techniques for their capstone history courses so that their faculty could concentrate on working with them on the intricacies of the subject matter and more in-depth research skills. However, most of the texts I looked at did not really teach students how to search in databases and how to think historically while performing those searches. None of the books did an adequate job of integrating the Internet into research either as a resource or as a presentation method. In my everyday role as a reference librarian, I also found students struggling to learn how to appropriately use the Internet for research. So, I decided to write the book I wish I had to teach the course.

This volume would not exist without the help of a number of associates, colleagues, and friends inside and outside of academia. Before I even had a book contract, Dean Judith Sessions and then Provost Ronald Crutcher granted me a 13-week leave to research and begin working on the text. Allan Winkler, of the history faculty at Miami University, encouraged me to undertake the project, even when I had doubts that anyone might use such a text. Cecelia Cancellaro of Idea Architects helped me to prepare a prospectus, refine chapters, and present my ideas to a publisher. Susan Ferber at Oxford University Press, more than an editor, kindly tolerated a first-time author who had so many questions and an often "less than polished text." She was kind and patient and shaped the text into a useable resource for many levels of researchers. Her guidance was invaluable. Lisa Grzan and Andrew Pachuta reshaped my text and made the book sound even better.

Along the way, many individuals read the manuscript and offered their critical advice and knowledge in their particular areas of expertise. Thanks to Charlotte Goldy, Michael Howser, Sylvia Hu, Cindy Jasper-Parisey,

Laura Reeves, Lisa McLaughlin, John Millard, Nancy Moeckel, Theresa Mudrock, Melissa Norris, Steven Norris, Carla Pestana, Sven Eric Rose, Lisa Santucci, Robert Schmidt, Helen Sheumaker, Aaron Shrimplin, Amy Stander, Rachel Vacek, Rob Withers, David Wolcott, Susan Wortman, William A. Wortman, Frances Yates, Judith P. Zinsser, and the anonymous readers for Oxford University Press. Special thanks to Michael Howser for preparation of the images for the book and to the Information Services Department in King Library at Miami University (Ohio). University libraries are open and staffed most days of the year (many holidays included), so my 13-week leave meant extra duty for all of the librarians in my department. Thank you. While I have benefited from the input of many, decisions about the content and style are mine alone.

   If you are an undergraduate student beginning your first major history research project, this book was designed for you. It contains research tips, explanations of how historians use sources of all types regardless of format (electronic, paper, or original manuscript). It will help you plan your research thoughtfully and logically. It is my belief that research, the foundation of any historical paper, project, or website, is central. In fact, for me it is more interesting than writing or presenting the findings. And if you have good skills, that research can actually be fun!

Introduction:
What It Means
to Be a Historian

Every day, history influences our lives. Unresolved issues and ill-resolved circumstances create turbulence and conflict, as well as unexpected opportunities for change in our world. As a student of history, you will be asked to assess the events of the past and their effects on the lives of people and nations past and present through a research paper or perhaps an oral presentation or a website.

For instance, if you decide to research the decline of the Ottoman Empire and the division and domination of the Middle East by European colonial powers in the late eighteenth and nineteenth centuries, you will need to locate appropriate secondary works, such as books and journal articles written on this topic by other historians. You must also locate primary sources such as British, German, and French government documents, as well as government documents from such countries as Egypt, letters and diaries of individuals involved in the process, and images. Weaving ideas and evidence that you have found in these resources into an argument, you will be able present your own interpretation of these events.

Whether you are using secondary works like books, journals, and magazines or primary sources like government documents, oral testimonies, letters, and diaries or the vast array of research material available through the Internet, this book will guide you through your research by giving you information and advice about how to locate, evaluate, and utilize the wide variety of sources available for historical research. In addition, you will learn strategies for focusing your thesis, organizing your research, and presenting your material effectively, convincingly, and professionally.

In the following chapters, you will learn

- questions to ask before, during, and after your research process, as well as questions to ask of your sources and their authors
- search strategies that can be used in both electronic and print indexes and to figure out what types of sources are appropriate for particular research questions
- how to find and use books, journals, and primary sources quickly and efficiently, as well as how to select the best ones for your topic

- how historians practice their craft and the nature of historical discourse and narrative
- how to find, use, and evaluate media (images, speeches, maps)
- guidelines for presenting your historical research in different formats: paper, oral presentation, and website

Chapter One discusses how historians do research and how scholarly information is published and disseminated. Chapter Two provides an overview of reference resources, which will provide background and factual information to guide you in learning more about your topic before beginning your research. Chapters Three and Four provide search techniques for finding books and journal articles and advice on how to use each in your research. Chapter Five suggests techniques for evaluating your sources. Not only will you need to find appropriate sources that complement and enhance your research topic, but you must also learn to distinguish quality research. Chapter Six discusses the use of primary sources and strategies for finding those sources. Chapter Seven focuses on the Internet, how to use it in your research and how to search efficiently through its wealth of good and marginal material. Chapter Eight discusses maps and their use in historical research. Learning to "read" a map is an important part of understanding certain parts of history. Chapter Nine looks at the uses of multimedia in historical research and suggests ways of integrating these forms into your research as well as techniques for evaluating these resources. Finally, Chapter Ten explores multiple ways of presenting your historical research, distinguishing among the research paper, the oral presentation, and the website as presentation formats.

Technology has ushered in significant changes to the study and practice of history. These changes compel the student of history to think about historical research more creatively and to become comfortable using both traditional and newer sources and methods. This book offers insights into the most effective search strategies and provides concrete suggestions and guidelines for research-related questions and concerns. Because of the quantity, questionable quality, and increased availability of both primary and secondary sources, history students must be more sophisticated than ever before about their research methods. Yet today, as in the past, practicing history can be fun; and this book will show you how to enjoy what you do as you conduct your research more effectively.

1

Historians and the
Research Process:
Getting Started

WHAT YOU WILL LEARN IN THIS CHAPTER:
- how scholarly information is communicated
- how to develop a topic and build an argument
- how to begin organizing your project and to take notes
- how to document your research

How Scholarly Information Is Communicated

The research process you are about to participate in is the result of a process of discourse and writing even older than Herodotus, Greek scholar credited as the father of history. Today, part of the discourse (the discussion and exchange of ideas) of historians' research processes includes presenting research at conferences, talking about topics on listservs and blogs, and writing journal articles and books. At conferences, other scholars interested in the same topic ask questions and discuss alternative interpretations. Similar activities occur online in listservs and blogs, although in a much less formal manner. In journal articles and books, a very formal written discussion takes place among the other historians' interpretations (secondary works), primary sources, and the author. Prior to publication, these printed works have been reviewed or "refereed" by other expert scholars knowledgeable on aspects of the subject. These experts have offered suggestions for improvement and ensure that the publisher of the material is printing responsible, accurate, viable historical research. Indeed, this book was read by anonymous reviewers, among other readers, who helped the author focus her thoughts.

With the advent of the Internet and technology enabling scholars and nonscholars alike to self-publish their work, this model of scholarly communication may slowly change to include forms other than the most common formats, the journal and the book. With its multimedia and hyperlinked format and the capacity for jumping around within text, as well as to other pages and websites, the Internet offers new opportunities for historical scholarship and discourse. However, often, the checks and balances used for quality control are not yet in place, making material more challenging to use effectively.

What Historians Do and How They Do It

Simply put, historians gather clues and evidence from the past in order to understand and reconstruct an image of a particular person, place, event, or time period. Then, using that image, historians interpret its meaning, not only for the past but also for the present. In other words, historians are interested in determining the significance of the past for the people who actually experienced it in light of how history continues to affect modern society. Historians strive to make meaningful connections between the past and the present.

The study of history is not unbiased, despite the best attempts and intentions of historians. History is not merely a collection of facts and dates but, rather, the unfolding and telling of a story from the past, which always involves a degree of judgment and interpretation. Each historian's past and present influence the questions he or she will ask about the topics of history under consideration. Each historian brings a unique perspective.

Formal and informal methods of practicing history have philosophical viewpoints and methodological patterns, which can be described as fitting into particular schools of historical study. Schools of history are fundamental ways in which historians approach historical questions. For instance, the Annales school, founded in 1929 in France, was a reaction to the traditional way of studying history through the analysis of biography, documents, and events. The historians of the Annales school instead embraced quantitative methodologies of studying history (using statistics) and incorporated material culture and social interpretations (the history of poverty and childhood, for instance) into their studies, which led to the growth of social history after World War II.[1] Other examples of schools of history include the Empiricists, the Marxists, and the Progressives. In addition to schools of history, there are methodologies of practice in history, such as microhistory, which involves looking at one small event and extrapolating information from it to make broad statements about regions or groups of peoples; women's history, which uses gender as a framework for looking at events or issues; and

Box 1.1 Early History Journals

Although other historical journals existed, the earliest, true modern scholarly historical journal was the *Historische Zeitschrift* founded in 1859 in Germany. It was the first to have the markings of rigorous scholarship and discourse that are recognized in modern historical journals, articles with clear documentation on a single thesis and approved by other historical scholars. Its support or patronage came from the Prussian monarch Maximillian, even though Germany had a highly developed university system. Quickly following this journal were the *Revue Historique* (1876), the *English Historical Review* (1886) and the *American Historical Review* (1886). Each of the major European nations and the United States copied the *Historische Zeitschrift* in professionalizing historical research and writing.

Source: Margaret F. Stieg, *The Origin and Development of Scholarly Historical Periodicals* (University, AL: University of Alabama Press, 1986), 3–4, 238.

oral history, which relies on interviews and verbal testimonies of individuals who experienced an event.[2] If you continue on to advanced study, additional categories and their distinctions will become clearer. For your purposes as a beginning researcher, it is important to know that these philosophies and methodologies influence historians' writings and research questions. See the bibliography at the end of the chapter if you wish to read more about the schools of history.

Historians build their arguments, their discourse, and their conclusions upon primary sources. Primary sources are the evidence that individuals, governments, organizations, and cultures or societies leave behind. Some examples of primary sources are a letter from a soldier written home to his sweetheart from the battlefield, a newspaper advertisement offering a reward for a runaway slave, a map detailing the layout of a village from twelfth-century China, a taped interview with a Holocaust survivor, and a battle-axe used in the Battle of Hastings. (Chapter Six describes, in greater detail, the nature of primary sources and how to find them.) Interpreting these remnants and artifacts can be challenging, requiring imagination as well as collaboration and discussion with other historians. Individual historians do not work in a vacuum. In fact, one of the central activities of historians is to engage in debate and discourse with other historians about the interpretation of the evidence they have collected.

Secondary works are the interpretations of a topic by other historians that draw on primary sources and other interpretive works to build an argument about a historical idea. Secondary works include books, such as *Pride, Faith, and Fear: Islam in Sub-Saharan Africa* published in 2003; journal articles, such as "The Body as Attire: The Shifting Meanings of Footbinding in Seventeenth-Century China" published in the *Journal of Women's History* in 1997; Internet sites, such as *Heritage: Civilization and the Jews* (http://www.pbs.org/wnet/heritage/) built to accompany the PBS series; and video series, such as *The Century* by ABC News and newscaster Peter Jennings on the history of the twentieth century.[3] Historians carefully study the work of their peers as they conduct their research in order to see interrelationships among these works and sometimes among the work of scholars in other disciplines. They also regularly present their findings for other scholars to debate in journal articles, books, letters to the editors of scholarly journals, e-mails on listservs, and conference papers.

Historians make clear where they are drawing on the work of others by citing these sources in notes, which appear at the bottom of the page or end of the chapter or work. Deciding what to footnote can be complex. A discussion later in this chapter will offer a bit more clarification. However, if you know that you are using an idea or words that are not your own, be safe and document your work with a footnote or endnote. Claiming someone's ideas as your own and falsifying evidence is intellectual theft and fraud. Historians properly document their sources.

Practicing History in the Electronic Age: Tips for the Information-Literate Historian

The advent of the computer, along with the accompanying new ways of keeping track of notes, has had a major impact on the way historians practice their craft. Some historians have likened this electronic revolution to the invention of the printing press. Historian Jeffrey Barlow outlines some of the challenges and advantages to historical evidence in the electronic age in his essay "Historical Research and Electronic Evidence: Problems and Promises." [4] Among the advantages the electronic age brings to the study of history, Barlow lists the following:

- Online access means more people can have access to historians' evidence, both primary and secondary, more easily. For example, many primary sources are freely available online. Many universities make their dissertations available electronically, although some may restrict access. Many journals can be delivered to your desktop through such services as *JSTOR* and the *History Cooperative*.

- Electronic discussion groups allow for the creation of a broader, more dynamic community. Instead of waiting for the next newsletter of a professional organization or research group, you can read a posting on a listserv and respond to it immediately. A paper placed on the Internet can have a public bulletin board attached for posting comments. Electronic book reviews such as those at *H-Net* can be written and posted more quickly than book reviews in paper journals.

- On the Internet everyone is equal. Because anyone can publish ideas, more and different ideas can be heard. Because of the lengthy and rigorous review process that print materials must go through, sometimes the publishing process can retard the dissemination of new ideas that are considered radical, controversial, or too off-beat. The Internet facilitates new and sometimes radical discussions that can have a positive impact on the study of history.

Despite these powerful advantages, the electronic age also poses some challenges to gathering historical evidence, as Barlow points out:

- Historic electronic documents can be unreliable, impermanent, and lacking in authority depending on who has prepared and posted them. They can be easily altered or outright manufactured. Libraries, by virtue of the fact that they have knowledgeable librarians who select and organize materials, have the ability to filter out unreliable material. Through peer review, publishers offer a degree of reliability by having other historians assess the scholarly quality of their work. However, most websites do not have these checks and balances. Also, web pages may disappear, whereas printed and electronic books and journals made available by publishers usually remain accessible in a library.

- Assembling, scanning, and creating an electronic collection are easy enough tasks for anyone to do, regardless of their subject expertise. Such collections can lack the organization and selectivity that a professional scholar and editor would provide in a printed collection. For instance, editors of a collection of letters will often decide which ones are significant and which are less relevant, as well as provide notes about their authors and the context in which they were written.

- Errors can easily and rapidly be picked up and repeated. Barlow cites the *Protocols of the Elders of Zion,* a document fabricated by the Russian secret police from a Russian novel that was purported to be evidence that Jews were plotting to take over the world. It was published throughout the twentieth century and continues to surface today on the

Internet as a primary source document. No scholar would include it in a published work as evidence that Jews were trying to colonize other nations, but an uninformed researcher might inadvertently do so if he or she believed certain websites.

- The Internet easily archives documents that are the result of plagiarism or intentionally present biased viewpoints.

While your research will not necessarily conform to a "school" of history, it will take place within the existing narrative and discourse of other historians' research. Selecting a viable topic that not only interests you but also adds to the historical literature is challenging and essential for a successful project.

Beginning Your Research

Where Do Viable and Interesting Topics Come From?

Whether writing a paper, creating an oral presentation, or planning an academic website, your topic selection is crucial. Keep a strong focus. Too much material covering too many ideas will dilute your argument and your readers' ability to follow it, resulting in jumbled facts and ideas. Even if you are creating a website and not attempting to lead your audience to a single conclusion, they should still be able to make sense of your argument and understand the significance of the material you are presenting. Far too often, topics are chosen based on the large amount of secondary works available. Overabundance of sources can lead to an unfocused project. Quantity and quality are not necessarily equivalent. However, having an appropriate number of focused sources for the length of your project is important. You cannot easily and adequately write a 25-page paper based on two books, nor can you manage to incorporate 50 sources into an eight- to ten-page paper.

When selecting a topic, it is best to begin with an idea that you are interested in and that exemplifies a larger phenomenon. For instance, you may be following the current debates on the changing family in twenty-first-century America and want to explore what families were like in a different place and time. Before making a decision about any topic, it is always a good idea to look at a subject encyclopedia article. This type of encyclopedia and other reference resources, discussed in greater depth in Chapter Two, are tertiary sources and compiled by summarizing existing research. If you are researching family life in ancient Rome, then an article such as "Motherhood, Roman World" in the *Encyclopedia of Women in the Ancient World* will acquaint you with the terminology of your topic, provide background information, and help you focus your thoughts, as well as provide a bibliography for further reading. Once you have selected a topic, do some preliminary searching in your library's online catalog (see Chapter Three) and one of the appropriate online periodical indexes (see Chapter Four). Check the availability of resources and the specific focused nature of some of these works you find. Before you are too set on your topic, this is a way to determine that it is viable and that there is sufficient and existing scholarship. Your professor will be asking you to write a paper or a project on a topic that is unique, so you must get to know the existing literature.

Developing a Question and Formulating an Argument

Having a viable topic, one that will have primary sources and secondary works to draw upon, is essential but not really the end point of your work. Many students stop at this stage of their research and write a paper or report on a topic. Historical research involves building on others' research as well as primary evidence but, most importantly, formulating a unique research question and developing an argument. The sample questions below are not yet refined enough to be considered paper topics or arguments, but they show the beginnings becoming ones.

RESEARCH QUESTIONS	NOT RESEARCH QUESTIONS
How did slaves preserve African cultures in their everyday lives?	*Slave trade*
Why did Christianity spread from Byzantium to Russia?	*Russian Orthodox Church origins*
What were medical practices in from the eighth to the tenth centuries, and how did they change?	*Islamic civilization and science*
What were the lives of Indian women in the seventeenth and eighteenth centuries in British-influenced India like?	*Women and imperialism*

Selecting and refining your question and argument are critical and constant processes throughout your research. An underdeveloped question usually leads to more difficulty in formulating an effective paper. Additionally, historians Henry J. Steffens and Mary Jane Dickerson suggest asking yourself the following basic questions to help you to more effectively focus your thesis or topic and your research process.[5]

1. *"What is this piece about?"* What is your central argument? You may have many issues to discuss, but if you have to boil your argument down to two sentences or describe your website quickly, what is it that you really want to convey to your audience?

2. *"Why am I writing this?"* Later, this book talks about intentional and unintentional biases and the fact that all historians have subconscious motives when they approach their research. You have a reason for selecting a topic. Understanding that reason is important and can help strengthen your research project.

3. *"Who am I writing this for?"* Who is your audience, aside from the professor who has assigned this project? If, for example, your project is a website, many people will see it. How will you take into account differences in gender, age, educational or knowledge level, and attitudes? You do not have to please everyone. In fact, trying to do so will result in a very ineffective project. However, identifying and thinking about your audience as you plan your website or paper is essential to its ultimate success.

Preliminary Organization: The Blueprint

Effectively presenting your research requires some preplanning. Chapter Ten will help you craft the final product, whether you have chosen a paper, presentation, or website. Early in your research you will want to outline your major areas of interest and points of argument. Regardless of your final format, you will still conceptualize your topic in sections or subcategories from which you will make logical links from one section to the next. Do not be afraid to draw organizational diagrams, maps, or charts to clarify those associations before beginning your research. In fact, for a website, diagrams are often conceptually easier to replicate electronically. Your organization will inevitably change, grow, collapse, and transform as you learn more about your topic, so do not become overly attached to keeping exactly the same scheme that you originally outlined. In addition, you may even get as far as the construction of the website or the writing of the paper and find that part of your argument is lacking and that you need to come up with more supporting primary evidence or secondary works for a particular section. As you begin writing your paper or constructing your website, you may discover new questions that need to be explored. This is a normal part of writing history. Just be careful to make sure that new ideas or sources relate to your research and do not distract from your focus.

The way you arrange your evidence will create different associations and thus present different analyses and perhaps even lead to different conclusions.[6] For instance, as Laurel Thatcher Ulrich researched the diary of Martha Ballard, a midwife in eighteenth-century Maine, she was able to assemble additional primary sources in such a way as to make that diary, previously judged trivial and colloquial, become a rich and exemplary source for the study of women's history. In her presentation of Ballard's diary, she utilized survey maps, tax records, court testimony, an eighteenth-century text on midwifery, as well as secondary sources including a history of Augusta, Maine, to present and interpret Ballard's life and role as a prominent member of her community. The resulting book, entitled *A Midwife's Tale: The Life of Martha Ballard, Based on Her Diary, 1785–1812*, weaves a wide variety of primary source evidence into an amazing piece of history (for more detail, see http://dohistory.org).[7] Current interest in women's history led producers to turn the story of this diary into a PBS program. Not only did the eighteenth century speak to the twentieth century, but this piece of history was translated from a traditional form, a printed book, to a more popular form, a television documentary, and to an enhanced piece of scholarship on a website.

In researching and analyzing *A Midwife's Tale*, Ulrich had to gather and organize a large amount of information from both secondary and primary sources and carefully distinguish her ideas from those presented in these other sources. It is important for you to do the same in your research.

Taking Notes

Once you have established your categories and subcategories, you must create a system to keep track of notes from your secondary works and primary sources. Carefully documenting the source and origins of the ideas you present is crucial. A simple method for doing this is to assemble a series of index cards coded to reflect the categories and subcategories you have identified. Have a main bibliographic card on which you record the relevant information (author, title, publisher, date of publication, date website viewed, etc.) for all the sources you are using. Then, as you take specific notes, mark the cards by title of the subcategory they belong to, for instance, Russian Revolution–causes, and the source of the information, usually the author's last name and date. A number of books exist to provide instruction on note-taking using paper notecards. Software also exists for note-taking. Some historians have used a program called *Scribe* (http://chnm .gmu.edu/tools/scribe/) that can be found on the website of the Center for History and the New Media at George Mason University. This free software will allow you to manage not only traditional notes but also digital images. Knowing what to write down for future use is essential for accurately presenting your own ideas and not inadvertently committing plagiarism, or taking someone else's words or ideas and claiming them for your own. Whether you are writing a paper or creating a website, you must be true to your sources. Blatant plagiarism can lead to a failing grade and even expulsion from school. Many schools have honor codes which explicitly prohibit plagiarism. Creating a website is no different from publishing a printed book. You have placed a document in the public domain and put your name on it. It must be your work with the proper acknowledgment of sources and ideas.

When taking notes, you can save yourself much agony if you distinguish among what you perceive as general knowledge, a paraphrase, or a direct quote. Paraphrases and direct quotes need to be attributed to their original authors and require documentation, usually in the form of a footnote or reference or some sort of documentation in a website. Knowing what is general knowledge and what needs to be documented can be difficult. The following guidelines will help.[8]

- *General knowledge.* What seems to be commonly known about your topic. It may be hard to tell at first because you may not know much about your topic. However, if you keep reading the same facts and assumptions over and over, that would be general knowledge. For instance, that the Great Wall of China was built in the third century B.C.E. or that the purpose of the *Domesday Book* (1086) was to survey and assess the value of the land and property in England for the purposes of taxation by William the Conqueror would both be considered general knowledge. Statistics should not be considered general knowledge and always require a footnote.

- *Paraphrasing.* Taking an author's words and substituting your own words for their ideas. You do not want to quote long passages of text by an author directly because of space constraints, so you summarize his or her argument or assessment. Using the original syntax of the author and plugging in the synonym of your choice is not really paraphrasing, and although it is not really a direct quote, it is not good writing practice. Either summarize in your own words an author's meaning or use the author's own words as a direct quote.

- *Quoting.* Using the author's exact words. Sometimes an author says something so eloquently that you want to keep the exact spirit of the original language. You may also be unable to paraphrase the text in any

Box 1.2 History of Documentation and Historical Scandals

Originally, history and scholarship were evaluated based solely on the author's reputation. Prior to the middle of the nineteenth century, footnotes as a commonly used and standardized format did not even exist. There were attempts to provide scholarly works with some form of documentation in the eighteenth century, but the primary purpose of the authors was often to teach political or moral lessons, not to interpret the past. Recent scandals, from questionable sources to outright plagiarism, have rocked the historical community and brought renewed attention to historical documentation. Both Stephen Ambrose and Doris Kearns Goodwin, acclaimed academics as well as popular scholars, have been accused of using passages in their works that are nearly identical to those written by other scholars. Debate has also raged for a number of years over the authenticity of Alex Haley's famous saga *Roots.* Journalist Phillip Nobile wrote an article in the *Village Voice* and produced a documentary for the BBC that examined Haley's alleged plagiarism of portions of Harold Courlander's *The African.* Courlander sued Haley, but the case was settled out of court. An even more recent case of potential academic fraud has surfaced with Michael Bellesiles and his examination of American gun ownership in *Arming America: The Origins of a National Gun Culture.* The controversy centers on the existence, or nonexistence, of some probate records Bellesiles claimed to use as his primary evidence. Columbia University found sufficient evidence of fraud to rescind the prestigious Bancroft Prize that had been awarded to Bellesiles.

For more information see:

Anthony Grafton, "Birth of the Footnote." *Lingua Franca,* Nov 1997:59–66. See also his longer work, *The Footnote, a Curious History* (Boston: Harvard University Press, 1997).

"Writing History," Jan 28, 2002, *Newshour with Jim Lehrer.* Transcript, http://www.pbs.org/newshour/bb/law/jan-june02/history_1-28.html (accessed October 1, 2005). David Kirkpatrick, "Historian Says Borrowing Was Wider than Known." *New York Times,* Feb 23, 2002, 10A:5. David D. Kirkpatrick, "As Historian's Fame Grows, So Do Questions on Methods." *New York Times,* Jan 11, 2002, A1:5. For a fuller examination of the recent scandals, see Jon Wiener, *Historians in Trouble: Plagiarism, Fraud, and Politics in the Ivory Tower* (New York: New Press, 2005)

Philip Nobile, "Uncovering Roots." *Village Voice* Feb. 23 1993: 31–38, and
the BBC documentary *The Roots of Alex Haley*.
Harold Courlander, *The African* (Boston: Little, Brown, 1960).
"How the Bellesiles Story Developed," *HNN (History News Network)*,
http://hnn.us/articles/691.html (accessed January 1, 2006).

other way, so directly quoting the author is your only way to convey
the idea.

Two of these cases, paraphrasing and quoting, require proper documentation or footnotes as they are not your words and ideas but a reflection of
others'. If you are unsure if your piece of information needs a footnote, it is
always best to document your source with a footnote or a hyperlink with the
source or a location. While you do not want to overburden your audience
with notes, it is better to err on the side of caution rather than making someone else's ideas look like your own.

Format for Documenting Sources

There are a number of ways and formats for providing documentation for
your sources, both primary and secondary. The *Chicago Manual of Style*
and its derivative, *A Manual for Writers of Term Papers, Theses, and Dissertations* (commonly known by the name of its author, Turabian), are generally the preferred citation guides for historians. These books will show
you what information you need and how to construct bibliographies and
footnotes/endnotes for any source you will use for your project. On rare oc-
casions, your professors or teachers may allow you to use Modern Language Association (MLA) or American Psychological Association (APA)
style.[9] You may also encounter these citation styles in some of the indexes
and databases you use for your research. If your project is a website, use
hyperlinks to create unique types of documentation. You can link to a
scanned image of a photograph, for example. Remember that copyright
laws restrict you from scanning the complete text of many secondary
source works. You may also need permission from an archive to scan and
mount some of your primary source materials on a website since many
archives retain publication rights. To obtain permission to use an image on
a website, you must identify and contact the producer or owner of the document, image, or book, not always a straightforward task.

The Changing Nature of Historical Research and What Remains the Same

Historians are gradually changing and expanding their methods of research to take advantage of materials available on the Internet, but the discipline is still grounded in the principle of discussion and discourse based on primary evidence and attribution of those sources. You must learn to practice these techniques of discussion and discourse, while navigating between a traditional print world and the newer electronic frontier. The following chapters will help you understand and utilize standard and new sources and technologies to conduct your research effectively and to present your findings.

FOR FURTHER READING

Study of History

Barlow, Jeffrey G. "Historical Research and Electronic Evidence: Problems and Promises." In *Writing Teaching and Researching History in the Electronic Age*: *Historians and Computers*, ed. Dennis A. Trinkle, 194–225. Armonk, NY: M. E. Sharpe, 1998.
How the Internet has changed historical research practices.
Brown, John Seely, and Paul Duguid. *The Social Life of Information*. Boston: Harvard Business School Press, 2000.
Simply, how information travels in the age of the Internet.
Burke, Peter, ed. *New Perspectives on Historical Writing*. University Park: Pennsylvania State University Press, 1992.
Contains essays that examine the shift to newer ways of "doing" history. Chapters include "History from Below," "On Microhistory," "History of Reading," "Oral History."
Fischer, David Hackett. *Historians' Fallacies: Toward a Logic of Historical Thought*. New York: Harper and Row, 1970.
Classic text that systematically points out problems in historical reasoning. Topics include fallacies of "question framing," "generalization," "false analogy," and "factual significance."
Grafton, Anthony. *The Footnote, a Curious History*, rev. ed. Cambridge, MA: Harvard University Press, 1997.
History of the use of footnotes in the discipline of history.
Green, Anna, and Kathleen Troup, eds. *Houses of History: A Critical Reader in Twentieth-Century History and Theory*. New York: New York University Press, 1999.
Basic discussion of the schools of history.
Guilderhus, Mark T. *History and Historians: A Historiographical Introduction*, 5th ed. Upper Saddle River, NJ: Prentice Hall, 2003.

Succinct discussion of historians and their craft, including the role of Western philosophical thinking.

Marwick, Arthur. *The New Nature of History: Knowledge, Evidence, Language.* Chicago: Lyceum Books, 2001.
In-depth discussion of the evolution of history as a discipline. Focus is on Western thought.

Munslow, Alun. *The Routledge Companion to Historical Studies.* London: Routledge, 2000.
More up-to-date than the *Dictionary of Concepts in History.* Will also give definitions and discussions of ideas commonly discussed by historians.

Myers, Robin, and Michael Harris, eds. *Fakes and Frauds: Varieties of Deception in Print and Manuscript.* Detroit: Omnigraphics, 1989.
Cites cases of forgery from the fifteenth to the twentieth centuries.

Ritter, Harry. *Dictionary of Concepts in History.* Westport, CT: Greenwood, 1986.
Dictionary that defines major schools and methodologies of historical study and research.

Stieg, Margaret F. *The Origin and Development of Scholarly Historical Periodicals.* University, AL: University of Alabama Press, 1986.
History of scholarly communication in historical periodicals.

Winks, Robin W., ed. *The Historian as Detective: Essays on Evidence.* New York: Harper and Row, 1969.
Classic set of essays by renowned historians that provide concrete examples of how to use and interpret primary source evidence.

Woolf, D.R., ed. *A Global Encyclopedia of Historical Writing.* New York: Garland, 1998.
Focus is on major historians and their writings. Many historians have influenced schools of history and trends in historical scholarship.

How to Do Research

Barzun, Jacques, and Henry F. Graff. *The Modern Researcher.* 6th ed. Belmont, CA: Wadsworth/Thompson, 2004.
The standard for designing and writing simple to complex research projects in all disciplines.

Henige, David. *Historical Evidence and Argument.* Madison: University of Wisconsin Press, 2005.

Marius, Richard, and Melvin E. Page. *A Short Guide to Writing about History.* 5th ed. New York: Pearson/Longman, 2005.

McDowell, W. H. *Historical Research: A Guide.* London: Longman, 2002.
Background about the nature of the discipline of history.

Steffens, Henry J., and Mary Jane Dickerson. *Writers Guide. History.* Lexington, MA: D. C. Heath, 1987.
Older guide but good for focusing questions when beginning a project.

Storey, William Kelleher. *Writing History: A Guide for Students.* 2d ed. New York: Oxford University Press, 2004.
Excellent guide for writing a paper. See especially the chapter "Building an Argument."

Weidenborner, Stephen, and Domenick Caruso. *Writing Research Papers: A Guide to the Research Process.* 6th ed. Boston: Bedford/St. Martins, 2001.
Step-by-step guide, from designing a research topic to creating a paper.

Style Manuals and Citation Guides

The Chicago Manual of Style. 15th ed. Chicago: University of Chicago Press, 2003.
David Warlich's Landmark Project. *Citation Machine,* http://citationmachine.net (accessed January 1, 2006).
Put the essentials of your citation in the form provided and you will receive a citation in APA and MLA formats.
Gibaldi, Joseph. *MLA Style Manual and Guide to Scholarly Publishing.* New York: Modern Language Association of America, 1998.
Publication Manual of the American Psychological Association. 5th ed. Washington, DC: American Psychological Association, 2001.

NOTES

1. Many books will outline these and other schools. This definition comes from Martha Howell and Walther Prevenier, *From Reliable Sources: An Introduction to Historical Methods* (Ithaca, NY: Cornell University Press, 2001), 110–112. Some other examples include Anna Green and Kathleen Troup, eds. *Houses of History: A Critical Reader in Twentieth-Century History and Theory* (New York: New York University Press, 1999); Arthur Marwick, *The New Nature of History: Knowledge, Evidence, Language* (Chicago: Lyceum Books, 2001); and Harry Ritter, *Dictionary of Concepts in History* (Westport, CT: Greenwood Press, 1986).
2. Peter Burke, ed., *New Perspectives on Historical Writing* (University Park: Pennsylvania State University Press, 1992).
3. Charlotte A. Quinn and Frederick Quinn, *Pride, Faith, and Fear: Islam in Sub-Saharan Africa* (New York: Oxford University Press, 2003); Dorothy Ko, "The Body as Attire: The Shifting Meanings of Footbinding in Seventeenth-Century China," *Journal of Women's History* 8 (Winter 1997): 8-27; Public Broadcasting Service, *Heritage: Civilization and the Jews,* http://www.pbs.org/wnet/heritage/ (accessed January 1, 2006); *The Century: Decades of Change.* Peter Jennings, prod. ABC News in association with the History Channel (Princeton, NJ: Films for the Humanities and Sciences, 1999), videocassettes.
4. Jeffrey G. Barlow, "Historical Research and Electronic Evidence: Problems and Promises," in *Writing Teaching and Researching History in the Electronic Age:*

Historians and Computers, ed., Dennis A. Trinkle (Armonk, NY: M. E. Sharpe, 1998), 206–215.

5. Henry J. Steffens and Mary Jane Dickerson, *Writers Guide. History* (Lexington, MA: D. C. Heath & Co., 1987), 6–14.

6. W. H. McDowell, *Historical Research: A Guide* (London: Longman, 2002), 10.

7. Laurel Thatcher Ulrich, *A Midwife's Tale: The Life of Martha Ballard, Based on Her Diary, 1785–1812* (New York: Knopf, 1990); Film Study Center at Harvard University and Center for History and the New Media at George Mason University, *DoHistory*, http://dohistory.org/ (accessed March 23, 2006). At dohistory.org, Ulrich discusses how puzzling the diary has been for many researchers, past and present. Some saw it as trivia or a source of genealogical history, while others in the later twentieth century found it only marginally useful for information on midwifery. See the book introduction, page 8.

8. Stephen Weidenborner and Domenick Caruso, "Quoting, Paraphrasing, and Summarizing," in *Writing Research Papers: A Guide to the Process*, 6th ed. (Boston: Bedford/St. Martins, 2001), 122–144.

9. See the bibliography at the end of the chapter for suggestions for style guides and citation manuals.

2

Reference
Resources

WHAT YOU WILL LEARN IN THIS CHAPTER:
- types of reference resources
- how to locate reference resources
- ways to find and use definitions, background information, and supporting material for your research
- specific reference titles, in print and online

What Are Reference Resources and When Are They Useful?

In Chapter One, you selected a topic and began to do some preliminary research, filling out a vague outline/categories of points that you might want to discuss in your argument. You formulated an argument, which may change as your research progresses. Understanding some basic background information about your topic helps you to consider how and where to begin your search for information and formulate your search strategy, as well as to design the structure of your paper, project, presentation, or website. Consulting some of the reference resources listed in this chapter will provide you with a broader perspective and make your search for resources more efficient. You will use this chapter's resources in several ways. Initially, you will want to consult encyclopedias and multivolume general histories to ground your topic in historical research and to become familiar with its scope and the terms associated with it. Then, you will want to browse through some of the bibliographies that will lead you to other secondary sources. Each type of resource has a function. Depending on the needs of your research, you may or may not need to consult the other types of resources listed in this chapter. These resources can be some of the most useful but underused tools in a researcher's repertoire, saving time as well as opening up new avenues of knowledge. However useful, these types of materials are not the foundation of a research project in the manner that primary sources, such as letters or diaries, are.

Reference resources are considered tertiary (third-level) source materials, generally in the format of a book or website, that provide background information and a succinct overview and analysis of a subject or concept. "Tertiary sources" means that these resources have been compiled from secondary sources. Unlike a secondary source book or journal article, reference resources are not intended to be read in their entirety but to be consulted to clarify terms and concepts associated with your topic, as well as to provide basic facts, statistics, and referrals to authoritative secondary sources. For instance, the article on steelmaking in the *Dictionary of the Middle Ages* would help you understand the level of technical knowledge of blacksmiths making armor in the fourteenth century as well as the form in which steel was transported (*stahlkuchen* or steel cake or bundles or garb) and the market conditions in the Rhineland.[1] From the article in the encyclopedia, you can gain knowledge about the history, process, and place of steelmaking, as well as keywords to search in a database. The article also suggests resources for further reading. Similarly, *International Historical Statistics: Europe 1750–2000* provides statistics on the social and economic fabric of European nations by including tables with such data as passenger traffic on railways by country and by year in the nineteenth century. [2]

You cannot construct an entire research project by stringing together encyclopedia articles, citing statistics, and adding some definitions from a dictionary, some quotes from a book review, and a chronology of events. To build your research paper or website in this way is to act merely as a reporter, not a researcher. To assemble summary information and facts without an underlying thesis or purpose is not contributing to scholarship, only repackaging information.

By definition, reference resources typically provide the following:

- summary information
- definitions
- associative and synonymous terms to make searching easier
- names of individuals associated with an event
- dates and places
- data
- facts
- maps
- timelines
- bibliographies and sources for further reading

- biographical information
- addresses and locations

How to Find Reference Resources

Finding useful reference resources can be challenging. Literally thousands of print, online, and website sources exist that provide reference information. Generally, print reference resources are easy to find and understand. Internet reference resources often try to be all things to all researchers by creating a full virtual library, including reference resources such as encyclopedic information and fact-based information as well as full text of primary resources and sometimes even journal-like essays written by the author of the page or provided by the sponsoring organization. While many reference resources exist, because they are so numerous, it is impossible to have a comprehensive list of sources for history. If you become familiar with the *types* of reference sources available, you can use your library's catalog to locate other relevant ones and search the Internet for others. Throughout this chapter you will find a list of selected reference resources that will be useful during your research process. Your librarian will also be able to suggest many titles as well as strategies for using these resources and ways of finding others.

Types of Reference Resources

You will use different types of reference resources to support different research needs at various stages of your research. At the beginning of your research, encyclopedias are often the most useful to get your bearings on a subject. When you have a narrower topic with some specific terms, multivolume general histories will help you set your topic in a broader historical context, while biographical resources will help you investigate individuals' roles. As your research progresses and you integrate primary sources and more complex secondary works, you will want to use dictionaries and chronologies to understand the meanings of specific words and terms in the time of their origin and through their evolution, as well as the climate in which your events occurred. There are many types of reference resources that can assist you in constructing a research question. Below are the major types of reference resources useful to historians.

Encyclopedias

Encyclopedias can be one of the most useful resources for a beginning, as well as an advanced, researcher. Very quickly, such works provide a broad overview of a topic as well as the essential facts, keywords, principal participants, and often a bibliography. Use the keywords and the names of principal participants as search terms (see Chapter Three for search techniques) and the bibliography as a basis for beginning your reading. Two types of encyclopedias exist, one general and one specialized (sometimes called "subject encyclopedias"). General encyclopedias, such as the *Encyclopaedia Britannica*, the *World Book Encyclopedia*, or the online *Wikipedia*, attempt to encompass and define the vast amount of human knowledge. Subject encyclopedias like the *Encyclopedia of North American Indians* or *The Encyclopedia of African History and Culture* provide focused, in-depth knowledge on some aspect of a subject, place, or time period. They use terminology that specialists, in this case historians, use to converse about a topic, providing vocabulary to use in your search strategy in online catalogs and periodical indexes described in Chapters Three and Four. Many times the entries will provide at their conclusion a bibliography of articles for further reading. These materials are often standard sources with which to begin your research. For the level of research you are doing, subject encyclopedias are the more appropriate type to use. Their articles are written and signed by professional historians and contain very specific subject matter that will more fully address your research topic than general encyclopedias.

Articles in subject encyclopedias are formatted in two ways. Sometimes you will find their articles arranged alphabetically like a dictionary. These entries are often, but not always, short and definition-like. For instance, *The Modern Encyclopedia of Russian and Soviet History* is arranged in this manner, with entries like "Kizil-Koba Culture," a series of settlements in the Crimea from the sixth to the ninth centuries B.C.E. Other subject encyclopedias are collections of lengthy subject-oriented entries that read like journal articles. "The Aristocracy of Inherited Wealth," a signed article by Ronald Story in the *Encyclopedia of American Social History*, is an example of this type of entry in such a subject encyclopedia. Conceptually, these two types of encyclopedias contribute to your knowledge about your subject in different ways. The alphabetic encyclopedia sets the context of a topic by defining a person, place, or concept. The topically arranged encyclopedia provides a broad, sweeping analysis that contextualizes and analyzes many aspects on a given subject. Each has signed articles, which means that someone with knowledge of the subject wrote the entry or article, which helps you evaluate the quality and accuracy of the information presented. Some subject encyclopedias focus on a culture (*The Encyclopedia of Islam*), a region or country (*The Encyclopedia of Latin American History and Culture*), a subject specialty or type of history (*St. James Encyclopedia of Labor History Worldwide*), or a time period (*Dictionary of the Middle Ages*).[3] Often, online encyclopedias do not follow the patterns of print encyclopedias because of the Internet's ability to provide unique hypertext access that a static print source cannot. Some electronic encyclopedias are free to the public and are labors of love by individual scholars or academic societies, while other online resources are fee-based and often replicas of printed encyclopedias. Judging the quality of online electronic encyclopedias is problematic because it can be difficult to tell the origins of the information and the abilities of the author to write the entry. Those collections developed by commercial publishers and requiring subscriptions have some authority built in through stringent publication and editorial policies and practices. The online version of the *Catholic Encyclopedia* is a copy of the published 1914 edition, which would exclude all of the reforms of Vatican I and II and the teachings of John Paul II. An encyclopedia of U.S. Civil War battlefield medicine created by a Civil War reenactor may or may not contain correct information. You will need to verify some of that information.

Box 2.1 *Wikipedia*

Established in 2001 as a communal, multilingual encyclopedia, *Wikipedia* (http://www.wikipedia.org/) allows anyone to create and edit an article about a topic of their choosing. A huge endeavor that includes over 3.7 million articles in 200 languages, *Wikipedia* would seem to be the fount of knowledge. Simple to search, the encyclopedia almost always produces results. However, there are some drawbacks to this online encyclopedia as an information resource. Because everyone can edit an article, theoretically to correct mistakes, many individuals do edit articles, sometimes correcting honest mistakes but also fighting turf and ideological wars. The entry for "global warming" is under constant flux as individuals who disagree on the effects and even the premise of the phenomenon alter it. Another article suggested that one of U.S. Senator Robert Kennedy's former assistants might have been connected to a conspiracy to assassinate the senator. While the articles are signed, the authors' credentials are varied. The ability of the authors to clearly explain the topic varies widely as well, sometimes emphasizing topics of lesser importance. A recent study by the magazine *Nature*, however, found that *Wikipedia* was only slightly less accurate for selected science topics than the *Encyclopedia Britannica,* finding 162 factual errors, omissions, or misleading statements in *Wikipedia* compared to 123 in the *Encyclopedia Britannica.* Still, the reliability of the information will remain an issue. As a researcher, you must remain cautious if you use this source.

Sources: Jim Giles, "Internet Encyclopedias Go Head to Head." *Nature*, Dec 15, 2005, 900–901; "Criticism of Wikipedia," http://en.wikipedia.org/wiki/Criticism_of_Wikipedia (accessed January 1, 2006); "Wikipedia," http://en.wikipedia.org/wiki/Wikipedia (accessed January 1, 2006).

The Internet and electronic publication of texts have allowed several major publishers to develop cross-searching capabilities among their many fee-based reference publications. Because they are online, these collections can be updated more frequently than books can be printed. For example, Oxford University Press has collected many of its *Oxford Companion* books in *Oxford Reference Online.* Not strictly history-related, these sources provide basic definitions and background information about a given topic. ABC-CLIO, a major publisher of history books, issues many of its reference publications as e-books. While there is as yet no mechanism to search across all e-books, your library may have electronic access to individual titles. Gale, another large publisher of reference materials, offers the *Gale Virtual Reference Library,* a service that aggregates many of its reference products. *NetLibrary,* a company that has licensed many printed books and made them available as e-books, has created a "reference center" consisting of 800 reference books from which your library may select specific titles. Your librarian can tell you if your college or school has subscriptions to these electronic resources. Below is a selected list of encyclopedias. New titles are published daily, so this is merely an attempt to list the best at the time of the publication of this book.[4] Consult with your librarian for new titles related to your subject.

Selected Encyclopedias

NORTH AMERICA

Dictionary of American History. Stanley I. Kutler, ed. 3d ed. New York: Scribner's, 2003. 10 vols. Also available online through *Gale Virtual Reference Library.*

Encyclopedia of American Cultural and Intellectual History. Mary Kupiec Cayton and Peter W. Williams, eds. New York: Scribner's/Gale, 2001. 3 vols.

Encyclopedia of American Political History: Studies of the Principal Movements and Ideas. Jack P. Greene, ed. New York: Scribner's, 1984. 3 vols.

Encyclopedia of American Social History. Mary Kupiec Cayton, Elliot J. Gorn, and Peter W. Williams, eds. New York: Scribner's, 1993. 3 vols.

Encyclopedia of Cleveland History, http://ech.cwru.edu/ (accessed January 1, 2006).

New Encyclopedia of Southern Culture. rev. ed. Charles Reagan Wilson gen. eds. Chapel Hill: University of North Carolina Press, 2006.

Encyclopedia of U. S. Foreign Relations. Bruce W. Jentleson and Thomas G. Paterson, eds. New York: Oxford University Press, 1997. 4 vols.

Encyclopedia of Women in American History. Joyce Appleby, Eileen K. Cheng, and Joanne Goodwin, eds. New York: M. E. Sharpe, 2002. 3 vols.

Canadian Encyclopedia: Year 2000 Edition. Toronto: McClelland & Stewart, 1999. 3 vols.

LATIN AMERICA

Encyclopedia of Latin American History and Culture. Barbara A. Tenenbaum, ed. New York: Scribner's, 1996. 5 vols.

MIDDLE EAST

Civilizations of the Ancient Near East. Jack M. Sasson, et al., eds. New York: Scribner's, 1995. 8 vols.

Encyclopedia of the Modern Middle East & North Africa. Philip Mattar, ed. 2d ed. Detroit: Macmillan, 2004. 4 vols.

EUROPE

Critical Dictionary of the French Revolution. François Furet and Mona Ozouf, eds. Cambridge, MA: Harvard University Press, 1989.

Dictionary of Modern Italian History. Frank J. Coppa, ed. Westport, CT: Greenwood, 1985.

Encyclopedia of European Social History: From 1350 to 2000. Peter N. Stearns, ed. Detroit: Scribner's/Gale, 2001. 6 vols.

Encyclopedia of the Third Reich. Christian Zentner and Friedemann Bedurftig, eds. Amy Hackett, trans. New York: Macmillan, 1991. 2 vols.

Modern Encyclopedia of Russian, Soviet, and Eurasian History. Joseph
Wieczynski and George N. Rhyne, eds. Gulf Breeze, FL: Academic In-
ternational, 1976–2000. 60 vols., 2 vol. suppl. Edward J. Lazzerini and
George N. Rhyne, eds. 1995. Former title: *The Modern Encyclopedia of
Russian and Soviet History.*

Encyclopedia of Russian History. James R. Millar, ed. New York: Macmillan,
2004, 4 vols. Also available online through *Gale Virtual Reference
Library.*

*Modern Germany: An Encyclopedia of History, People, and Culture,
1871–1990.* Dieter K. Buse and Jürgen C. Doerr, eds. New York:
Garland, 1998.

Europe 1450 to 1789: Encyclopedia of the Early Modern World. Jonathan
Dewald, ed. New York: Scribner's, 2004. 6 vols.

AFRICA

*Africana: The Encyclopedia of the African and African-American Experi-
ence.* Kwame Anthony Appiah and Henry Louis Gates Jr., eds. 2d ed.
New York: Oxford University Press, 2005.

Encyclopedia of Africa South of the Sahara. John Middleton, ed. New York:
Scribner's, 1997. 4 vols.

Encyclopedia of African History and Culture, rev. ed. R. Hunt Davis, ed.
(orig. ed. Willie F. Page, ed.) New York: Facts on File, 2005. 5 vols.

ASIA

Cambridge Encyclopedia of China. Brian Hook, ed. 2d ed. New York:
Cambridge University Press, 1991.

Encyclopedia of Asian History. Ainslie T. Embree, ed. New York: Scribner's,
1988. 4 vols.

Kodansha Encyclopedia of Japan. Tokyo: Kodansha, 1983. 9 vols. and suppl.

Encyclopedia of Modern Asia. David Levinson and Karen Christensen,
eds. New York: Scribner's, 2002. 6 vols.

AUSTRALIA

Australians: A Historical Library. Broadway, N. S. W., Australia: Fairfax,
Syme, and Weldon Associates 1987. 11 vols.

WORLD, REGIONAL, CULTURAL, OR TOPICAL

Encyclopedia Judaica. 2d ed. New York: Macmillan, 2006. 20 vols. Also
available online [forthcoming].

The Encyclopaedia of Islam, new ed. E. Van Donzel, B. Lewis, and Ch.
Pellat, eds. Leiden: Brill, 1954–. 111 vols. Also available on CD-ROM.
An Encyclopedia of World History: Ancient, Medieval, and Modern, Peter
N. Stearns, ed. 6th ed. Boston: Houghton Mifflin, 2001.
Ecole Initiative, http://www2.evansville.edu/ecoleweb/ (accessed January 1,
2006).
Encyclopedia of North American Indians. Frederick E. Hoxie, ed. Boston:
Houghton Mifflin, 1996. 1 vol.
ehNet:Encyclopedia of Economic and Business History,
http://www.eh.net/encyclopedia/ (accessed January 1, 2006).

BY TIME PERIOD

Civilization of the Ancient Mediterranean: Greece and Rome. Michael
Grant and Rachel Kitzinger, eds. New York: Scribner's, 1988. 3 vols.
Brill's New Pauly Encyclopaedia of the Ancient World. Hubert Cancik and
Helmut Schneider, eds. Boston: Brill, 2002. In progress.
Oxford Classical Dictionary, 3d ed. rev. Simon Hornblower and Anthony
Spawforth, eds. Rev. Oxford: Oxford University Press, 2003. Also
available at *Oxford Reference Online*.
Dictionary of the Middle Ages. Joseph R. Strayer, ed. New York: Scribner's,
1982–1989. 12 vols. and suppl. New York: Scribner's, 2003.
Encyclopedia of the Renaissance. Paul F. Grendler, ed. New York: Scribner's,
1999. 6 vols.
Oxford Encyclopedia of the Reformation. Hans J. Hillerbrand, ed. New York:
Oxford University Press, 1996. 4 vols.
ORB: The Online Reference Book for Medieval Studies, http://www
.the-orb.net/encyclo.html (accessed January 1, 2006).

Bibliographies

Bibliographies can provide a collection of resources on your topic and save
some of the lengthy searching in other databases and catalogs. In the field
of history, they are often a combination of encyclopedia, bibliography, and
guidebook and offer an overview of the literature that exists about a broad
topic, such as the U.S. Confederacy or the Renaissance, including references to standard texts. Sometimes they offer a how-to-do-research feature
on the subject, with an overview of past and current scholarship, as well as
the locations of other secondary and major primary source collections.
Some bibliographies, like *The American Historical Association's Guide
to Historical Literature*, break history into periods and broad topics and

devote a chapter to each of these.[5] The chapter contains a short two-to-three-page discussion of the topic and its scholarship followed by a lengthy bibliography of classic and current secondary and primary resources.

Bibliographies can focus on a more specific subject, cover a more restrictive time frame, or attempt to be more comprehensive. For instance, when issued annually as a printed book, *The Eighteenth Century: A Current Bibliography* attempts to index everything published on the eighteenth century in all disciplines for that year. Some bibliographies collect sources on a very focused subject and are issued only once, for instance, *China During the Cultural Revolution 1966–1976*, which gathers together a large portion of the English-language literature on the Cultural Revolution.[6] Although these types of bibliographies are valuable, be careful not to rely totally on their contents as the literature they index can become dated.

Selected Bibliographies

SELECTED GENERAL BIBLIOGRAPHIES OF RESOURCES, INCLUDING HISTORY

New Walford Guide to Reference Resources. Vol. 1, *Science and Technology*; Vol. 2, *Social and Historical Sciences, Philosophy, and Religion*; and Vol. 3, *Generalia, Language and Literature, the Arts.* 8th ed. London: Facet, 2005–. Previous title *Walford's Guide to Reference Materials*, published by the Library Association.

Guide to Reference Books. Robert Balay, ed. 11th ed. Chicago: American Library Association, 1996.

SELECTED HISTORY-SPECIFIC BIBLIOGRAPHIES

The American Historical Association's Guide to Historical Literature. Mary Beth Norton, ed. 3d ed. New York: Oxford University Press, 1995. 2 vols.

Handbook for Research in American History: A Guide to Bibliographies and Other Reference Works. Francis Paul Prucha, ed. 2d ed. Lincoln: University of Nebraska Press, 1994.

A Bibliography of British History, 1914–1989. Keith Robbins, comp. and ed. Oxford: Clarendon, 1996.

A Bibliography of English History to 1485. E. B. Graves, comp. Oxford: Clarendon, 1975.

Bibliography of British History: Tudor Period, 1485–1603. Conyers Read, comp. 2d ed. Totowa, NJ: Rowman and Littlefield, 1978.

Bibliography of British History: Stuart History, 1603–1714. G. D. Davies and M. F. Keeler, comps. 2d ed. Oxford: Clarendon, 1970.
Bibliography of British History: The Eighteenth Century, 1714–1789. S. Pargellis and D. J. Medley, comps. Oxford: Clarendon, 1951.
Bibliography of British History, 1789–1851. L. M. Brown and I. R. Christie, comps. Oxford: Clarendon, 1977.
Bibliography of British History, 1851–1914. H. J. Hanham, comp. Oxford: Clarendon, 1976.
The Eighteenth Century: A Current Bibliography. New York: AMS Press, 1978– Annual.
European History, http://www.library.yale.edu/rsc/history/european/ (accessed January 1, 2006).
Reference Sources in History: An Introductory Guide. 2d ed. Ronald H. Fritze, Brian E. Coutts, Louis Vyhnanek, comps. Santa Barbara, CA: ABC-CLIO, 2004. Also available online through ABC-CLIO.
The Labyrinth: Resources for Medieval Studies, http://labyrinth.georgetown.edu (accessed March 23, 2006).
Stanford University Library Guides, http://library.stanford.edu/depts/hasrg/index.html (accessed March 23, 2006).
Yale University Library Subject Guides, http://www.library.yale.edu/guides/ (accessed March 23, 2006). Both Stanford and Yale libraries maintain an excellent list of history-related web guides that also include reference-like resources.

Multivolume General Histories

Sometimes you may need information that establishes a broader historical and theoretical context for your historical research. Whereas encyclopedias generally provide shorter summary bits of information, multivolume general histories provide sweeping, synthesizing scholarly narrative and analysis of topics, nations, regions, and eras. These types of sources examine the standard, accepted historical thought, including interpretations by many of the major, prominent historians past and present, but do not include current, cutting-edge historical theory. Below is a list of the major sets.

Selected Multivolume General Histories

New Cambridge Medieval History. Rosamund McKitterick, ed. London: Cambridge University Press, 1995–.
New Cambridge Modern History. G. R. Elton, ed. 2d ed. London: Cambridge University Press, 1990–.

Cambridge Ancient History. 3d ed. London: Cambridge University Press, 1970–.

Cambridge History of . . . and *New Cambridge History of* . . .: Cambridge University Press has a large number of histories that begin with these titles. Searching your library's catalog with these titles will bring a list of results.

Longman Companion to. . . . Chris Cook and John Stevenson, gen. eds. (Longman Companions to History Series). London: Longman.

General History of Africa. London: Longman, 1981–1993. 8 vols. Also known as *UNESCO History of Africa.*

History of Humanity. S. J. De Laet, ed. London: Routledge, 1994–.

Series Overviews

These two new series combine historiography with an overview of a place, era, or technique of analysis. They are slightly different from the sources above but can be used in the same manner.

Writing History . . . Stefan Berger, Heike Feldner, Kevin Passmore, eds. London: Hodder Arnold, 2004–. Series so far includes *Writing Gender History* (Laura Lee Downs, ed.), *Writing Medieval History* (Nancy Parnter, ed.), *Writing Early Modern History* (Garthine Walker, ed.).

Palgrave Advances in . . . New York: Palgrave/Macmillan, 2005–. Critical commentary on recent scholarship.

Biographical Resources

Much of history is told through the lives of individuals. Understanding and interpreting their actions and philosophies helps you to understand how they participated in and shaped the world and events around them. Until relatively recently history was written through the study of the lives of predominantly white male leaders and a few women, such as the Egyptian ruler Cleopatra and the British queen Victoria. Biographical information is collected in a number of ways. Often, these characteristics are the points around which a biographical dictionary is organized.

- *Profession/avocation.* It is helpful to know why a person is important, which usually implies a profession, for instance, author, politician, physicist, etc. However, a profession does not always equate with employment. Individuals can also be important for nonemployment activities in which they engage, for instance, reformers (civil rights, suffrage, temperance).

- *Nationality or region.* Countries want to be able to identify their significant citizens. National identities are formed, in part, by identifying the people who "belong" to a particular country. Sometimes dictionaries are organized by regions as well.

- *Gender, ethnicity, or race.* Famous women as well as African Americans and other minorities are often grouped together in biographical dictionaries. Many of the individuals in these groups have experienced similar struggles and likewise have been left out of many of the standard biographical sources.

- *Dates lived/flourished.* It is useful to know who was living at the same time and in the same era. For this reason, certain biographical dictionaries are organized to group together information about people who lived in a particular era.

Knowing how biographical information is organized will help you search for it. For instance, if you wanted information on John Singleton Copley, an American painter, you might look for information in *The American National Biography* as you know his nationality to be American.[7] You would find approximately three pages of information describing his life, followed by a short bibliography telling you where his papers are located and suggesting two book-length biographies you might wish to read for further information. Because Copley is a painter, you could also look for information in an encyclopedia on painters or American painting, such as *Grove Dictionary of Art. From Renaissance to Impressionism: Styles and Movements in Western Art 1400–1900.*[8] This assumes you know the approximate date your artist lived.

Biographical resources come in several formats: (1) *indexes* to biographical dictionaries and full-length biographies, (2) biographical dictionaries, and (3) full-length biographical books or monographs found through your library's online catalog. The most common way to locate information on an individual is to look for a biographical dictionary by country of origin. Your search results would give you both biographical dictionaries to the country as well as full-length biographies about the people who were citizens of that country. The subject heading to use in your library's online catalog is "[country]–Biography–Dictionaries (France–Biography–Dictionaries)." Also, you can look for a biographical directory by profession, for example, chemists or perhaps, more broadly, scientists or a bit more specifically, female scientists in the nineteenth century.

While not strictly a *type* of reference resource, another good source of biographical information is obituaries. Published in newspapers, journals, and magazines upon an individual's death, these articles highlight the facts and relationships of the person's life and, when appropriate, list major works and accomplishments. See Chapter Four for periodical and newspaper indexes. These indexes include references to obituaries. Some of the indexes and dictionaries listed below also include references to obituaries.

The possibilities, as well as your search strategies, for finding biographical information are nearly endless. The sources listed here attempt to be very broad in their coverage.

Selected Biographical Resources

DICTIONARIES AND COMPREHENSIVE RESOURCES

American National Biography. John A. Garraty, Mark C. Carnes, eds. New York: Oxford University Press, 1999 and suppl. 2002–. 24 vols., Also available through online subscription. Individuals who influenced American history but were not necessarily of American birth or citizenship. To be included in the print version, individuals must have died by 1996.

Oxford Dictionary of National Biography. H. C. G. Matthew and Brian Harrison, eds. London: Oxford University Press, 2004. 60 vols. Also available through online subscription. Individuals who influenced British history but were not necessarily of British birth or citizenship. Good for locating figures in British colonies. To be included in the print version, individuals must have died by 2001.

Notable American Women 1607–1950. Edward T. James, ed. Cambridge, MA: Harvard University Press, 1971. *Notable American Women: The Modern Period.* Barbara Sicherman, et al., eds. Cambridge, MA: Harvard University Press, 1980. *Notable American Women: A Biographical Dictionary Completing the Twentieth Century.* Susan Ware, ed. Cambridge MA: Harvard University Press, 2004.

Dictionary of Literary Biography. Detroit: Gale, 1978–. Also available online in *Biography Resource Center.* The term "literary" refers to individuals who write. The focus of the series is primarily on fiction writers of many formats (poetry, drama, novels, etc.) but also includes other types of writers such as historians.

Current Biography. New York: H. W. Wilson, 1940–. Three- to four-page biographies of contemporary individuals who are important and influential in all areas of life (politics, sports, entertainment, science, etc.). Coverage is international, so you could find, for example, a biography of Pol Pot during the Vietnam era.

Contemporary Authors. Detroit: Gale Research, 1967–. Also available online in *Biography Resource Center.* Short biographies that include bibliographies for all types of writers, including nonfiction.

Biography Resource Center. Farmington Hills, MI: Gale Group, 2004. Online subscription. A collection of biographical dictionaries and other biographical resources. Individuals included may be historical or more contemporary.

The following "Who's Who" sources provide basic biographical data on prominent American and British individuals, living and deceased. Many countries issue biographical sources titled *Who's Who.* While they tend to list living people only, a resource that was published 50 years ago would contain historical biographies.

Who's Who. London: A&C Black, 1849–.

Who Was Who. London: A&C Black, 1897–.

Who's Who in America. Chicago: Marquis Who's Who, Inc., 1899–.

Who Was Who in America. Chicago: Marquis Who's Who, Inc., 1607–.

Dictionnaire de Biographie Française. Paris : Letouzey et Ané, 1930–. Similar to the *American National Biography* and the *Oxford Dictionary of National Biography* but in French, and parts are much older. Still in progress.

Neue Deutsche Biographie. Herausgegeben von der Historischen Kommission bei der Bayerischen Akademie der Wissenschaften. Berlin: Duncker & Humblot, 1953–. Similar to the *American National Biography* and the *Oxford Dictionary of National Biography* but in German, and parts are much older. Still in progress.

A&E Biography, http://www.biography.com/ (accessed January 1, 2006).

Dizionario Biografico Degli Italiani. Alberto M. Ghisalberti, ed. Rome: Istituto Della Enciclopedia Italiana, 1960–[in progress]. Italian biographical dictionary.

Dictionary of National Biography. S. P. Sen, ed. Calcutta: Institute of Historical Studies, 1972–1974. For India. Would be a bit dated.

Australian Dictionary of Biography. Melbourne: Melbourne University Press, 1966–2000.

Dictionary of Canadian Biography. Toronto: University of Toronto Press, 1966–, http://www.biographi.ca/EN/ (accessed January 9, 2006).

INDEXES TO OTHER BIOGRAPHICAL RESOURCES

Biography and Master Genealogy Index. Detroit: Gale Research, 1975–. Also available online through subscription. Indexes biographical dictionaries.

Personal Name Index to The New York Times Index. Succasunna, NJ: Roxbury
Data Interface, 1976–. Also available through the *New York Times Historical* if your library subscribes to that database. Indexes a large number of years by individuals' names. Refers to the print newspaper index.
Biography Index. New York: H. W. Wilson, 1946–. Also available online. Indexes selected journal, magazine, and newspaper articles and interviews.

Chronologies

Chronologies can serve a number of purposes for your research. Sometimes
as you read your primary sources, you will find allusions to other contemporary events. Chronologies can help you place primary sources in their contemporary context because they list events in order of the date they occurred
and suggest the cultural influences that potentially impacted the individuals
and groups you are analyzing. Sometimes these reference sources will categorize social, scientific, and political events in separate lists. For example, for
someone studying the period between 1750 and 1850, it could be relevant and
potentially important to know that Ludwig van Beethoven (1770–1827), the
German composer, was a contemporary of Napoleon (1769–1821), Shaka the
Zulu king (1787–1828), Jane Austen (1775–1817), and Thomas Jefferson
(1743–1826) and that Joseph Priestly (1733–1804) isolated oxygen in 1774.

Selected Chronologies

The American Chronicle: Year by Year Through the Twentieth Century.
    Lois Gordon and Alan Gordon eds. New Haven, CT: Yale University
    Press, 1999.
American Decades. Detroit : Gale Research, 1994–.
American Eras. Detroit: Gale Research, 1997–.
World Eras. Detroit: Gale Research, 2001–.
Chronology of World History. H. E .L. Mellersh and Neville Williams, eds.
    Santa Barbara, CA: ABC-CLIO, 1999. 4 vols.
Day by Day: the Forties. New York: Facts on File. Also Fifties, Sixties,
    Seventies, Eighties, and Nineties.
Handbook of British Chronology. E. B. Fryde, D. E. Greenway, S. Porter,
    I. Roy, eds. 3d ed. London: Royal Historical Society, 1996.
Hyperhistory Online, http://www.hyperhistory.com/online_n2/History_n2/
    a.html (accessed January 1, 2006).
The Timetables of History. Bernard Grun. New York: Simon & Schuster, 1991.
Web Chronology Project, http://www.thenagain.info/WebChron/ (accessed
    January 1, 2006).

BBC History Timelines, http://www.bbc.co.uk/history/timelines/ (accessed January 1, 2006).

Dictionaries, Etymologies, and Word Origins

Words and language are central to historical research. If a word or phrase is central to your topic, look it up in one of these dictionaries. Meanings change over time, and your understanding of a definition may be tainted by your modern perspective (e.g., "nationalism" or "middle class" or "capitalism"). Whether examining the language of a fourteenth-century legal document describing land ownership or trying to discern the nuances of a modern historian's usage of words, understanding the origins of words and their historical development (*etymology*) is critical to your analysis. Knowing when and where a particular phrase or word came into common usage and the evolution of that usage provides an intellectual context for your research. A plethora of dictionaries and etymologies exist. On slang alone, there are volumes for American slang, southern U.S. slang, "underworld" and criminal lingo, and common language used by the army and navy, as well as slang in other languages. The source for the origins and usage of most words in the English language is the monolithic *Oxford English Dictionary* (OED). Available in print and online, the OED tells you the part of speech of the word, its definition, its origin, and its change in usage over time. Citing and dating the first documented use of the word in a sentence within a published work, the OED provides and establishes when and by whom words entered into common usage and, conversely, when they became seldom used.

To find a slang or etymological dictionary, use your library's online catalog and search by the subject "English Language" (or other language). Then limit by words in the subject dictionaries and what you wish to look for, for instance, "slang." This will locate dictionaries like *Soviet Camp Speech*, which details prisoners' language in Soviet detention camps.[9]

Selected Dictionaries, Etymologies, and Word Origins

Oxford English Dictionary. J. A. Simpson and E. S. C. Weiner, eds. 2d ed. New York: Oxford University Press, 1989. Also available online through subscription.

A Dictionary of Slang and Unconventional English: Colloquialisms and Catch Phrases, Fossilized Jokes and Puns, General Nicknames, Vulgarisms and Such Americanisms as Have Been Naturalized by Eric Partridge. Paul Beale, ed. 8th ed. London: Routledge, 2002.

Box 2.2: *Oxford English Dictionary*

The *Oxford English Dictionary* (OED) is considered the authority on the changes in uses of words. The OED developed from an 1859 proposal by the Philological Society of London to take words from quotes from significant works dated 1250–1858. Samuel Johnson (1709–1784), author of the first substantial dictionary (*Dictionary of the English Language*, 1755), included in his definitions a sentence that used the word. The editors of the OED established a system whereby the general public sent subeditors 4 3 6 cards that contained prospective words used in the context of a sentence with a citation. The whole process nearly became unmanageable, with the first edition of the dictionary not completely published until 1928. A similar project begun in Germany in 1852 by Jacob (1785–1863) and Wilhelm (1786–1859) Grimm, the *Deutsches Wörterbuch*, was not completed until 1960. In many cases, slang or cant, "the vulgar tongue," is left out of these dictionaries. So despite their comprehensiveness—the OED has over 475,000 words—you still may not find the word you are looking for!

*Sources:*James Rettig, "The *Jewel in the Crown*: The *Oxford English Dictionary*," in James Rettig, ed. *Distinguished Classics of Reference Publishing* (Phoenix: Oryx Press 1992), 180–197; K. M. Elisabeth Murray, *Caught in the Web of Words: James A. H. Murray and the Oxford English Dictionary* (New Haven: Yale University Press, 1977).

New Dictionary of American Slang. Robert L. Chapman, ed. New York: Harper & Row, 1986. (rev. ed. of *Dictionary of American Slang*. Harold Wentworth and Stuart Berg Flexner, comp., eds. New York: Crowell, 1975.)

Online Etymology Dictionary, http://www.etymonline.com/ (accessed January 1, 2006).

Statistical Resources

Adding clarity and specificity to your argument, statistics can be invaluable in providing data to support your argument without your having to crunch numbers yourself or do involved quantitative research. Finding just the right statistic to support your theory, however, can be challenging.[10] Thinking about what source may have produced or collected the statistics you desire will often help you figure out how to search for them. Because they need to count things and people for fiscal and political reasons (to tax and disburse monies, for instance) governments and organizations are frequent compilers of statistics. Thinking about the likely producers of the data and then searching your library's online catalog as well as *Worldcat* (a large database of library holdings worldwide, see Chapter Three for a full explanation) for publications produced by those agencies is useful. Look for those agencies as authors in your library's catalog and then limit your search by words in the subject "statistics." (See Chapter Three for a fuller explanation of search techniques.) For instance, use a country as an author and then limit your search by statistics in the subject to find a statistical abstract for that country. For example, searching for "Brazil" as an author and then limiting your results by words in your subject "statistics" you might find in your library *Anuario Estatistico do Brasil*, an abstract of statistics which began publication in about 1908.[11] Basic statistics such as population, crime rates, health statistics and such do exist for most countries; but be aware that you may not be able to find the exact statistic you desire for the time you need. Remember that while these figures provide a wealth of information about how a government categorizes its citizens, they may disguise much about the citizens themselves. Use statistics in conjunction with other primary sources.

Selected Statistical Resources

Abstract of British Historical Statistics. B. R. Mitchell. Cambridge: Cambridge University Press, 1962.

Annuaire Statistique de la France. Paris: Institut National de la Statistique et des Etudes Economiques, 1878– Annual.

China Facts and Figures Annual. Gulf Breeze, FL: Academic International Press, 1978– Annual.

ADS History (Great Britain), http://hds.essex.ac.uk/gbh.asp (accessed January 1, 2006).

Historical Statistics of Canada. F. H. Leacy, ed. 2d ed. Ottawa: Statistics Canada, 1983, http://www.statcan.ca/english/freepub/11-516-XIE/sectiona/intro.htm (accessed January 1, 2006).

Historical Statistics of Japan. Tokyo: Nikon Tokei Kyokai (Japan Statistical Association), 1987–1988. 5 vols. Also available on CD-ROM (Tokyo: Japan Statistical Association, 1999).

Historical Statistics of the States of the United States: Two Centuries of the Census, 1790–1990. Donald B. Dodd, comp. Westport, CT: Greenwood, 1993.

Historical Statistics of the United States, Millennial Edition: Colonial Times to the Present. Washington, DC: Government Printing Office, 2006. Also available online through subscription. (New York: Cambridge University Press, 2006).

How Much Is It Worth Today? http://eh.net/hmit/ (accessed January 1, 2006).

International Historical Statistics: Africa, Asia, and Oceana 1750–2003. B. R. Mitchell. 5th ed. New York: Palgrave Macmillan, 2003.

International Historical Statistics: The Americas 1750–2000. B. R. Mitchell. 5th ed. New York: Palgrave Macmillan, 2003.

International Historical Statistics: Europe 1750–2000. B. R. Mitchell. 5th ed. New York: Palgrave Macmillan, 2003.

Russia and Eurasia Facts and Figures Annual. Gulf Breeze, FL: Academic International Press, 1993– Annual.

Second Abstract of British Historical Statistics. B. R. Mitchell and H. G. Jones. Cambridge: Cambridge University Press, 1971.

Statistical Abstract of the United States. Washington, DC: GPO, 1879– Annual. Vols. for 1878–1902 issued by the Bureau of Statistics, (Department of the Treasury; 1903–1911 by the Bureau of Statistics, (Department of Commerce and Labor; 1912–1937 by the Bureau of Foreign and Domestic Commerce; 1938– by the Bureau of the Census.

United States Historical Census Data Browser, http://fisher.lib.virginia.edu/collections/stats/histcensus/ (accessed January 1, 2006).

Book Reviews

Understanding others' thoughts on a work, whether published in the 1800s or last week, can help you with your own comprehension and critical assessment of the work's significance. Book reviews provide relatively short critical overviews and discussion of a book's thesis and analysis. More than a mere summary, a review in a scholarly journal will usually compare the text of the book to related titles in the field as well as assess the primary evidence in the notes and bibliography of the book. As stated earlier, an important part of the practice of history is discussion of ideas with one's peers. Book reviews are one way of furthering that discourse. As a new scholar, book reviews can help you to develop a critical eye while reading your research materials. You can compensate, a bit, for your lack of depth of knowledge on a topic by reading others' commentaries. Book reviews also help you understand the intellectual climate of a time period. Looking at book reviews of Margaret Mead's *Coming of Age in Samoa* (1928) tells us as much or more about Western civilization's views on adolescence in the late 1920s as it does about indigenous cultures in Samoa.[12]

The easiest way to locate book reviews of a specific title is to use an index. Begin by determining the first publication date of your book. This tells you if you will be able to use an online index or if the book was published before the coverage of most online indexes. If you will be using a print index, knowing the publication date of your book tells you in which volume to begin searching for references to reviews. For print indexes, be sure to check several years as a book review may take some time to show up in an index. In addition to the sources listed below, most periodical indexes listed in Chapter Four will also index book reviews. There will be some overlap in journal coverage between periodical indexes, but in each case, some unique journal titles will result from your search. Most of the sources below will require you to look up the journal that contains the review. In some cases, the full text may be attached to an online index. *H-Net* (http://h-net.org) contains reviews of select history titles online.

Selected Sources of Book Review Resources

Book Review Digest. New York: H. W. Wilson, 1905–. *Book Review Digest Plus*. New York: H. W. Wilson, 2002–. Also available online through subscription. http://www.hwwilson.com/Databases/brdig.htm (accessed March 26, 2006). Fee based online.

Book Review Index. Detroit: Gale Research, 1965–.

Combined Retrospective Index to Book Reviews in Humanities Journals, 1802–1974. Evan I. Farber, ed. Woodbridge, CT: Research Publications, 1983–1984. 10 vols.

Combined Retrospective Index to Book Reviews in Scholarly Journals, 1886–1974. Evan I. Farber, ed. Arlington, VA: Carrollton, 1979–1982. 15 vols.

H-Net Reviews, http://www.h-net.org/reviews/ (accessed January 1, 2006). History net is the online organization of professional historians. One section of the website contains book reviews.

Directories

Directories simply provide addresses and contact information for associations, historical societies, archives, and libraries that you may need to contact about some aspect of their collections. Also, you may need to find out further information about programs or grants that these types of institutions offer. Many organizations now have websites, so you can often find online information previously available only in printed directories.

Selected Directories

Directory of History Departments, Historical Organizations, and Historians.
    Washington, DC: American Historical Association, Institutional Services
    Program, 1990–, http://www.theaha.org/pubs/directory/index.cfm
    (accessed January 1, 2006).
World of Learning. London: Europa Publications 1956–. Included in each
    country's listing are addresses and contacts for museums, historical
    organizations, and universities.

Using the Internet as a Reference Resource

The Internet is perhaps the best and the worst reference resource available
today. It has the ability to connect you to an established authority in the field
you are studying as well as to a self-proclaimed authority who knows very
little. There are several websites set up to act as reference sites, containing
the online equivalent of a shelf of printed reference resources. *Bartelby.com*
(www.bartelby.com) contains a plethora of sources such as the *Columbia
Encyclopedia* (2001), the *Encyclopedia of World History* (2001), *Roget's II:
The New Thesaurus* (1995), *Bartlett's Familiar Quotations* (1919), and
more. You can search all of these sources simultaneously or individually for
information. The problem with many free services such as *Bartelby* is that
these online replicas of print sources are often out of date. Other websites,
such as the *Internet Public Library* (http://www.ipl.org), offer a different approach by attempting to operate as a library, linking to websites as well as to
volunteer researchers who will answer your questions, just as a librarian
would. Some of these services answer questions mechanically, based on how
you have asked the question and how others have asked that question, using
natural language processing, for example, Ask.com (http://www.ask.com).
Still other services will also provide answers from real people, for a fee, such
as the one offered by *Google* (http://answers.google.com/answers/main).
This service, staffed by many screened and trained researchers, allows you to
ask a question, say how much you are willing to pay for information, and wait
to see if anyone will answer. You are not guaranteed a response. These services
can be useful, but remember that your public, school, and college libraries can
usually provide better information for free. Your local library and librarian also
are attuned to your professors', teachers', and classes' needs in ways these
other services are not. Many libraries offer numerous ways to contact a librarian. You could send an e-mail message, engage in an online chat, initiate an In-
stant Messaging session or make a telephone call, or simply walk into the library. Personalized, professional service can be delivered to you quickly and
efficiently in a variety of ways, but you must first make your needs known.

Case Study ▪ Using Reference Resources to Understand Herodotus

You will use several types of reference resources to find out about people and places mentioned in a passage of Herodotus' *Histories*.

Herodotus Histories Book V.49.1–51.3

49. . . . . It was in the reign of Cleomenes that Aristagoras the despot of Miletus came to Sparta; and when he had audience of the King (so the Lacedaemonians say) he brought with him a bronze tablet on which the map of all the earth was engraved, and all the sea and all the rivers. Having been admitted to converse with Cleomenes, Aristagoras spoke thus to him: "Wonder not, Cleomenes, that I have been so zealous to come hither for such is our present state that the sons of Ionians should be slaves and not free men is a shame and grief to ourselves. . . . Now, therefore, we beseech you by the gods of Hellas, save your Ionian kinsmen from slavery . . . I show you; . . . therein . . . lies that Susa where lives the great king, and there are the store houses of wealth and; take that city, and you need not fear to challenge Zeus for riches. . . ." 50. . . . . Cleomenes asked Aristagoras how many days' journey it was from the Ionian Sea to the king. Till now, Aristagoras had been cunning and fooled the Spartans right well; but there he made a false step; for if he desired to bring the Spartans way into Asia he should never have told the truth. . . . (From *Herodotus: With an English Translation by A. D. Godley*. London: William Heinemann, 1921)

What can you learn from this passage using reference resources?

- *Herodotus*. Greek historian who lived c. 484 to sometime after 424 B.C.E. Considered the "father of history," he published his *Histories* about Greece's defeat of the Persian king Xerxes around 445 B.C.E. (From Edwin Yamauchi. "Herodotus." *Encyclopedia of Historians and Historical Writing*. Chicago: Fitzroy Dearborn, 1999.)
- *Aristagoras, tyrant of Miletus*. Deputy tyrant of Miletus c. 505–496 B.C.E. who initiated the Ionian Revolt against the Persians. (From "Aristagoras," in *Oxford Classical Dictionary*. 3d rev. ed. London: Oxford University Press, 2003.)
- *Miletus*. Modern-day Turkey, coastal city of Asia Minor. Largest city in league of 12 Ionian cities. Destroyed by Persians in 494 B.C.E. Rebuilt and allied with Athens in the Peloponnesian War. In 499 B.C.E. the Ionian Revolt was started here by one of the cities ex-tyrants, Aristagoras. (For a long, detailed archaeological history, see G. Kleiner, "Miletos" in

Princeton Encyclopedia of Classical Sites. Richard Sitewell, ed. Princeton, NJ: Princeton University Press, 1976, and Percy Neville Ure, "Miletus," *Oxford Classical Dictionary*. 3d rev. ed. London: Oxford University Press, 2003.)

- *Cleomenes*. King of Sparta, reigned c. 520–490 B.C.E. Vigorous in his interference in foreign affairs, especially concerning Athens. Refused to support the Ionian Revolt. (From Paul Anthony Cartledge, "Cleomenes, (1)I *Oxford Classical Dictionary*. 3d rev. ed. London: Oxford University Press, 2003.)

- *Susa where lives the great king*. City in Italy. In this case, you would want to use the bibliography attached to the article in the *Oxford Classical Dictionary* and look up the book *The Royal City of Susa*, R. Tallon, ed. (1992). (From "Susa," in *Oxford Classical Dictionary*. 3d rev. ed. London: Oxford University Press, 2003.)

If you wanted to set the context for the entire account, you might wish to read the following articles:

Shalom Perlman. "Interstate Relations." In *Civilization of the Ancient Mediterranean*. Michael Grant and Rachel Kitzinger, eds. New York: Scribner's, 1988.

J. K. Anderson. "Wars and Military Science: Greece." In *Civilization of the Ancient Mediterranean*. Michael Grant and Rachel Kitzinger, eds. New York: Scribner's, 1988.

Also unique to classical and many literary texts are commentaries, line-by-line, or passage-by-passage discussions of the text. In this case, you may want to consult the following:

W. W. How and J. Wells. *A Commentary on Herodotus: With Introduction and Appendices*. London: Oxford, 1967.

NOTES

1. Norman J. G. Pounds, "Steelmaking," in *Dictionary of the Middle Ages*. (New York : Scribner's, 1982).
2. "Table F3: Passenger Traffic on Railways," in *International Historical Statistics: Europe, 1750–2000*, 5th ed. B. R. Mitchell. (New York: Palgrave Macmillan, 2003).
3. Thomas S. Noonan, "Kizil-Koba Culture," in *The Modern Encyclopedia of Russian and Soviet History*, Joseph L. Wieczynski, ed. (Gulf Breeze, FL:

Academic International Press, 1976), now titled *The Modern Encyclopedia of Russian and Soviet and Eurasian History*; Ronald Storey, "The Aristocracy of Inherited Wealth," in *Encyclopedia of American Social History*, Mary Kupiec Cayton, Elliott J. Gorn, Peter W. Williams, eds. (New York: Scribner's, 1993); Richard C. Martin, ed. *Encyclopedia of Islam and the Muslim World*. (New York: Macmillan Reference USA, 2003); Barbara A. Tenenbaum, ed. *Encyclopedia of Latin American History and Culture*. (New York: Scribner's/ Macmillan Library Reference USA, 1996); Neil Schlager, ed. *St. James Encyclopedia of Labor History Worldwide: Major Events in Labor History and Their Impact* (Detroit: St. James Press/Thomson Gale, 2004); Joseph R. Strayer, ed. *Dictionary of the Middle Ages* (New York: Scribner's, 1982).

4. *NetLibrary Reference Center*, http://legacy.netlibrary.com/help/reference _center.asp (accessed January 1, 2006).

5. Mary Beth Norton, ed. *The American Historical Association's Guide to Historical Literature*, 3d ed. (New York: Oxford University Press, 1995).

6. Tony H. Chang. *China During the Cultural Revolution, 1966–1976: A Selected Bibliography of English Language Works* (Westport, CT: Greenwood, 1999).

7. Emily Ballew Neff, "Copley, John Singleton," *American National Biography*. (New York: Oxford University Press, 2000), http://www.anb.org/articles/17/17-00180.html (accessed January 1, 2006).

8. Jane Turner, ed. *Grove Dictionary of Art. From Renaissance to Impressionism: Styles and Movements in Western Art 1400–1900* (New York: St. Martin's Press, 2000). Also available online, *Grove Art Online*, http://www.groveart.com (accessed January 1, 2006).

9. Meyer Galler. *Soviet Camp Speech* (Jerusalem: Magnes Press, The Hebrew University, 1994).

10. For the flexibility of statistics, see Darrell Huff, *How to Lie with Statistics* (New York: Norton, 1954).

11. Ministerio da Agricultura, Industria e Commercio, Directoria Geral de Estatistica, *Anuario Estatistico do Brasil* (Rio de Janeiro: 1908–).

12. Margaret Mead, *Coming of Age in Samoa: A Psychological Study of Primitive Youth for Western Civilization* (New York: W. Morrow & Company, 1928).

3

Finding
Monographs and
Using Catalogs

WHAT YOU WILL LEARN IN THIS CHAPTER:
- how to define and identify a book or monograph
- how to use subject headings and understand how they differ from keywords
- how to select your search terms and enter them in an online catalog
- how to use an online catalog and the contents of its records effectively

---

What Is a Book? The Changing Nature of Monographs

A book is a book is a book, right? The traditional form of the book, a narrative with an introduction, a body or discussion, and a conclusion, is still the major, standard means of scholarly, and even nonscholarly, written communication. This linear layout of text allows the author to lead the reader through the evidence, arriving together at one or several conclusions. However, this format has not always predominated. Originally, written texts were papyrus rolls that were rolled and unrolled and read aloud to groups. Little attempt was made to draw the text to a conclusion. Instead, the purpose of the document was to record the facts and the story so the narrative could be publicly debated and discussed. Around the fourth century C.E., the codex became the form we now recognize as a book. With pages to turn, the layout and purpose of the printed text changed radically as a result. With the establishment of universities around the twelfth century C.E., monographs (or books) evolved to contain interior organization, such as chapters and subheadings, identifiable named authors (instead of the unnamed "eyewitness" or no attribution at all), documentation or footnotes, and an essay structure that includes a conclusion. Further, this structure encouraged the book to become more tightly focused on a single subject, allowing the author to lead an individual reader through an argument.

With the advent of the Internet, in the era that has been called the "late age of print," these assumptions as well as the linearity of the book text have been challenged by alternative methods. A website seldom leads visitors to a single conclusion. Rather, much like the early papyrus rolls, such a site must satisfy a number of different types of users. With its use of hypertext, a website allows every visitor to experience the site in a unique way, drawing his or her own conclusions, and no longer comes to a single end.[1] This phenomenon will be further described in Chapter Ten on presenting your research.

Historians and publishers are experimenting with new ways of delivering scholarship digitally. A substantial number of monographs are now being replicated in electronic form, and a few are being issued only in electronic form. Such subscription projects as *NetLibrary* (http://www.netlibrary.com/) and the *History E-Book Project* (http://www.historyebook.org/) provide online access to databases of monographs selected by participating publishers. In each case, you are able to search through subject headings to retrieve monographs, just as with a library catalog. The added value of each of these services is that you can also search for keywords throughout the *full text* of all of the works contained in each of the databases. The texts in the *History E-Book Project* are all historical in some manner, whereas *NetLibrary* contains a finite number of e-books from all disciplines, including history. Although these projects are expanding, you as a researcher will still primarily be dealing with traditional printed monographs, found through a library catalog.

When Are Books the Right Choice for Information?

In this chapter, we look at books, or monographs, as secondary works, those materials that provide analysis or interpretation of primary sources and other secondary works. You will need both books and journal articles to know the field of research for your topic, as well as to enter into the discussion with other historians and to discover what research has not been done and how your unique topic fits into this large body of research. To omit important works from experts in the field is a serious flaw in your research. However both forms, book and journal, serve a particular role. Monographs and journal articles will be the core secondary sources for your research. While many types of books are published, the standard type of secondary book in history is the scholarly monograph. Intended for an academic audience, it is an extensive, in-depth discussion of a topic by an individual, or perhaps coauthors. The scholarly monograph is distinguished from other types of books, such as a collection of essays by many scholars around a single topic, a collection of essays by one scholar on many topics, or a *feschrift* (a collection of essays in honor of a scholar). Because of their length, monographs are able to thoroughly examine large topics intensively, make extended arguments, and raise many questions around a diversity of issues. By comparison, a journal article is usually limited in page length and, thus, often narrower in scope, distilling the major points of an argument. In fact, journal articles are an excellent source for organizing and focusing a paper topic. Chapter Four will discuss the uses of journal articles further. In monographs, the secondary works cited as documentation in the bibliography or the notes tend to be at least several years old, even when the book has just been published. Journal bibliographies tend to be more up-to-date, in part because journals publish articles more frequently and because journal article topics tend to be more cutting-edge. Scientists tend to publish their groundbreaking research in professional journals since the information is deemed time-sensitive and can be disseminated much more quickly in journals than in monographs. Sometimes historians publish parts of their research in journal articles before writing a larger analysis in the form of a book. For instance, Mary Kupiec Cayton wrote an article in *The American Historical Review* in 1987 entitled "The Making of an American Prophet: Emerson, His Audiences and the Rise of the Culture of Industry in Nineteenth Century America." [2] Two years later, she published a book, *Emerson's Emergence: Self and Society and the Transformation of New England, 1800–1845*, which in part considers not only the role Emerson's public lectures had on his reception but also his audiences' influence on his message. [3]

Using the building blocks of primary resources, a book will take a broad topic that spans a number of years and examine its impact in-depth. For instance, the book *Tempered in the Revolutionary Furnace: China's Youth in the Rustication Movement,* by historian Yihong Pan, examines the experiences of a few dozen of the seventeen million urban, educated, middle school Chinese students sent to the countryside to experience rural life and boost agricultural production between 1953 and 1980.[4] Using oral histories and other primary sources, coupled with secondary works including other historians' interpretations of the period, Pan provides new insights into the reasons many of these students as adults led protests in 1978 and 1979 that forced the Chinese government to abandon this program. Compared to an article, the topic of the book is fairly broad, covering a number of years and incidents. Yet, in its 284 pages, it is able to explore the topic of the rustication movement comprehensively, in a way that a journal article could not.

How to Use a Book Artfully

While it is often best to read a book cover-to-cover to examine the author's argument from inception to conclusion, it may be that the information or analysis you need is contained in a portion of the text. In order to determine this, always use the book's navigational tools to the fullest. Look carefully at the table of contents. In it, you will find information that will help you identify the parts of the book that are most relevant to your research. Many online catalogs now include a book's table of contents in the catalog records,

---

Box 3.1 Defining and Refining Your Topic Using Monographs

As you do your research, you will be constantly refining and defining your topic. Because monographs usually cover such a breadth of subject, you will use them to begin to see the directions your topic can take. Remember, you cannot fully examine every aspect of a topic in the pages allotted by your teacher or professor or the website space you will design. To help focus your topic and your thoughts, reflect on how the book was classified in the *Library of Congress Subject Headings* (LCSH). LCSH was designed to classify knowledge in connection to other ideas and may help you to understand the context of your topic in a broader scheme of knowledge. Also look at tables of contents in some of the books that best fit your topic to see how the material is subdivided. Further, look at the bibliographies at the end of what you think are key chapters and select some of those sources to read. Called "snowballing" or "pillaging," you are looking into the same writings, or discourse, that other historians have examined to research your topic. This is an excellent way to begin to build a list of resources, to test the viability of your broad topic, and to find out what has been published on a subject. However, do not limit your research to sources you find in bibliographies. This could limit your research by recycling and duplicating the same ideas, preventing you from discovering new theories. Be sure that you also look for monographs and journal articles through catalogs and periodical indexes.

so in some cases you can browse the contents without even having the book in your hands. The index at the back of the book is also an important navigational tool. A good index can pinpoint the information you seek. Even if only one chapter of the book pertains to your research, it is still wise to read the introduction and conclusion of the book as well as the section in which you are interested. This will help you to understand the fuller context of the material you select and the author's overall argument. To find monographs, you need a catalog, usually a library's catalog.

Finding Monographs and Using Catalogs

A catalog, in its most basic definition, is a description or listing of a collection of materials. A library catalog simply provides a description of that library's holdings and other materials to which the library has access, including book titles, journal titles (but not their contents, e.g., not the individual article titles), video titles, children's book titles, government documents, special materials (like manuscript collections) and even CD-ROMs, electronic monographs, full-text journals, and sometimes websites. (Some libraries do omit certain types of material from their online catalog, such as U.S. government documents.) The online catalog may also contain materials that are full text, online, which can be delivered to your desktop and are not physically located on the shelves in, or even owned by, your library. If you are unsure about the contents of your library's online catalog, ask your librarian.

Online catalogs provide a number of ways to access a library's collection. Understanding how the catalog operates will reduce your research time as well as help you discover some amazing information. Skillful use of a library's catalog will provide you with quality resources for your paper or project. Inability to make that catalog give you results that match your topic can add to your research time and frustration.

In any library catalog (online, the printed card drawers, or even those catalogs of library collections that are printed in book form), you can search for a book by the subject, author, or title. For author, you must search by the last name first. For titles of monographs, you must search for the beginning of the title, dropping the initial article but using all of the articles within the title. For instance, the book *Women of the Pleasure Quarters: The Secret History of the Geisha*, by historian Lesley Downer, would be searched by entering "women of the pleasure quarters" in the title field.[5] You need not be concerned with capitalization of words.

Keyword vs. Subject Searching

When you begin your research, your search strategy will take the form of either a keyword or a subject search.

- *Keyword.* A keyword search makes an *exact* match of the word that you type in the search box. The computer will be searching through some combination of the titles, notes, table of contents, and subject fields of the catalog record. For example, if you search for the keywords "children and history," the results *might not* include a book entitled *A History of Childhood in the Middle Ages* because you asked the catalog to look for the word "children," not "childhood." You would only find that book listed in your results if the word "children" was listed somewhere in the online record, maybe in the subject headings field.

- *Subject.* A subject search performs a search through an approved, controlled list of words and phrases. Most college and university library catalogs use the *Library of Congress Subject Headings* as a source for approved subject headings. Using a standard word or set of words, a subject heading, helps collect synonymous words and ideas under one term or phrase. Using the same example, a search for the word "child" would not find monographs using the word "teenagers." However, you could select the subject headings "Adolescence–United States–History" or "Teenagers–United States–History" or "Children–United States–History" and focus your topic, as well as eliminate those monographs that would technically meet your criteria but not be on your topic. In this case, you need to select the word or phrase that the *Library of Congress Subject Headings* list uses, which is not always precisely the wording you would naturally use.

Guessing a subject heading can be difficult, so unless you are confident of a subject heading, it is best to begin with a keyword. The subjects that have been assigned to that particular book are listed in the catalog record for the monograph and hyperlinked at the bottom of the screen of the catalog record.[6] The smart research strategy is to look at several relevant monographs in your results list and search on the subject headings that are attached to these records. Begin to manipulate these subject headings. Many times these subject headings will suggest additional terms and concepts. Often, they will pinpoint a smaller, highly relevant number of monographs and other materials. Using these subject headings will save you time in your research and will produce more efficient, precise results.

Box 3.2 *Library of Congress Subject Headings*
and Controlled Vocabulary

The *Library of Congress Subject Headings* are a voluminous set of
books (some libraries have these online) containing agreed-upon
words and phrases used in most university catalogs that describe library materials. Designed to classify and arrange the materials in the
Library of Congress in 1898, these subject headings merely attempted
to classify knowledge into standardized words and phrases so that catalog librarians would always use the same word or words to describe
materials instead of choosing synonymous words and phrases. For example, the terms "doctor," "physician," and "surgeon" can be synonymous, yet "doctor" can also mean "professor." While other countries
use the Library of Congress system, other classification schemes are
also in use. This standardizing of subject headings is called "controlled vocabulary." You will encounter similar systems in many periodical indexes.

Source: Lois Mai Chan. *Still Robust at 100: A Century of Library of Congress Subject
Headings. LC Information Bulletin* Aug 1998, http://www.loc.gov/loc/lcib/9808/lcsh-
100.html (accessed August 2, 2005).

Keyword Searching

When doing a keyword search, it is best to begin by performing a little word
association. In the example above, you would need to think of both the
words "children" and "childhood." You might even come up with other related words, such as "youth" or "adolescent" or "adolescence." You must
remember that the computer and the catalog are not doing the thinking for
you. It is your job to think of associative or synonymous words. In fact, it is
possible that the first words that come to mind are not the words that best
reflect your topic. Language is political, and point of view is critical. For instance, if you were doing a subject search for monographs and materials on
the Vietnam War, you would find that "Vietnam War" is not a subject heading because, technically, the United States never declared war on Vietnam.[7]
The correct subject heading is "Vietnamese Conflict 1961–1975." If you do
a keyword search in the catalog, common language in book titles often
refers to this "action" as the "Vietnam War" and that solves, in part, your
dilemma. Then, as suggested above, you could use the subject headings in
the catalog records of the monographs you have identified to find more
monographs and other materials in the catalog.

To compensate for this problem of exact word matching in keyword searching, you can use two techniques: truncation and Boolean searching. The use of truncation, sometimes called "wild cards," allows you to search for many forms of a word in one step. In our example of children and childhood, you could enter the search with an asterisk (*) (sometimes $ or ! is used) after the root word, in this case "child*." Using "child*" will give you the results "child," "children," "childhood," "childlike," and "children's." However, it will not give you results that contain the words "teenager" or "youth." To expand your search to include those terms, you would want to use Boolean searching and use "and" or "or" between words that are synonymous. For instance:

child* or youth or teenage*

Then combine this idea with history using a Boolean "and" to combine concepts

(child* or youth or teenage*) and history

This particular search is too broad, unless you are in a smaller library, so you would want to limit it further by adding a geographic specification, for instance, "United States." Chapter Four on journals will discuss Boolean searching in more depth as it is especially useful in searching periodical databases.

Subject Searching

Sometimes, you may know the exact subject heading and will want to begin with a subject search. If you are looking for biographies or histories of a place, the subject headings of these works are automatically the person or place name. For example, to find biographies on Mahatma Gandhi, you would look under his last name, "Gandhi," as a subject. The subjects on Gandhi will then be subdivided by categories such as "Bibliography," "Correspondence," "Philosophy," and "Views on life." Individuals who have pseudonyms are now found under both their commonly known names, for instance "Twain, Mark," as well as their real names, "Clemens, Samuel Langhorne." It is always best to check both names. Likewise, buildings and historic sites will be found under their names. Cities, provinces, states, countries, and other political divisions will have subject headings under their names. For instance, the subject heading for Berlin is "Berlin (Germany)." Usually, political divisions are followed by their larger political unit (e.g., cities by province or state) and then have other subject subdivisions attached after that (e.g., "Sydney N.S.W.," for New South Wales in Australia, or Kuala Lumpur Malaysia"). However, many times the subject headings are complex: the subheadings that directly follow the main heading in the string do not always include the word "history" even though that is what the results will cover. Additionally, when "history" is a subheading, it is not always the first subheading in the string. Some examples are shown below:

British–Travel–Germany–History–20th century

Interfaith marriage–Germany–Berlin–History–20th century

Architecture–England–London–History

Households–England–History–To 1500

In the example above, if you had entered "England–History–Architecture" in the subject field in your catalog, you would not get any search results because the order of the words matters in subject headings. One way around this problem is to do a simple subject search and then to limit the results by selecting words in the subject "history." This allows the word "history" to appear in any order in the string of the subject subheadings. The subject headings above are regular ones found in the *Library of Congress Subject Headings* list. However, there are "form subject headings" that can be commonly applied to many subjects. Limiting by these can be useful in narrowing your topic. You can use words for types of reference resources, such as encyclopedias, statistics, etc., as subheadings to find those kinds of sources. Limiting by other common words in the subject, or subject subheadings, is also productive, for example, "Africa, West–Civilization" or "Palestine–Antiquities." A selected list is shown below.

Social life and customs	*Politics and government*	*Antiquities*
Civilization	*Bibliography*	*Philosophy*
Pictorial Works	*Description and Travel*	*Dictionaries*

How to Read an Online Catalog Record

Even though online catalogs have different appearances, the essential information in your library's online catalog record is the same as that contained in every other online catalog record worldwide. The book has a bibliographic citation, that is, the author, title, publisher, and place and date of publication. In addition to these, the record will indicate the number of pages as well as any illustrations (illus. or ill.) or maps. Sometimes the table of contents is included. At the end of the record are the Library of Congress subject headings assigned to this particular book. Also on the screen somewhere are an indication of the location of the book, the call number, perhaps the floor number or library (if your campus has multiple libraries) in which the book can be found, as well as information on whether the book is on the shelf or checked out. The call number will begin with either a letter or a number. Most academic libraries use the Library of Congress call numbering system, an alphanumeric system (a combination of letters and numbers) that organizes materials into broad, related categories. History is often classed under "D" (world history), "E" (U.S. history), and "F" (Latin American, local U.S., and Canadian history). However, because of the interdisciplinary nature of history, you will find history monographs with call numbers throughout the Library of Congress classification system. For example, *Branches of Heaven: A History of the Imperial Clan of Sung China*, by John W. Chaffee (Cambridge, MA: Harvard University Press, 1999), has the call number DS751.3.C35 1999 for Chinese history. The full Library of Congress classification system can be seen at http://www.loc.gov/catdir/cpso/lcco/lcco.html. See Figure 3.1 for an example of a local catalog record.

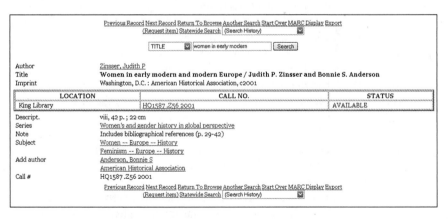

Figure 3.1. An example of a record from a local library's online catalog. Along the left side of the screen, the record fields are clearly labeled. When you search for a keyword, typically, you are searching through the words in the author, title, imprint, series, note, subject, and added author fields. When you search for a subject, you are searching only in the subject field. Notice also that the subjects are hyperlinked allowing you to directly search those subjects. *Record courtesy Miami University (Ohio) Libraries.*

Box 3.3 Book Reviews and Discourse

Book reviews are a useful tool for focusing your thoughts as well as discovering what others think about the quality of other historians' work. This form of discourse, in which the writers of the reviews are critiquing the author's research and argument, will help you not only to understand what the author intended with his or her work but also to look at the execution of the book's argument and its research flaws. A book review will compare one particular work to other important works on a similar topic, not only leading you to other resources but also helping you to judge their quality.

Finding Monographs and Using Catalogs Outside of Your School

While you should begin your research at your college or university, you may find that you have selected a topic in which your library's collection is not very strong. You may need to look at other libraries' collections and request materials through interlibrary loan. Interlibrary loan is a service offered by most libraries that allows monographs and other types of materials to be borrowed between libraries, as well as providing photocopies of journal articles from other libraries' collections. This process may involve fees, takes time, and can have borrowing restrictions, so be sure to consult your librarian.

The greatest challenge is identifying those monographs and sources that you need and that your library does not own. Many libraries subscribe to a database called *Worldcat* that is used by libraries worldwide to share cataloging. In essence, when you use this database you are searching the holdings of thousands of libraries simultaneously. However, resist thinking of *Worldcat* as a database that contains *every* book *ever* written, in *every* library. It does not. But it is a huge database that can help you find resources that you could never find otherwise.

Because *Worldcat* is an online catalog, it functions in much the same way as your library's online catalog. It contains monographs, titles of journals (not their contents), motion pictures and videos, sound recordings, electronic resources, manuscripts, and even selected Internet sites that libraries have deemed quality resources for inclusion in their catalogs. You can search by author, title, keyword, and subject. You can limit by type of publication (serials, sound recordings, monographs, even Internet resources), date, language, and format (large print, microform). Some of the terminology is different (author phrase and subject genre phrase, e.g.), but you are basically doing the same kind of searching as in your home library's online catalog. You should begin with an advanced search option. Of the three choices of search level you are given in *Worldcat* (basic, advanced, and expert), the advanced level gives you the most guidance and will help you to know exactly where in *Worldcat* (author, title, subject, or other limits) you want to search. In the tabbed navigation bar toward the top of the *Worldcat* screen, select Advanced Search, if that is not your library's opening search screen.

In the search portion of the screen, you will find a series of boxes in which you will enter your search words. Next to these boxes are drop-down boxes from which you will select where you want *Worldcat* to look for your search terms. Because librarians also use this database, it will have some unusual choices in these drop-down boxes. For instance, under the general category of Subject, you will have the choice of Subject Phrase, Named Person Phrase, and Genre/Form Phrase, to name a few. Under the general category of Title, you will have the choice of Title Phrase, Series Title, and Series Title Phrase. Although the differences are significant to librarians, do not worry about them as a beginning researcher. When searching for a title, author, subject, and keyword, use the general category (such as Author) and you will be searching all the variations listed in the drop-down box. Remember, though, the distinction between keyword and subject still applies in *Worldcat*, as in any database you will search. If you wish to limit your search, you can check the boxes that appear below the main search box and limit your search by date, by serial (journal, magazine), etc. You can choose to rank your results by relevance or by date (currency). The default is relevance, meaning that items judged as more appropriate for your topic by the database are ranked highest. Sometimes that means the items have more of the keywords in the record or in the subject field instead of the title field (Fig. 3.2).

Your results in *Worldcat* will be grouped by type of resource, with monographs, serials, archival materials, maps, etc. all collected separately toward the top of the screen in tabs. An individual record also has the same functionality as your local online catalog, with the subject headings hyperlinked. The results will tell you what libraries own your item. Keep in mind that, unless it is a manuscript, your library probably will be able to request a copy from another library through interlibrary loan (Fig. 3.3).

If you know that a particular library is strong in a particular subject area, you may want to search that library's online catalog directly. For instance,

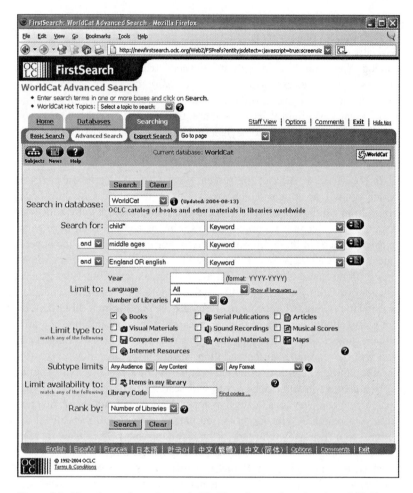

Figure 3.2. The advanced search page in *Worldcat*. Screen shot taken from OCLC's FirstSearch® service. *Used by permission of OCLC. FirstSearch® and* Worldcat *are registered trademarks of OCLC Online Computer Library Center, Inc.*

if you live in Ohio but are doing a project on the history of the Pacific Northwest, you may want to use the University of Washington's catalog to locate materials because it is a research library and its collection of Northwest regional history would be more substantial than that in most Midwest libraries. Most universities allow outside users to search their catalogs. One of the lists of catalogs below will enable you to link to and search other libraries' catalogs.

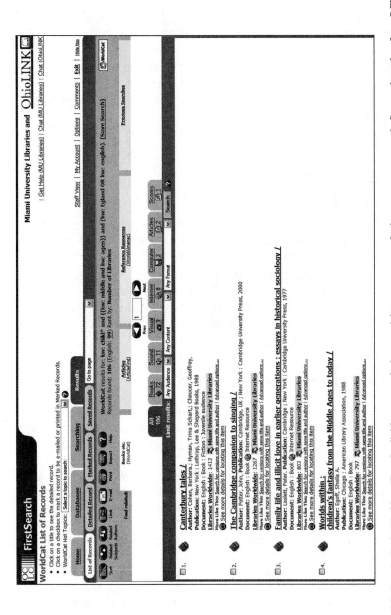

Figure 3.3. Results list in *Worldcat*. The tabs divide your results by material type so you can further narrow your search. Screen shot taken from OCLC's FirstSearch® service. *Used by permission of OCLC. FirstSearch® and Worldcat are registered trademarks of OCLC Online Computer Library Center, Inc.*

SEARCH TIPS
1. Connect to your library's online catalog.
2. Begin with a keyword search.
3. Find a title of a good source which reflects your topic.
4. Look at the subject headings linked to the record.
5. Use those subject headings to connect directly to that heading in the catalog.
6. Check *Worldcat* or another library's catalog.

Sources for Catalogs

- Your library's catalog

- *Worldcat*. FirstSearch, http://www.oclc.org/firstsearch/content/worldcat/ (accessed August 2, 2005). Large online catalog of libraries, primarily in the United States but also in other countries around the world.

- *Libweb*, http://sunsite.berkeley.edu/Libweb/ (accessed August 2, 2005). Online listing of over 6,600 homepages from libraries in over 115 countries. Easier to navigate than *Libedex* (http://www.libdex.com/), with indexes by type of library (public, academic, and national) as well as by country.

Where Else Can I Find Monographs?

The online catalogs above are your best source for finding monographs. There are, however, a few other ways to find monographs. You can use an online collection of e-books or subject bibliographies that will lead you to printed monographs.

If your library has access to the *ACLS History E-Book Project* (http://www.historyebook.org/), you may look in this collection to find useful monographs. The project contains over 1,000 secondary work monographs, with new titles added each year. Titles are selected by a board of learned societies, university presses, and the University of Michigan for their importance to the field, availability for electronic conversion, and fit with the existing e-book collection. While 1,0001 monographs may seem large, it is still a small collection compared to a library, so it may not contain anything on your topic. To search this database, use the subject or title search in the Basic Search, located under the Search button on the navigation bar on the main and most underlying pages. Only if you have a unique word or phrase should you use the full-text search at this point because you will find massive amounts of text and many references to books if you are not very specific with your search. As the project increases in size, you may find many of the monographs it contains useful and the advanced methods of searching, Boolean searching for instance, more useful.

You might think of searching the major online booksellers for research monographs, expecting them to behave like a catalog and a library. Although many scholars are big fans of Amazon.com and BarnesandNoble.com, these are not library catalogs. Their subject control is spotty. Their keyword searching is not fine-tuned, often leaving you with a plethora of results you did not want and without the results you need. The ranking of results is based on an odd algorithm that has more to do with sales and popularity than with your search criteria or appropriateness to your subject. After all, their purpose is to sell books. Also, you have no idea what is in the database, what is missing from the database, and why. They have an interest in telling you what is in print and out of print, but they cannot match the collection of a long-established library. Finally, the companies all have excellent customer service, but they do not have trained librarians who are connected with your professors and courses, have knowledge of the discipline of history, or know exactly what you need.

Case Study ▪ Finding and Using Monographs: The Spread of Islam in Western Africa

Your topic is the spread of Islam in western Africa, including the nations of Mali and Ghana. In this part of the world, Islam spread through the work of missionaries and traders, rather than through conquest.

1. Begin by dividing your topic into concepts.

CONCEPT I	CONCEPT II	CONCEPT II
Islam	West Africa	Missionaries
		Traders

2. List associative or synonymous words.

CONCEPT I	CONCEPT II	CONCEPT II
Islam	West Africa	Missionaries
Islamic	West African	Traders
Muslim	Mali	
	Ghana	

3. Decide which words will best reflect your topic and do a keyword search. Use truncation (*).

islam* and (mali or ghana)

and limit by words in the subject "history."

4. Select a relevant source in your results list: *Islam in West Africa: Religion, Society, and Politics to 1800*. Nehemia Levtzion. Altershot, UK: Variorum, 1994.

5. Look at the subject headings assigned to the book and use some to search for more monographs and materials on your subject. "Islam–Africa, West–History".

6. You may wish to combine the terms "missionaries" and "trade" in some way with either or both "West Africa" and the two country names to gain a broader insight on the influences of these two activities.

7. If you need more information, do the same or similar searches in *Worldcat* or another library's catalog.

NOTES

1. Jay David Bolter, *Writing Space: Computers, Hypertext, and the Remediation of Print*. 2d online ed. (Mahwah, NJ: Lawrence Erlbaum Associates, 2001), 77–120.

2. Mary Kupiec Cayton, "The Making of an American Prophet: Emerson, His Audiences and the Rise of the Culture of Industry in Nineteenth Century America," *American Historical Review* 92 (June 1987): 597–620.

3. Mary Kupiec Cayton, *Emerson's Emergence: Self and Society in the Transformation of New England, 1800–1845* (Chapel Hill: University of North Carolina Press, 1989).

4. Yihong Pan, *Tempered in the Revolutionary Furnace: China's Youth in the Rustication Movement* (Lanham, MD: Lexington Books, 2002).

5. Lesley Downer, *Women of the Pleasure Quarters: The Secret History of the Geisha* (New York: Broadway Books, 2001).

6. These are linked to other records with the same subject heading in the catalog. The catalog will perform a search on this subject heading and generate a list of those items assigned the same subject heading.

7. In catalogs, librarians will alter subject headings as historical usage changes. For example, over the years the subject heading for African Americans has changed from "Negroes" to "Afro-Americans" to the current "African Americans."

4

Finding Journals, Magazines, and Newspapers: Using Indexes

WHAT YOU WILL LEARN IN THIS CHAPTER:

- the differences between journals and magazines and when to use each
- the differences between general and subject-specific periodical indexes
- how to select an appropriate periodical index
- how to search in a periodical index

This chapter will teach you, first, to define and distinguish journals, a staple of historical secondary research, from magazines and newspapers and, second, how to find, use, and construct a search in a specialized periodical index. Locating appropriate and on-topic journal articles can be difficult because there are so many and because their indexing is not as easily accessible as a book. Not listed in online catalogs, individual journal articles must be discovered through selecting one or more of the appropriate specialized indexes for your field of study.

Using a Journal Article Artfully

Journals are essential components of your secondary works and of the historical discourse and scholarly exchange of ideas. Often, they provide a more focused examination of some aspect of your topic and supply a very specific, detailed bibliography that will point you to other valuable secondary works and primary sources. Not just an essential part of secondary source research, journal articles can offer an excellent model for the structure of your paper. Look at the introduction and conclusion and then examine how the subsequent paragraphs line up the discussion and evidence to support the ideas presented in the beginning. By the end of the article, did the author achieve her or his purpose? Because of their length, journal articles must be well organized, keep their argument focused, and have the proper mix of evidence, both primary and secondary sources, directly related to the topic. For instance, in the article "Is Smoking Permissible in Islamic Law? Answers from Arabic manuscripts in the Beinecke Collection," Felicitas Opwis uses three seventeenth- and eighteenth-century Arabic primary source legal texts supported by scholarly secondary works to examine tobacco's use in secular society and the conflicts between secular and religious authorities. Likewise, Scott Levi in his article "The Indian Merchant Diaspora in Early Modern Central Asia and Iran" uses selected contemporary published travel accounts from the sixteenth to the twentieth centuries to examine the roles Indian agents had on the foreign economies of central Asia, Iran, the Caucasus, and much of Russia where they lived and worked.[1] In both of these cases, the topics are focused and the primary source evidence is limited and focused. The primary and secondary evidence is interwoven and directly related. The bibliographies from journal articles such as these can lead you to primary and secondary sources that you may wish to use in your research. You may wish to provide a different interpretation, but the bibliography will help you discover sources that you may not have known about.

What Are Periodicals (or Journals or Magazines)?

You will want to make sure you can distinguish a journal article from other types of periodical articles. Periodicals, another important type of secondary work, are materials that are issued "periodically," that is, more than once, usually at regular intervals—for example, quarterly or monthly. This category includes journals, magazines, newspapers, and annual reviews. Unlike full-length books, periodicals include short articles that focus on narrower, more concise subjects. Because they are published frequently, periodicals generally contain up-to-date, timely research. Each type of periodical has a very specific intent:

- *Journals.* The audience for journals is academics, specialists, and researchers in the field on which the journal focuses. Often, this is a narrow audience. Some examples are *Oral History Review, Early American Review*, and *Nineteenth Century Feminisms*. Journals provide one way for researchers to communicate with one another. The language in these articles can be quite specialized and sometimes less accessible to general readers. The frequency of publication is usually quarterly or less. Articles generally contain many footnotes and a bibliography of sources.

- *Magazines.* Magazines are read by the general public and reflect the culture, ideas, and politics of the day. The language used is more accessible to all levels of readers. These publications usually contain images and either report or provide summary information on research or topical issues. They usually contain little or no documentation, such as footnotes, bibliographies, or complicated tables of statistical evidence. Magazines are usually published more frequently than journals: monthly, weekly, or twice-monthly. Magazines are considered primary sources because they report on events and reflect public attitudes and opinions.

- *Newspapers.* Newspapers are generally published daily with the intent to report the happenings of the city, town, and nation in which they are issued. They view the world's news from their particular location or perspective or publish stories from a worldwide wire service or other newspapers for news from other places. Frequently, newspapers do in-depth reporting on issues relevant to their particular area. Newspapers are usually more suited for primary source research. However, some major newspapers will provide background information for historical events and places that may prove useful to your research. They contain little documentation, such as footnotes, bibliographies, or complicated statistical evidence.

- *Annual Reviews.* Published once a year, annual reviews attempt to survey the evolution of scholarship within a discipline during a particular year. Annual reviews are more prevalent in the sciences and the harder social sciences, such as psychology and education, than in the humanities and history.

For the purposes of this chapter, most of our discussion will revolve around journals and magazines, the resources that index them, and the ways they can be used for historical research.

Journals vs. Magazines

Journals are the medium that scholars use most often to communicate new research findings, ideas, and conclusions. By contrast, magazine articles are written by journalists trained in research and reporting techniques who are not typically specialists in any one specific discipline. These journalists gather their information by interviewing professional researchers and practitioners and by researching and reading some of the scholarly journal articles that you might use for your own research. For example, if a journalist were writing an article on Martin's Hundred, a plantation located outside of Jamestown, Virginia, and chartered sometime around 1618, he or she could consult journal articles and books written about the settlement as well as interview the archaeologists who excavated the site. The journalist would not actually be doing the archaeological digging and interpreting of the artifacts found. The archaeologist might publish his or her findings in a journal. Upon completion, the journalist's article, which is a synthesis and explanation of the investigation, goes to an editor, who makes corrections and adjustments and decides the final shape the article will take. This editor also has the power to decide whether or not to publish the finished article. While the journalists and editors at history-oriented magazines like *Smithsonian* and *National Geographic*, as well as more general magazines such as *Time* or *Newsweek*, are educated and informed, their purpose is to speak to a broad, general audience interested in history and other subjects, as opposed to a specialized and high-level audience. This does not mean that these magazines are inaccurate. It just means that their content is often too general to be used as the basis of your secondary historical research.

The physical appearance of magazines is also distinctive. Glossy photographs adorn the cover as well as the interior. Such magazines contain paid advertisements, helping them remain affordable to a wide readership. Their subjects are broad and their headlines sometimes even sensationalized. For instance, an article about mummies in a glossy magazine called *Archaeology* was titled "The Well Dressed Dead," while a related article in a journal called *European Neurology* was titled "Myotonic Dystrophy in Ancient Egypt." [2]

Journal articles have a very different purpose and, consequently, different identifying qualities. The publishing process is structured so that scholars review, or referee, other scholars' work. Scholars submit articles to a journal, often on a specialized, focused topic. The articles are then sent to several other experts in the field to read and judge the accuracy of the scholarship. These readers, or referees, will often suggest changes or point out flaws in the authors' reasoning or arguments. The editor of the journal then decides whether to send the article back to the author for revision or to reject the article for publication. A journal article is judged by its scholarly merit as opposed to its ability to appeal to a mass audience. For an example of the review process, see the March 1997 issue of the *Journal of American History*, where the journal printed all of the reviewers' comments with the original journal article.[3]

Journal articles, like scholarly monographs, have notes, either at the bottom of each page or at the end of the article. Detailed charts, diagrams, and tables of statistics are sometimes included in this documentation. This material, along with other cited primary sources, serves as the foundation of the author's research and findings and supports the author's analysis and interpretation. The material is presented in such a way that other scholars can integrate those sources into their own research. In this way, historical research can be cumulative. The chart below outlines the differences between journals and magazines.

JOURNALS	MAGAZINES
Signed article by author. Author is usually scholar in the field who is an expert.	*Articles often unsigned. Articles often written by journalists or nonspecialists in the field about which they are writing.*
Language is technical and aimed at a specialized audience, usually those who also study in the field. Uses the jargon of the discipline.	*Language is simpler and aimed at a general audience. Anyone who is interested could read and understand the article.*
Documentation in the form of notes, footnotes, and bibliography.	*Has no documentation but often mentions sources in the article.*
May contain complicated charts and graphs.	*Glossy photographs and simple charts or graphs.*
Articles have been through a scholarly referee process, selected by a journal editor, and reviewed by specialists in the field.	*An editor has approved articles.*

In December 2003, the traditional format of the journal was subjected to an experiment in the *American Historical Review*. The journal published an article solely in electronic format that sought to rearrange the traditional journal article from its usual linear format to a more hypertext layout. This journal article, "The Differences Slavery Made: A Close Analysis of Two American Communities," challenged that linear format by operating much like a web page that allowed the readers to jump between introduction, summary of argument, points of analysis, and methods. [4] The introductory "page" (Fig. 4.1) was similar to a journal article but enhanced by hyperlinks to tables, maps, and footnotes. The methods section provided a description of the technical aspects of the data collection and production of the maps. In a separate tool bar section, readers could select evidence, historiography (bibliography), and tools. These three sections are essentially bibliographies of the primary and secondary sources used in the articles with links to the actual sources and links back to the text in the analysis. This article could be read in the traditional manner or broken into bits and reassembled, in whatever manner readers desire to build their own understanding of the argument. Although complex, it is the beginning of electronic scholarship. The American Historical

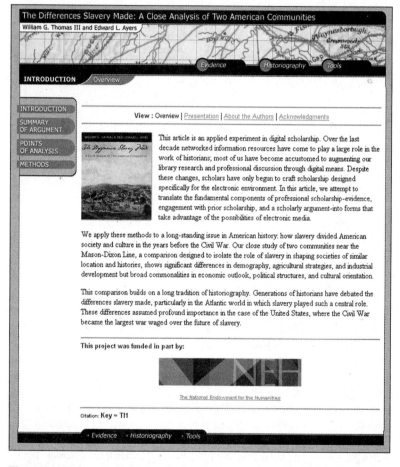

Figure 4.1. Front navigation page of "The Differences Slavery Made: A Close Analysis of Two American Communities," an electronic scholarly article published in the *American Historical Review*. *Used by permission of the* American Historical Review, *William G. Thomas III, and Edward Ayers.*

Association has encouraged other scholars to publish electronic projects. You can view these projects at http://www.historycooperative.org/ahr/elec-projects .html, if your library has a subscription to the *History Cooperative*.

Journals usually include letters to the editor as well as book reviews, two modes in which scholars continue their discussion and historical debate. Letters to the editor comment on previously published articles and the quality of their historical interpretation, while book reviews, written by other researchers who are working in the field, evaluate the scholarly contributions of published books.

Commentary Periodicals

A third type of periodical exists, which is relevant to historical research and falls between the categories of journal and magazine. This periodical is often considered a journal even though it has the characteristics of a magazine. Sometimes called "commentary magazines," these publications contain political and social commentary that offers insightful analyses of events and issues. For example, you can read an article written in *The Nation* on March 15, 1919, by playwright, critic, and actor Robert Benchley entitled "The Making of a Red," a parody on the hostility toward supposed communists in the entertainment community. The 1919 article is a primary source. In the January 21, 2002, issue, the same magazine published an article by Benjamin Barber, political philosopher, author, and former advisor to President Clinton, entitled "Beyond Jihad vs. McWord: On Terrorism and the New Democratic Realism." The article, as with Barber's book of a similar title, takes a capitalistic market focus while contrasting liberals' international interdependence approach with conservatives' war response to terrorism. Usually, the articles contained in these publications are opinion pieces or personal accounts based on learned analysis of primary and secondary source material. Often written by well-known and respected political commentators, these are definitely not the kind of glossy, mainstream articles that journalists write for general magazines. Because they reflect the conservative, liberal, and moderate political and social opinions of the time in which they were written, these commentary articles can also be primary sources and can be used in your own research to document certain areas of thinking and debate. Many of these magazines have been published since the early part of the twentieth century and provide a useful intellectual history of Western philosophical thought.[5] Yet, because they are opinion-based and usually contain few footnotes, charts, or other scholarly documentation, they may not be considered scholarly journal articles by your professor.

Even so, these articles can be excellent sources for you as you conduct your research. You can use them to help clarify and formulate your own opinion, as well as to understand other points of view and other approaches to your research topic. Some examples of commentary magazines/journals follow.

TITLE	DATE OF FIRST PUBLICATION	POLITICAL POINT OF VIEW
The Nation	1865	Liberal
The New Republic	1914	Liberal
The Progressive	1929	Liberal
The American Spectator	1932	Conservative
National Review	1955	Conservative

The Role of Newspapers in Secondary Historical Research

Newspapers tend to be most useful as primary sources, reporting events and other primary source data. Chapter Six contains information on using newspapers as primary sources. However, newspapers can occasionally be used as secondary works when they publish stories on historical sites, anniversaries of historical events, or new archaeological discoveries that provide background information. In these cases, the newspaper is functioning more like a magazine than a journal, lacking documentation and complicated charts and graphs. Older newspapers are most often used as primary sources, providing evidence about people and events in particular eras. Before using a newspaper article as a secondary source, check with your professor.

How to Find Articles: Designing a Search and Using an Index

The best method for finding journal articles is to use a periodical index. If you have mastered your college or university's online catalog, learning to use a print or online index is just an expansion of that knowledge. Most major indexes to journals and magazines, as well as the journals you seek, are not available for free via the Internet. (An exception is the *Directory of*

Open Access Journals, which provides free full-text access to scholarly journals, see http://www.doaj.org. None of these journals' contents is likely to be included in a periodical index, nor will they be accessible through an Internet search engine.) However, many journals, subscription or free, can be accessed, usually online, through your library's subscription. Because of the interdisciplinary nature of history, a wide variety of potentially relevant indexes is available. In the section below, you will learn how to find the right index for your topic.

Before using a periodical index, it is best to make sure your topic is well-defined and organized and that you understand the relationship of the components or concepts of your topic. As you know, journal articles are often more specific than books, so the terminology that you use to search for those articles must be more precise than the words you used in your online catalog search. Divide your topic into its essential ideas or concepts and play word association with those ideas. For instance, if your topic is "the participation of women in the scientific revolution of the sixteenth through eighteenth centuries in Europe," you would think of the following search terms:

CONCEPT I	CONCEPT II	CONCEPT III	CONCEPT IV
Women	*Science*	*Sixteenth century*	*Europe*
		Seventeenth century	
		Eighteenth century	

Remember that the way *you* may think of your topic is not the way *others* may describe it. You will want to think of synonyms and other words that are close in meaning and reflect your topic. You will want to list similar concepts together, even if you do not use all of these words in your search. For instance, in this example, you may think of the following:

CONCEPT I	CONCEPT II	CONCEPT III	CONCEPT IV
Women	*Science*	*Sixteenth century*	*Europe*
Gender	*Math*	*Seventeenth century*	*France*
Female	*Mathematics*	*Eighteenth century*	*England*
	Botany	*Early modern*	*Great Britain*
	Chemistry	*Enlightenment*	*Germany*
	Physicians		*Italy*
	Surgeons		
	Medicine		
	Physics/Physicist		

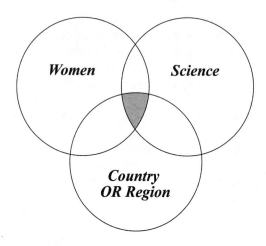

Figure 4.2. Boolean diagram that represents your concepts divided into sets.

Once you have made your list, think about the association of concepts, one to another. Must the list of journal articles you are seeking include *all* of the concepts you have listed or just a couple? You are beginning to use Boolean logic when you think this way, creating sets and linking them with the Boolean operators, either "and" or "or" (see Fig. 4.2).

The Venn diagram in Figure 4.2 would be written as a search statement in a database, as follows (capitals do not matter):

women and (scientist* or botan* or chem* or surgeon* or physician*) and (europ* or england or english or france or french)

Use parentheses to group your concepts and synonyms, or sets, together. This tells the database how to search for your topic, considering first the words in the parentheses and then connecting the concepts as a whole. You would enter this search statement as a keyword search in a periodical index or database. Remember, the * (sometimes $ or ! in some databases) is truncation or a wild card, as you learned in Chapter Three. When doing a keyword search, you must account for spelling variations and forms of your words. So, "botan*" will find "botany" as well as "botanist," "botanical," "botanically," etc. Your search statement has asked for some form of the word "botany" (or "surgeon," "physician," "england," "europe" or "european") to appear in the database record. The article listings that result must have one of the words in their title, abstract, or subject headings/descriptors corresponding to each of the sections of your search statement that you have separated by an "and." Results of this search will include articles such as the following:

Weber, A. S. "Women's Early Modern Medical Almanacs in Historical Context." *English Literary Renaissance* 33 (Oct 2003): 358–402.

Jacob, Margaret C., and Dorothee Sturkenboom. "A Women's Scientific Society in the West: The Late Eighteenth-Century Assimilation of Science." *Isis* 94(2) (2003): 217–252.

Findlen, Paula. "Becoming a Scientist: Gender and Knowledge in Eighteenth-Century Italy." *Science in Context* 16 (2003): 59–87.

Tosi, Lucia. "Marie Meurdrac: Paracelsian Chemist and Feminist." *Ambix* 48 (July 2001): 69–82.

Klairmont-Lingo, Alison. "Women Healers and the Medical Marketplaces of 16th-Century Lyon." *Dynamis* 19 (1999): 79–94.

Evenden, Doreen. "Gender Differences in the Licensing and Practice of Female and Male Surgeons in Early Modern England." *Medical History* 42 (April 1998): 194–216.

The better your search statement, the more useful your resulting list of journal articles will be. Throughout the course of your research you will refine and even repeat the same search in the same and in different databases. The more you learn about your topic, the more you will recognize relevant articles that previously seemed irrelevant.

SEARCH TIPS
1. Divide your topic into concepts.
2. List synonyms and associated terms.
3. Indicate relationships of terms using the Boolean operators "and" or "or."
4. Use parentheses to make associations in your search statement.

Using an Online Database: *Historical Abstracts* and *America: History and Life*

Search statements can be used in a variety of online periodical databases. You can use general periodical indexes, such as *Academic Search Premier*, *Reader's Guide to Periodical Literature*, or *Infotrac*, and/or specialized, discipline-centered indexes such as *Historical Abstracts* or *America: History and Life*. (An Internet search engine generally will not index journal articles, the exception being *Google Scholar*. *Google Scholar* is not truly an index and has many limitations, which are discussed later in this chapter.) General indexes try to cover a large number of journal articles in a wide variety of disciplines, including history. Often, these general indexes include magazines as well. Because of this "one size fits all" approach, the subject headings lack professional terminology that an index designed for practitioners in the field would have. Using a specialized index will not only save you time but also directly connect you to the appropriate historical literature, eliminating the guesswork as to the quality and acceptability of the article and publication. The search engine *Google* is attempting to create a separate index of academic materials useful for research called *Google Scholar*. Part of the problem with *Google Scholar* is that the coverage is limited to the connections it can make with publishers and others that supply full-text articles, preprint articles, and conference publications. This conglomeration of resources is only a small portion of what is available and may miss key resources for your topic just because *Google* did not have a contract with that publisher. Search results are arranged on a sort of cited-reference search, what others have cited in their works, as well as the usual *Google* ranking algorithm. *Google Scholar* is not able to provide the subject control or the limiting capabilities that a subject-specialized index can. This often results in huge numbers of results. It is a suitable resource if you need just a couple of items and your search strategy is not too complex or too general. While it may still prove to be a powerful research tool, as yet it is not adequate for an advanced researcher. With the exception of some of the contents of *Google Scholar*, articles are not freely available on the Internet. Even *Google Scholar* does not completely link to full text. You must rely on your library to pay for online journal subscriptions.

For more precise and quicker results, use a subject-specialized index designed for history journals that uses the language of historians, such as *America: History and Life* or *Historical Abstracts*. These indexes cover "modern" history, roughly 1450 to the present, but also include articles with background information prior to the fifteenth century. *America: History and Life* indexes U.S. and Canadian history, while *Historical Abstracts* covers the rest of the world. Both are multilingual but with a heavy preponderance of English-language articles and have been issued in both electronic/online as well as paper formats. The focus of this discussion is on the electronic version. However, the print versions are also very useful if that is what your library has. Do not ignore these indexes at your library just because they are not electronic! Print or electronic, they are the best way to connect to the scholarly, historical journal literature.

Like most indexes and catalogs, these indexes have both keyword and subject access. The subject access is not as useful as in many other indexes because subject assignment can be imprecise and somewhat irregular. As a novice searcher, it is best to use the keyword search and your newfound Boolean searching skills. Both of these indexes have extra features that will help you refine your search even more.

Entering a Keyword Search in *Historical Abstracts*

Enter your search in the keyword box, using * for truncation as necessary (Fig. 4.3). A keyword search statement for the concept of mothers and family in World War II era Germany could look like the following:

(nazi* or german*) and (mother* or famil*)

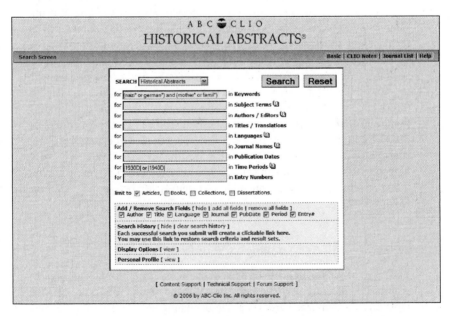

Figure 4.3. Main search screen for *Historical Abstracts*, one of the major online databases for history. Enter your search in the Keyword box. A unique feature to this database as well as its companion database, *America: History and Life*, is the ability to restrict the time period the articles cover. In the example above, we have limited by the decades of the 1930s amd 1940s. ©*2006 ABC-CLIO. Reprinted by permission, all rights reserved.*

Your search is asking for articles that include some form of the word "nazi" (including "nazis," "nazism," etc.) and "mother" or "family" (including "mother," "mothers," "motherhood," "family," and "families") in the title, subject, or abstract fields. Your search, however, is also asking for the more general concept of "german" (as well as "germans" or "germany") and some concept of "family" or "mother." Remember that in Boolean logic, your search results must only match one word from *each* set. Articles may have this broader view of family history in Germany without specifically including some form of the word "Nazi" and thus not directly covering the period of the 1930s and 1940s. In this case, you may want to restrict your search by the time period the articles cover (e.g., the 1930s and 1940s), specify that they be written in English (unless you read German), and perhaps further limit the type of publication to journal articles. Remember, if this does not produce the desired results, you must approach the search from a different viewpoint. Always have at least one other way to think about your topic. A librarian and your professor will help you with this.

When using *Historical Abstracts* or *America: History and Life*, it is important to know about these databases' unique feature that allows you to further limit your general search by historical period. As discussed above, your search may yield articles outside of your desired time period. Using only the search words "german*" and "women*" could provide you with articles on the eighteenth and nineteenth centuries, when what you need is information about the 1930s and 1940s. This is when the special date-limiting feature in *Historical Abstracts* can be useful. You can limit your results by decade or by century (or even by exact date, although that is usually too restrictive). In this example, you would select the decades 1930s and 1940s. Selecting the entire twentieth century would be too broad as you would retrieve results that would examine German family life before the rise of the Nazis, as well as in East Germany during the Cold War (Fig. 4.4).

What You Will Get: Looking at Your Results

The result of your search will be a list of citations, customized to your search criteria. In the case of *Historical Abstracts*, the results are listed with the most recently published articles at the beginning and the oldest at the end. Each citation consists of the basic information needed for you to locate the article as well as an abstract, or summary, telling you what the article covers; a list of the descriptors/subject headings assigned to that article; the time period covered by that article; and the primary sources used to write the article (Fig. 4.5). In most cases, *Historical Abstracts* and *America: History and*

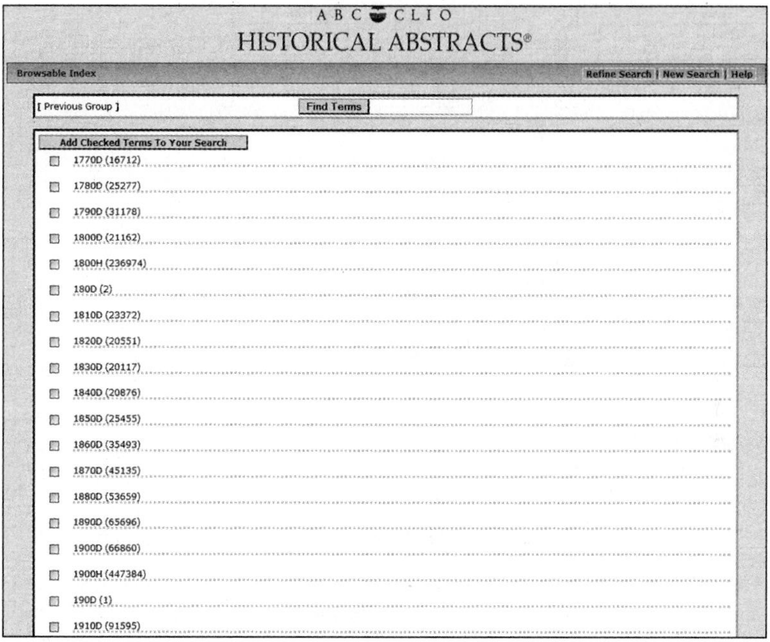

ABC CLIO
HISTORICAL ABSTRACTS®

Browsable Index   Refine Search | New Search | Help

[Previous Group]   Find Terms

Add Checked Terms To Your Search

- ☐ 1770D (16712)
- ☐ 1780D (25277)
- ☐ 1790D (31178)
- ☐ 1800D (21162)
- ☐ 1800H (236974)
- ☐ 180D (2)
- ☐ 1810D (23372)
- ☐ 1820D (20551)
- ☐ 1830D (20117)
- ☐ 1840D (20876)
- ☐ 1850D (25455)
- ☐ 1860D (35493)
- ☐ 1870D (45135)
- ☐ 1880D (53659)
- ☐ 1890D (65696)
- ☐ 1900D (66860)
- ☐ 1900H (447384)
- ☐ 190D (1)
- ☐ 1910D (91595)

Figure 4.4. Screen with listing of time periods. Clicking in a box restricts the focus of your articles to that time period. "H" restricts articles to the whole century and "D," to the whole decade. ©2006 ABC-CLIO. *Reprinted by permission, all rights reserved.*

Life will provide only the citation and abstract and you must locate the article. Your library may have links from the citation in these two indexes to the full text of journals. If not, you will need to look up the journal title in your library's online catalog to see if your library subscribes to it in paper, electronically, or not.

Part of being a good researcher is recognizing good results from your search. Good results fit your topic, are not too general, and are not too many in number to make it impossible to read them all within the time constraints of your research. If your search results in an extremely long list of citations, it probably means that your search terms were too broad. You may be willing to sort through hundreds of bibliographic citations to find those that reflect your needs, but it is better to refine your search using the special capabilities of these databases. As a general rule, between 25 and 50 citations is a good-sized list. Anything over 100–150 exceeds a manageable, browseable list.[6] With any larger yield, add additional search terms or limits to restrict your search statement or rethink your search terms entirely. In the case of

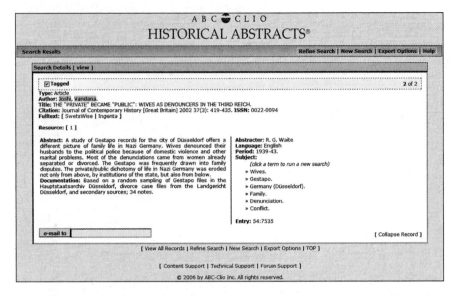

Figure 4.5. One of the results from your search. Provided is the title, author, and page numbers of the article as well as the name, date, and volume of the journal. An abstract, or summary of the article is also provided. The abstract might provide you with other terms and names individuals to search for. Notice the documentation note at the bottom. That tells you that the references consist of primary sources and what those primary sources are. ©2006 ABC-CLIO. *Reprinted by permission, all rights reserved.*

Historical Abstracts or *America: History and Life*, if you have too many citations, you can restrict your historical time period even further, add additional keywords to your search, or limit your results to those that are written in English or those written in the last 5 years. If you have too few results, you need either to expand your search by adding other search terms and linking them with "or" or to rethink your choice of terms and keywords. Perhaps there are better, more common, or more descriptive words that reflect your topic. Going back to your word lists when you divided your topic into concepts may help you think of other words to use. If you have tried to expand your search several ways, using new terms each time, it is possible that you have a unique topic on which little has been written. If you suspect this to be the case, you may wish to check with your professor or a librarian.

By its nature, history crosses many disciplines and many other disciplines publish articles on their own history. Searching in other related indexes may be useful. In historical research, or in fact any research, ignorance and poor search techniques are no excuse for not discovering the works of other scholars who have written on your topic. Look at Selecting Other Indexes, below, to find periodical indexes other than *Historical Abstracts* and *America: History and Life*.

Other Ways to Use an Online Index

Online indexes and databases have other features that may be helpful in performing your search. *Historical Abstracts* and *America: History and Life* both allow you to browse through author, article title, journal title, and subject sections of the database. This can be very useful if you are unsure about the spelling of an author's name or if an author uses initials instead of a first name. If you have selected a subject heading that is not used in the database, this feature allows you to select your search words from a list. Sometimes looking through a list of subject headings will suggest words or terms that had not occurred to you. Some indexes other than these two main history ones have more elaborate subject indexing systems, similar to the *Library of Congress Subject Headings* used in the online catalog. This kind of browsing search is often more effective in those indexes.

SEARCH TIPS
1. Use the keyword search.
2. Use truncation and Boolean search techniques.
3. Limit your search by time period.
4. Expand or limit your search to produce an acceptable number of results.
5. Use other special sections of the index as appropriate (author or title index or browse by author, title, or subject).

Selecting Other Indexes

Because history is such an interdisciplinary subject, you will often find periodical indexes aimed at other disciplines very useful for certain topics. Ancient historians use *L'Année Philologique* because *Historical Abstracts* and *America: History and Life* do not encompass the time period they study. If your topic looks at some aspect of medical history, in addition to the historical indexes discussed above, you would benefit by searching medical indexes like *Medline* (the free general public version is called *PubMed* [http://www.pubmed.gov]) or *PsychInfo*. A selected list of the subject-specialized indexes for other disciplines can be found at the end of this chapter. However, you can also look in your institution's online catalog to find out what is available, in print and possibly online. Generally, these indexes are listed in the catalog using very broad subject headings. In the medical example above, the subject heading to use is "Medicine–Periodicals–Indexes." If your topic is in social history, you might want to do a search in your online catalog under "Sociology–Periodicals–Indexes." You would find the subject-specific specialized index, *Social Sciences Index*. The subheading "Bibliography" is also sometimes used, for example, "Education–Bibliography–Periodicals."

E-Journals and Electronic Collections of Journals

While using a periodical index is perhaps the most efficient way to locate the best history journal articles, e-journals and collections of e-journals offer a possible second alternative when searching for scholarly articles. Digital collections such as *JSTOR* and the *History Cooperative* provide full text of many journal articles and allow for searching the full text. These collections, while useful, should not be confused with a periodical index. While many scholars think of them as an index, they have no subject access, only keyword searching. So, if article authors used the word "negroes" in their 1911 research and "Afro-Americans" in their 1977 research and "African Americans" in their 1990 research and you use the keyword search "blacks," you would likely miss significant scholarship. If your search words are too general, you will literally get thousands of results because you are searching through every word of the text of the articles. In the case of *JSTOR*, articles from the most recent 2–5 years are not included. Called the "moving wall," this means if you use JSTOR as an index and restrict your research to its contents, you will be excluding current scholarship. However, in the case of the *History Cooperative*, you can search only through recent issues of history journals. The purpose of *JSTOR*, *History Cooperative*, and other collections of full-text journals is to provide the full text of a selected list of journals based on a contractual agreement with the journal publishers. Sometimes this means the publisher will not allow the current issue(s) to be supplied or will not provide digitized versions of older issues. While the reasons for this are numerous, a periodical index simply provides a timely reference to the article's existence in a journal because none of these contractual or copyright issues affects the indexing of articles. But when you have a focused concept or unique term, searching these large full-text repositories can be beneficial. Also, access to a single journal title will allow you to browse quickly and efficiently through the table of contents for its issues. Browsing the table of contents of a very focused journal, for instance, *History in Africa* or *Renaissance Quarterly*, will allow you to catch topics related to your research that you may not have come across with your choice of keywords or subjects in your index searches. (Remember too that you can browse the table of contents of a print journal just as you can that of an online journal.) Your search strategy should integrate the search capabilities of both periodical indexes and full-text journal repositories. Both provide useful research articles.

Case Study ▪ Searching for Periodical Articles: Canton Trade System

Explore the following topic: the Canton Trade System (1760–1843), a series of trade regulations used by the Chinese to give domestic traders, known as *cohong*, an advantage over trading tea and textiles with such foreign companies as the British East India Company.

1. Divide your topic into concepts.

CONCEPT I	CONCEPT II	CONCEPT III	CONCEPT IV
China	*Trade*	*Europe*	*1760–1843*
		British East India Company	

2. Think of other related words.

CONCEPT I	CONCEPT II	CONCEPT III	CONCEPT IV
China	*Trade regulation*	*Europe*	*1760–1843*
Cohong		*European*	
		British East India Company	
		Britain	
		British	
		Portugal	
		Portuguese	

3. Select *Historical Abstracts* and perform a keyword search. Enter your search as follows:

(china or chinese) and trade

Remember $ or * or ! is truncation and will give you any number of characters after the root word. In this case, "chin*" is too short of a word and you will get too many results that would match your request but not be related to the word "China." After you receive your results, you will want to limit them by decades and probably by English, unless you read Chinese.

4. Aim for a list of not more than 70 results. A bibliography of 25–50 articles is ideal.

5. Depending on the quantity and quality of your results, you can add some of the words in your list above. For instance, at the time of the writing of this book, "Canton Trade System" yielded no results, but the phrase may be used by an author in the future. The word "Europe" was not used because articles would usually be written about a specific country, in this case probably Britain or Portugal. You could add those words if your results list is too large.

Selected Historical Indexes

These indexes apply to history and either cover time periods not covered by *America: History and Life* or *Historical Abstracts* or are created for a very specific time period of history.

Royal Historical Society Bibliography. 1900–, http://www.rhs.ac.uk/bibl/ (accessed September 2, 2005). Subject matter covers the Roman period of the British Isles published from 1900 to the present. Journal articles, books, and other publications, including *Annual Bibliography of British and Irish History. Writings on British History*.

L'Année Philologique; Bibliographie Critique et Analytique de L'Antiquité Gréco-Latine. Paris: Société d'édition "Les Belles Lettres." 1924–. Former title: *Dix Années de Bibliographie Classique* . . . 1914–1924. Also available online through subscription http://www.annee-philologique.com/aph/ (by subscription) and on CD-ROM titled *The DCB: Database of Classical Bibliography*. Atlanta: Scholars Press, 1995– (1974–1989). Index for classical history, literature, art, religion, folklore, early Christian texts, papyrology, and science. Access by subject, classical author, or text. Published in 1995, the CD-ROM covers publications from 1974 through 1989.

Diotma, http://www.stoa.org/diotima/ (accessed January 1, 2006). Index covering issues about women and gender in the ancient world.

TOCS-IN (Tables of Contents of Interest to Classicists), 1992–, http://www .chass.utoronto.ca/amphoras/tocs.html (accessed January 1, 2006). Searchable list of table of contents of journals in classical studies.

ITER: Gateway to the Middle Ages and the Renaissance, 1784–, http://www .itergateway.org/ (accessed January 1, 2006). Citations to books, journal articles, and essays concerning the Middle Ages and Renaissance studies.

Feminae: Medieval Women and Gender Index, http://www.haverford.edu/ library/reference/mschaus/mfi/mfi.html (accessed January 1, 2006). Index to journal articles, book reviews, and essays in books concerning gender issues but focusing on women and the Middle Ages. Excludes single-author monographs. Coverage is since about 1990 but not for all titles in the database.

Early Modern Women Database, http://www.lib.umd.edu/ETC/LOCAL/ emw/emw.php3 (accessed January 1, 2006). Web resources for Europe and the Americas ca. 1500–1800.

Viva: A Bibliography of Women's History in Historical and Women's History Journals, http://www2.iisg.nl/viva/ (accessed January 1, 2006). Multilingual bibliography from history and women's studies journals as well as selected articles from *Africabib*. Covers 1975 to the present.

Annual Bulletin of Historical Literature. London: Historical Association. 1911–. Also available online through subscription, http://www.abhlo .com/splash (accessed March 26, 2006). Annual bibliography, classified by historical subject and era, providing access to recent scholarship.

International Medieval Bibliography. Leeds, UK: University of Leeds, 1967–. Also on CD-ROM and available online by subscription, http:// www.leeds.ac.uk/ims/imb/index.html (accessed March 26, 2006). Covers all aspects of medieval life (450–1500) and culture, including literature, politics, history, religion, and philosophy. Lists articles, *festschriften*, conference proceedings, monographs, and collected essays.

Isis: Current Bibliography of the History of Science and Its Cultural Influences. Chicago: University of Chicago Press, 1913–. Index to history of science journals. Since 1975, Isis is included in the electronic database *History of Science, Technology, and Medicine*.

C.R.I.S.: The Combined Retrospective Index to Journals in History, 1838– 1974. Washington, DC: Carrollton, 1977–1978. 11 vols. Index to journals of interest to historians. Index is an enhanced keyword title list; that is, words in the title, with extra significant words added, are listed in a column.

Internationale Bibliographie der Zeitschriftenliteratur. Munich: K. G.
Saur, 1896–. Also available online through subscription. Covers general
academic journals in all fields but focuses on the social sciences and
humanities. Especially good for European-language journals.

Selected Periodical Indexes of Use to Historians

ABZU, http://www.etana.org/abzu/ (accessed January 1, 2006). Index to
books, journal articles, conference proceedings, book reviews, and
websites on the Middle East. Some are full-text and some, condensa-
tions of the texts.

Africa Bibliography. Manchester: Manchester University Press, 1984–.
Indexes articles, books, and essays. Arrangement is by country or region.

Africabib.org, 1974–, http://www.africabib.org (accessed January 1, 2006).
A compilation of a series of databases: *Bibliography of Africana Periodical Literature Database; African Women's Database; Women Travelers, Explorers and Missionaries to Africa 1763–2004: A Comprehensive English Language Bibliography; DISA: Digital Imaging Project of
South Africa—South Africa's Struggle for Democracy: Anti-Apartheid
Periodicals, 1960–1990.* Indexes books, journals, and conference proceedings. Access is by broad subject heading, keyword, or author/title.
You must select and search each database separately.

American Bibliography of Slavic and East European Studies. Urbana-
Champaign, IL: American Association for the Advancement of Slavic
Studies, 1956– Annual, http://gateway.library.uiuc.edu/absees (accessed
March 26, 2006). Annual comprehensive listing of journal articles,
books, book chapters, book reviews, dissertations, online resources, and
selected government publications produced in the United States and
Canada. Has full-record keyword searching. Also available in print.

Annual Egyptological Bibliography. Leiden: E. J. Brill, 1947–, and some
years available online. http://www.leidenuniv.nl/nino/aeb.html (1992–,
accessed January 1, 2006). You must search in each individual year and
then by very broad subject unless you wish to pay for a subscription.
Some libraries may subscribe.

Applied Science and Technology Index 1913, http://www.hwwilson.com/
(accessed January 10, 2006). Applied sciences, such as inventions, mechanical technology, industrialization, etc. Index to journal articles.

Art Abstracts. Bronx, NY: H. W. Wilson, 1929–. Also available online
through subscription, http://www.hwwilson.com/ (accessed January 10,
2006). Journal articles, yearbooks, and museum publications. Useful
for art histories, painting, and sculpture.

Arts and Humanities Citation Index. Philadelphia: Thompson ISI, 1977–, also available online through subscription, http://scientific.thomson.com/products/ahci/ (accessed January 1, 2006). All humanities, including history. Part of the *Web of Science.* Unique system that will also index footnotes. You can find a source that you like and trace what other articles have cited it. Online is a subscription.

ATLA Religion Database. Chicago: American Theological Library Association, 1960–, also available online through subscription, http://www.atla.com/products/titles/titles_rdb/titles_rdb_a.html (accessed January 1, 2006). Indexes journal articles, book reviews, and essays in religion and theology from the American Theological Society. Online is the union of two print indexes, *Religion Index One* and *Religion Index Two.*

BHI: British Humanities Index. London: Library Association, 1962–, also available online through subscription, http://www.csa.com/factsheets/bhi-set-c.php (accessed March 26, 2006). General humanities index with international coverage.

Bibliography of Asian Studies. 1969–, also available online through subscription, http://www.aasianst.org/bassub.htm (accessed January 1, 2006). Multilingual, nearly comprehensive index to all aspects of Asian studies. Includes books, reference works, conference and symposia proceedings, and journals.

Black Studies/Kaiser Index to Black Resources, also available online through subscription, http://biblioline.nisc.com/scripts/login.dll (accessed January 1, 2006). Bibliography and index of journals, magazines, newspapers, newsletters, pamphlets, reference books, and reports on black life outside of Africa and published 1948–1986. Created by the Schomburg Center for Research in Black Culture of the New York Public Library. Check with your library to see if they have a subscription.

EconLit/Economics Literature/Journal of Economic Abstracts. Evanston, IL: American Economic Association. 1963–, also available online through subscription, http://www.econlit.org/ (1969–, accessed January 1, 2006). Business and economics focus. Good for journals and papers on economic history.

Film Literature Index. Albany, NY: Filmdex, 1963–, also available online through subscription, http://webapp1.dlib.indiana.edu/fli/index.jsp (accessed January 1, 2006). Popular and scholarly film and television periodicals.

Geobase (1980–, accessed January 1, 2006) available through First Search by subscription, http://newfirstsearch.oclc.org/. Includes journals, books, monographs, reports, and theses in human and physical geography.

Historical geography is a field of study that would include information for historical research.

History of Science, Technology, and Medicine. Research Libraries Group, 1975–, http://www.rlg.org/en/page.php?page_ID5 192 (accessed January 1, 2006). Database that includes journal articles, conference proceedings, books, book reviews, and dissertations on the history of science and technology and allied historical fields. Electronic equivalent of *Isis Current Bibliography of the History of Science, Current Bibliography in the History of Technology, Wellcome Bibliography of the History of Medicine,* and *Bibliografia Italiana di Storia della Scienza.*

Index to Black Periodicals/G. K. Hall Index to Black Periodicals. Boston: G. K. Hall & Co, 1950–. Indexes the black magazine and journal press. This index has had various titles, so you may need assistance finding all of them in your library.

Lexis-Nexis. Dates vary by publication, http://www.lexis-nexis.com (accessed January 1, 2006). Full-text collection of newspapers and magazines. Many titles reach back into the 1970s. This is probably more useful as a primary source.

Medline/Index Medicus. Washington, DC: National Library of Medicine, 1953– /1879– http://www.ncbi.nlm.nih.gov/entrez/query.fcgi. (accessed March 26, 2006). Index to medical journals that would include the history of medicine. Online as PubMed

Middle East Abstracts and Index. Pittsburgh: Northumberland Press, 1978–. Also available on CD-ROM. Index that addresses all aspects of Middle Eastern life. Indexes journal articles, editorials, government documents, press releases, annual reports, speeches, news conferences, books, theses, and dissertations.

MLA International Bibliography. New York: Modern Language Association of America, 1956–. Also available online through subscription, http://www.mla.org/bibliography (accessed March 23, 2006). Literary criticism journals. Literature and history are often tied together.

Music Index. Detroit: Information Coordinators 1949–. Also available online through subscription, http://www.hppmusicindex.com/ (accessed May 15, 2006). Critiques of music, composers, and culture in journals.

OCLC Public Affairs Information Service (PAIS). 1913–. Also available online through subscription, http://www.csa.com (accessed March 28, 2006). Foreign affairs, political history. Index to journals, policy papers, and government, international, and organizational documents.

Philosopher's Index. Bowling Green, OH: Philosophy Documentation Center, Bowling Green State University. 1940–. Also available online through subscription, http://www.philinfo.org (accessed March 29, 2006). Index to journals, articles, books, and essays that would include ancient intellectual history.

Psychological Abstracts/PsychInfo/Psych Abstracts. Washington, DC: American Psychological Association, 1927–. Also available online through subscription, http://www.apa.org/psychinfo (accessed March 28, 2006). Journals, books, and book chapters on the development of psychology.

Women's Resources International. Baltimore: NISC, 1972–. Available online through subscription, http://www.nisc.com/factsheets/qwri.asp (accessed March 24, 2006). Broad range of women's issues, including history.

NOTES

1. Felicitas Opwis. "Is Smoking Permissible in Islamic Law? Answers from Arabic Manuscripts in the Beinecke Collection," *Yale University Library Gazette* (2001 Suppl): 178–184; Scott Levi, "The Indian Merchant Diaspora in Early Modern Central Asia and Iran," *Iranian Studies* 32 (Fall 1999): 483–512.
2. "The Well Dressed Dead," *Archaeology* 57 (May/June 2004): 16; Giacomo Cattaino and Laura Vicario, "Myotonic Dystrophy in Ancient Egypt," *European Neurology* 41 (1999), 59–64.
3. Some flaws are quite evident in the Organization of American Historians' brave experiment. The article itself was not a typical journal article. The nature of the article led some of the reviewers to guess the writer's identity, destroying the usual anonymity of the author during the review process. If you want to follow the debate, you can also see the article Adam Shatz. "Strange Fruit," *Lingua Franca* August 1997: 18–20. Still, the exercise is useful to understand how the review process works.
4. William G. Thomas III and Edward Ayers, "The Differences Slavery Made: A Close Analysis of Two American Communities," *American Historical Review* (December 2003), http://www.vcdh.virginia.edu/AHR/ (accessed January 1, 2006).
5. For a less historical list, see Arts and Sciences Library, University at Buffalo (SUNY), *Commentary and Opinion Journals*, http://ublib.buffalo.edu/libraries/asl/guides/jour_comment_opinion.html (accessed January 1, 2006).
6. Some historians will browse large numbers of search results before deciding on a topic in order to survey the breadth of research activity on a topic. But this is surveying the topic at a preliminary stage of your research process, when you are not really into the core of your focused research topic. If you are not careful, you can be distracted by too many citations.

5

Evaluating Your Sources

WHAT YOU WILL LEARN IN THIS CHAPTER:
- how to decide if the resources you have found are reliable and of good quality

---

Why Evaluate Your Sources?

Using reliable sources as a foundation for your research is necessary to achieve effective results and produce the best possible research paper or project. It is also essential if you want your work to be taken seriously by your professors and teachers, as well as other historians and researchers. In the previous chapters, you have learned how to find secondary sources for your research. This chapter explores how to distinguish quality research from substandard research, a crucial task for a researcher. This can be difficult when you are not an expert in the field and have not spent your life studying a particular geographic area or period of history. However, to be a critical researcher, you must reflect upon the accuracy, value, and authority of your sources.

This chapter provides the basic criteria and some solid research techniques to help you evaluate secondary works. Other chapters will offer more detailed criteria and guidelines for evaluating specific resources: primary resources and Internet resources in Chapters Six and Seven, maps in Chapter Eight, and images in Chapter Nine. While basic evaluation strategies can be applied to all types of resources, techniques used for evaluation of primary sources and Internet resources differ from those used for secondary works because for primary sources you must have some knowledge of the time in which they were created and for Internet resources you must have an understanding of website navigation and function.

Basic Evaluation Criteria

The list below summarizes a number of commonly used evaluation criteria and is not exclusive to history. Asking these questions will help you assess the value of your research.

- *Author authority.* Who is the author, and what is his or her affiliation? Most journal articles and many books have biographical information on the author at the bottom of the first page or at the back of the book. Is the author from a reputable institution or organization? Does that institution or organization reflect a political viewpoint through which the author's research might be filtered? Is the author a practicing historian in the topic of history about which he or she is writing? For instance, is this person a historian with a strong economic background in writing on the military–industrial complex and the Vietnam War, or is he or she a chemist by day with an interest in Vietnam-era economics? Perhaps he or she is not a scholar at all. Look at the publisher or website affiliation. In other words, consider why you should trust this scholar's authority. You can also look for other sources of biographical information on this individual by using some of the biographical sources listed in Chapter Two.

- *Audience and purpose.* Understanding the audience for which the author wrote the text is important. Is it for other scholars or practitioners who will understand the same professional concepts and terminology? Even if you do not yet fully understand what they mean, can you understand the context of such words and phrases as "neocolonialism" or "nihilism"? Can you tell by the language of the book or journal article that the target is a more general audience? If so, is the content scholarly enough to be useful for your research? Checking footnotes and documentation, below in this list, can help you make this determination. (See the section on footnotes and documentation, below in this list, for a better understanding of what you can learn from these citations.) Remember, the best way to understand an author's purpose is to read the introduction of a book or journal article, where the argument is usually spelled out quite clearly.

- *Accuracy and completeness.* Since you have already planned the search strategy you will employ as you consult your institution's online catalog, as well as one or two periodical indexes, you already have an idea about the scope of your topic. Use this knowledge to think about issues that should logically be addressed by the works you are employing as sources. Has the author covered all of the necessary topics? If important issues or themes are excluded, this may affect your research and signal problems with your sources. Then, as you read the text, consider if the author supplies the evidence and discusses the topics she or he promises. If not, this could be a red flag that the work is not of the best quality. Compare content across all sources. If one of your sources does not consider many of the same issues, authors, and pieces of evidence that your other sources do, this may be a clue that it is not reliable. That does not mean an author must agree with all of your other sources, but all of the authors should enter into the same debate. To further understand a book's audience, you can also look for book reviews to see what other scholars thought about the texts you are using. See Chapter Two for sources on finding book reviews and biographical information.

- *Footnotes and documentation.* Look at the footnotes and documentation. If little documentation is presented in the form of references to primary sources, charts, or graphs, you should look at the source with a very critical eye. An important component of presenting research is to identify findings and include proof for what you have found and where you have found it so that others may replicate and judge your results. As with scientific fields in which other scientists replicate experiments to see that they get the same results, if you look at another historian's work and cannot replicate the research process based on the documentation, that may signal problems with her or his research process. A footnote or an endnote should contain all of the information necessary to find the "data" or item it refers to in the text. You should be able to go back and look up the referenced journal article, for instance, and see on a particular page what your original source was quoting or referencing. If the footnote references a primary source, that source should be clearly identified, so even if you cannot go to the archive and look at the source, you understand what it is and when it was produced.

Perspective and Bias: Historians and Interpretation

We believe in a fair society that reports news and research in a factual and objective manner. Yet, varying perspectives and biases are part of life and part of research. When you formulate your research query, you do so with your twenty-first-century sense of curiosity and knowledge. All good historians have a perspective that influences their choice of research topics and the manner in which they plan their investigation and compile their primary sources. Sometimes this perspective can cause quite different analyses to emerge. An example of this phenomenon can be seen in the work of two scholars of Nazi Germany, Christopher Browning and Daniel Goldhagen. Based on a Hamburg police battalion's participation in the killing or deportation of Polish Jews in 1941 and 1942, Browning wrote a book entitled *Ordinary Men: Reserve Police Battalion 101 and the Final Solution in Poland.*[1] Based on the same primary sources, Goldhagen wrote a book entitled *Hitler's Willing Executioners: Ordinary Germans and the Holocaust.*[2] Just by looking at the two titles, it becomes evident that the two historians have a very different interpretation of similar evidence. Neither scholar disputes the facts about the atrocities committed. Browning believes the motives of the German soldiers were rooted in allegiance to their country and their fellow soldiers. In a time of war, they would follow their orders. Goldhagen believes that not just the soldiers but most Germans were "eliminationist anti-Semites." While the debate has became quite heated and is more complicated than can be discussed here, it is evident that these two scholars framed their research questions differently and that their investigations were influenced by their own perspectives. Goldhagen not only is of Jewish background but also had family members victimized in the Holocaust. Browning came of age in the 1960s during the Vietnam and Watergate eras, when the motives of the U.S. government engaged in war were questioned. Neither book is based on sloppy research, but both authors have perspectives colored by their pasts. You, as a historian and researcher, must realize that research is never just compiling the factual information but requires interpretation and that you need to be critical about how others' perspectives shape their interpretations.

Scholarship or Propaganda?

As you conduct your secondary source research, you must carefully evaluate information to distinguish sources that have been created with the *intent* to deceive or to sway opinion. *Propaganda* is defined as "the spreading of ideas, information, or rumor for the purpose of helping or injuring an institution, a cause, or a person."[3] Propaganda uses half-truths or takes facts out of context so that those who read or view it will draw erroneous or oversimplified conclusions. Propaganda is not always evil, although it is often thought to be so; but it must be recognized for what it is. Below is a table that contrasts scholarship and propaganda.[4] Remember that propaganda would be considered a primary source as it reflects attitudes and opinions at a given period of time. Be sure the sources you find for your secondary sources (and the research you produce) fit in the scholarship column.

SCHOLARSHIP	PROPAGANDA
Describes the limits of data	*Has excessive claims of certainty (we have the only way or the right view)*
Presents accurate descriptions of alternative views	*Makes personal attacks/ridicules*
Presents data that do not favor preferred views as well as data that support these	*Presents emotional appeals*
Settles disputes by use of generally accepted criteria for evaluating data	*Distorts data unfavorable to preferred views*
Looks for counterexamples	*Suppresses contradictory views*
Uses language in agreed-upon ways	*Suppresses contradictory facts*
Updates information	*Appeals to popular prejudices*
Admits own ignorance	*Relies on suggestion (e.g., negative innuendo)*
Attempts to discuss general laws/principles	*Devalues thought/critical appraisal*
Finds own field/area of investigation difficult and full of holes	*Transforms words to suit aims*
Relies on critical thinking skills	*Magnifies or minimizes problems to suit the purpose*
	Presents information/views out of context

Case Study ▪ Evaluating Sources: Holocaust Historians

As discussed in this chapter, Christopher Browning and Daniel Goldhagen interpreted primary source evidence quite differently in their two books about a German battalion in World War II. The following will help you put into perspective how you as a scholar might evaluate such information:

Shatz, Adam. "Browning's Version: A Mild-Mannered Historian's Quest to Understand the Perpetrators of the Holocaust." *Lingua Franca* 7 (Feb 1997): 48–57.

Shandley, Robert R., ed. *Unwilling Germans?: The Goldhagen Debate*, with essays translated by Jeremiah Riemer. Minneapolis: University of Minnesota Press, 1998.

Using the questions posed in this chapter, ask yourself:

1. How did each scholar's background affect his perspective? How did this background guide the framing of the questions asked of the primary source data and the conclusions drawn?

2. Were the audiences and purposes of each book the same? By reading the *Linga Franca* article, do you think one of the scholars might have had a more general audience in mind? Was the purpose of each of the books to speak to a different segment of a scholarly audience? Do you think other scholars' perspectives influenced their analyses of this debate and, thus, the reception of these two scholars' research?

3. Did either author include or ignore evidence included by the other? This may be discussed by other scholars in their examinations of the books. It may be useful to browse the original texts and look at the bibliographies and footnotes. You may also want to read book reviews.

NOTES

1. Christopher R. Browning, *Ordinary Men: Reserve Police Battalion 101 and the Final Solution in Poland* (New York: HarperCollins, 1992).
2. Daniel Jonah Goldhagen, *Hitler's Willing Executioners: Ordinary Germans and the Holocaust* (New York: Alfred A. Knopf, 1996).
3. "Propaganda," *Merriam-Webster Collegiate Dictionary* http://www.m-w.com/dictionary/propaganda (accessed January 1, 2006).
4. Sonia Bodi, "Scholarship or Propaganda: How can Librarians Help Undergraduates Tell the Difference?" *Journal of Academic Librarianship* 21 (Jan 1995): 21–25.

6

The Thrill of Discovery: Primary Sources

WHAT YOU WILL LEARN IN THIS CHAPTER:
- how to differentiate many types of primary sources
- how to search for primary sources
- how to locate and use archives
- how to evaluate primary sources

Primary sources, or primary evidence, are the foundation of historical research. Whether it is a collection of personal letters of one of the first African-American surgeons, plaster casts of the remains of former residents at Pompeii that captures them in their moment of death, or an archive of vintage radio broadcasts, primary sources are what excite and compel historians to pursue their craft and are the material from which historians formulate questions. Identifying and appropriately using primary sources often present the greatest challenges to novice and skilled researchers alike. To be an effective researcher, you must be able to identify the variety of primary sources and understand the relationship among them. Integration of government documents, photographs, and oral histories, if these are available, can help you to form a more balanced analysis and assessment of a past event or situation.

This chapter first defines and then provides categories of primary sources to help you imagine the types that exist for your research. As each category of primary source is explored, search tips to find primary sources as well as major collections, both in print and online, will be included. Primary sources can be found in manuscript, print, and online forms. Chapter Seven will explore the Internet, which can be quite valuable for primary sources (although it can be used for research in a variety of ways well beyond primary research). These two chapters can be used together in your search for primary materials. In conclusion, a list of criteria to evaluate your primary sources is provided. Just as with secondary sources, you must evaluate the quality and accuracy of your primary sources. Much of the time, you will have to try to think like someone in another century to understand the perspective and intent of individuals who existed in different environments and possessed different knowledge from you. Doing so will allow you to develop search and evaluation strategies to help you find, utilize, integrate, and evaluate primary sources in your research.

Definitions

Distinguishing a primary source from a secondary source is essential. Below are characteristics of each.

- *Primary sources* are items that are directly associated with their producer or user and the time period in which they were created. Examples include diaries, newspaper articles, government documents, clothing, photographs, oral interviews, and news broadcasts.

- *Secondary works* are analyses and interpretations based on primary sources and other sources, which can include other secondary works such as books and journal articles, and tertiary sources, such as encyclopedia articles.

These definitions can become confused, however, when a secondary text becomes a primary source because the analysis it presents is actually an example of the intellectual and cultural thought of the time in which it was written. For instance, Denis Diderot's *Encyclopédie, ou, Dictionnaire raisonné des sciences, des arts et des métiers* was an attempt by the philosophers and intellectuals of the eighteenth century to compile the known information about the world into a set of volumes. In the eighteenth century, Diderot's *Encyclopédie* was useful as a secondary work, a text that compiled and interpreted the world's knowledge. Many scientific advances and changes in cultural attitudes have occurred in the intervening centuries, transforming this encyclopedia from a secondary work of the eighteenth century into a primary source in the twenty-first century. The volumes tell us what eighteenth-century intellectuals knew and how they perceived their world.

Nature and Categories of Primary Sources

When looking for primary sources, it is necessary to think about the variety and types of sources available. There are many ways primary sources can be categorized. Thinking of them in the following categories will help you search for them:

- *Public records.* Governments are and have always been in the business of keeping a myriad of records in order to define their populations, create policies and procedures, and otherwise maintain civil order. Generally, these records were never intended to be published, are unique copies, and were for the internal operation of the government. Census records, court records, some statistics, wills, local administrative records, and tax records are all examples of public records. Sometimes church records may count as public records as the Catholic Church was a governing body during certain eras and in certain regions.

- *Official records.* To operate, governments have laws and guidelines, the documentation of which becomes a valuable official record that provides a wealth of information. Usually, these records are published and more than one copy exists. These records are intended to make citizens aware of the rules and regulations as well as the actions of their civil government. Sometimes the differences between public and official records are slight. Examples of official records include laws, civil codes, legislative hearings, and treaties.

- *Personal documents.* Individuals have always generated amazing amounts of documentation that can teach us a great deal about their lives and societies. Diaries, letters, e-mail correspondence, oral histories, financial records, and household accounts are all incredibly rich research sources. With the advent of e-mail, personal correspondence on paper has declined, along with some of these other types of primary sources historians have been used to examining. Instead, researchers will need to incorporate artifacts and other material to discover the daily lives and thoughts of ordinary people.

- *Artifacts/relics.* Individuals leave behind "stuff," including material possessions and general debris, such as refuse. Analyzing what items humans produced, used, consumed, and discarded provides insight into the lives of the vast majority of humankind, few of whom leave any written or other personal records to be studied. Examples include furniture, paintings, tools, machines, clothing, textiles, firearms, cooking tools, farm implements, music, and art.

- *Business and other organizations' documents.* Corporations and other organizations, such as unions, civic clubs, charities, and churches, produce materials that document their activities as well as the roles and identities of their workers, members, constituents, and clients. Shipping manifests, inventories, financial records, meeting minutes, and production schedules can provide insight into a business, its goods, and its influence, for example, on the local economy, society, and labor pool.

- *Images.* Photographs, posters, paintings, engravings, icons, and videos are valuable records of events but also serve as chronicles of changes in the texture of individuals' lives. Families grow and change. Cities and buildings damaged by war and decay fall apart and are rebuilt. Images provide glimpses not only of dress and decoration but also of values. How was a middle-class home decorated in Victorian England? What did Red Square look like in revolutionary Russia? How did illuminated Bibles reflect medieval culture? How did propaganda films reflect Nazi ideology? Chapter Nine explores visual and audio media as primary sources.

- *Architecture, city plans, and maps.* A city's map, neighborhoods, and mix of architectural styles indicate how individuals rich and poor relate as a society. Maps indicate how traffic flowed and how land was used. Rural land uses, environmental history, and landscape archaeology all tell us how individuals relate to the land and the importance of land in their society. Documents that provide this kind of information include photographs, city plans, blueprints, house drawings and house plans, as well as maps. Actual buildings also provide information about their past.

- *Media and other public communication.* News and its path of communication have certainly changed over time, but its significance as a primary source has not. With the rise of commercial and industrial societies, individuals as well as governments and commercial interests needed to effectively find and disseminate information. What they have left behind is vast amounts of fertile material for study, including newspapers, magazines, learned societies' publications, television news broadcasts, broadsides, and radio broadcasts.

- *Literary texts.* The text of a novel, essay, poem, play, short story, or religious work is a primary source. Written in a specific time and place, these works reflect the culture and thought of an era and location, even if the work is critical of the status quo or set in another time. Historians sometimes analyze popular novels alongside other primary source material in their research.

Planning Your Project with Primary Sources

Now that you have a sense of the variety of primary sources, a bit of planning before you begin your search is wise. You will need to be attentive to what materials are available locally and those that may require interlibrary loan, assistance from an archive at a distance, or even a trip to that archive. You should locate and request these materials or at least correspond with the archivist early in your research, even if it turns out that you will not use those sources. When querying an archive, do not ask for everything on, for example, the Battle of Gettysburg; instead, ask a more specific question, such as, does the archive have information on a specific person from the town or battle? Be prepared for a bit of a wait and for a possible trip. Most repositories and archives do not have the staff or the finances to describe collections in detail, to search through many boxes for specific material at the request of an individual researcher, or to photocopy large amounts of material to send to you. If your project must be finished within a semester or less and you are unable to travel to the archives, you must quickly determine how central certain pieces of primary evidence are to your research. Acquiring primary materials can take time, and you do not want to be caught short in your effort to obtain and analyze important sources.

Locating Primary Sources

Considering these categories and examples of primary sources helps you to imagine the kinds of primary evidence that might exist to support your research question. Sometimes your research question arises from your curiosity about a primary source. But then you may also need to locate additional primary sources that will effectively support your thesis. As you read secondary works and discover primary sources, you will refine your research questions, causing you to search for more supportive evidence in the form of additional primary and secondary sources. As a beginning researcher, you may have difficulty selecting a topic and keeping yourself focused as you begin to discover so many related resources. Asking the following questions will help you think about what kind of evidence to look for and how to link your evidence directly to your research question.

SEARCH TIPS
1. What types of primary materials might have been produced? Remember to think about both printed materials, such as documents, as well as physical representations of culture, such as artwork and architecture.
2. Who would have produced these primary sources?
3. Who would have used and/or critiqued these primary sources?

4. When would these primary sources have been produced?
5. Would these primary sources have been published, unpublished, or represented in another form (an audiotape of an interview, e.g.)?
6. What would historians of that period have used to do their research?
7. Why does this source still exist? Why was it important enough for someone to preserve?

Fixing the "authorship" in a specific place and time, as well as identifying the types of resources you hope to find, will help you to figure out where to look for sources. Published sources (magazines, books, etc.) are the easiest to find because they have been cataloged and multiple copies were produced (and likely saved). Locating artifacts, personal documents, and audio and video images is often more challenging as these are one-of-a-kind materials and often uncataloged.

In searching for primary sources, you must think like the people who lived in the place and time you are studying. This means that you must consider their language, terminology, and way of life. For instance, important differences between British and American English will affect the way you must search in current and historical catalogs and indexes. For instance, while Americans refer to "Queen Anne's War," the British call this same military action the "War of the Spanish Succession." Information about African Americans is often indexed under the archaic term "negro," bars are found under "saloons," housekeeping is found under "domestic economy," and "mental hygiene" is used to explore mental illness. Medicine and illnesses always present a challenge. "Hysteria" was a common diagnosis given to women in the past, but it actually refers to a very nonspecific ailment, making it much more difficult to locate primary source documents.

Before you begin your search, take a quick look at a subject encyclopedia, like those discussed in Chapter Two, to get an overview of a topic. This will give you a number of terms, definitions, and associations that will make your search for primary sources as effective as possible. Additionally, reading a journal article or two or at least the introduction of a book on your topic will help to refocus your twenty-first-century mind.

Much of the primary source material you find will be in the traditional printed format, either in a published book or in a manuscript. Some manuscripts, however, have been filmed, reproducing many pages on microfiche (a 4 3 6 inch piece of film) or microfilm (a roll of 35 mm film). Some primary source material is also available in digital form via the Internet, but since the digitizing process is time-consuming and expensive, a large portion of this material is still available only in print, microfilm, or microfiche. See Chapter Seven for a more complete discussion of how to locate, access, and interpret online primary source materials.

Dividing primary sources into published and unpublished sources will help you define your search strategy. Published sources will be the easiest to locate through your library. These were mass-produced, so, at least at one time, more than one copy existed. You will probably be able to locate a copy to borrow through interlibrary loan or find a microfilmed copy of your printed primary source. Unpublished sources are typically one-of-a-kind items and often held in a single location, such as a museum or archive, although some may have been microfilmed or digitized and made available on the Internet. Documents, diaries, business records, parish records, an individual's papers, and photographs are all examples of unpublished primary sources. Before visiting a museum or archive, you should contact the curator or archivist to find out about the collection. Sometimes copies can be made of the items you want. More often, archives receive high volumes of requests, so if you do not know fairly clearly what you are looking for and where it might be, they will be unable to assist you. They will not search through boxes of manuscripts looking for your evidence. Here are some general characteristics of the types of institutions and organizations that hold primary sources:[1]

- *Archives.* Archives hold official documents of official bodies. Federal and state/provincial archives hold materials relating to the activities of the country or other civil unit. For example, the National Archives holds an original copy of the U.S. Declaration of Independence.

- *Local historical societies.* Historical societies hold documents of local interest, individual and family papers, local council minutes, local company records, and church and parish records, if not held by the church. For example, the Wisconsin Historical Society has a database for local history topics (http://www.wisconsinhistory.org/genealogy/).

- *Museums.* Museums contain artifacts, relics, and sometimes supporting documentation, such as the papers of the archaeologists or perhaps the painters whose works they collect. The Louvre (http://www.louvre .fr/llv/commun/home_flash.jsp?bmLocale5 en) holds famous paintings such as the Mona Lisa.

- *Universities.* As institutions of higher learning, universities can have a combination of all of the above and function as all of the above. Special collections may exist at different institutions. For example, the University of Sussex holds some papers of the British novelist and critic Virginia Woolf.

- *Libraries*. Libraries tend to hold published primary source material, such as old books, but can have unpublished materials. Usually, they have a special library within the library or on campus for these materials.

Knowing the nature of an institution helps you determine which ones are likely to hold the types of sources you are looking for. However, lines can blur between these types of institutions, especially in small towns. The local university or public library may be the repository for all of the local history as well as the current and primary source printed materials. Local historical societies may have archival materials, and archives may have information about the city in which they are located as well as papers of individuals who have lived in the town. Sometimes an institution may hold the primary source material simply because it has the ability and space to preserve it, even though the institution does not appear a likely source for the item. Contact more than one organization when looking for primary sources for your research.

Published Sources for Mass Consumption

Of all of the types of primary sources for which you will search, printed and published primary sources are the easiest to locate and to obtain. The invention of moveable type by Johannes Gutenberg in 1455 made the printed word more affordable and thus more easily disseminated. Since Gutenberg's invention, society has not stopped printing information and news for mass consumption. Prior to Gutenberg, book production was laborious as each individual copy was handwritten or block-printed and considered as much a piece of artwork as a container of knowledge. Post-Gutenberg, books were valued more for their content and owned by a larger number of literate individuals. With improved printing and transportation, journals and newspapers became the primary means of public communication for centuries. Newspapers not only provided political news but also fostered debate, announced what goods were entering various cities and ports, and reported births and deaths. Journals allowed scientific societies and specialized audiences to exchange new discoveries and debate ideas. Magazines channeled some of those ideas to the masses, reported fashion and news, serialized novels, published other fiction and poetry, and provided all manner of entertainment and general knowledge to their readers. When looking for published primary sources to use in your research, it is important to remember that each of these types of sources will require different approaches and search strategies.

Books as Primary Sources

The major tool for finding primary source books or monographs is your library's online catalog. Remember, a book is considered a primary source only if the author was involved in a particular event, lived during or close to the time period you are studying, or expressed the intellectual ideas of a particular era. For example, Nicholas Culpeper's book *A Directory for Midwives: or, A Guide for Women* . . . [2] contained sections on the formation of the child in the womb, cures for diseases, miscarriages, and "suckling" directions. This edition, "newly correct from many gross errors," gives us an idea about the depth and limits of the reproductive knowledge of the seventeenth century, but it is clearly outdated for a modern-day obstetrician or a basic sex education class.

Locating published primary source books is quite similar to finding secondary source books. Because you will be looking for older materials, you will want to use broader subject headings and keyword searches in the catalog. The more you work with an online catalog, the easier it will become to use. Despite libraries' and archives' best efforts, many institutions have uncataloged materials. Checking with your librarian or archivist may reveal valuable collections that will not turn up in your library's catalog. The following search tips need not be executed in order, but individual tips can be helpful, depending on the information you know about your topic. You will want to try several of these techniques in more than one catalog at various points in your research.

SEARCH TIPS

1. Search by keyword. Use the keyword search in your library's online catalog. Think as broadly as you can and use Boolean operators to link similar concepts together. For instance, "obstetric*" or "midwi*" (for "midwifes" or "midwives"). Often, online catalogs as well as databases have a method to limit or narrow your search by the date of publication. Look for the limit button, enter the date or dates that define your time period of interest, and let the computer do the search for you!

2. Search by corporate author. Try to figure out the identity of the author of your primary source. *Corporate author* means not an individual but a group of some type, perhaps a government, an organization, or a company. This can be difficult to determine at times. Such official bodies produce documents in the organization's name even if individuals associated with the official body

write them. If you are looking for documents by the African National Congress, for example, enter that phrase as an author. Sometimes guessing the official name of an organization is tricky. Most online catalogs will help you, for instance, giving you a referral from "Nazi Party" to the Nationalsozialistische Deutsche Arbeiter-Partei.

3. Search by keyword and limit your search by words in the subject headings. Remember, a keyword search is for the exact word or words in the book title, subject headings, and sometimes the content notes of the catalog record. After you have done a broad keyword search, limit your search by using one of the following terms in the subject headings: "Diaries," "Personal Narratives," "Sources," "Documents," "Statistics," "Antiquities," or "Correspondence." For example, a keyword search with "women and medieval and japan" with a limit of "correspondence" would find *Letters of the Nun Eshinni: Images of Pure Land Buddhism in Medieval Japan.*[3]

4. Search by very broad subject. Often, primary source materials are assigned very general subject headings, have titles that might seem strange to twenty-first-century researchers, and will not be readily found by some of the methods described. You can do a broad search, such as "Women–United States," and use the catalog's limiting ability to narrow the search to those entries that also have "Periodicals" in the subject. For example, doing a subject search for "Women's Rights" and limiting the search to "Periodicals" could turn up Amelia Bloomer's magazine *The Lily: A Lady's Journal Devoted to Temperance and Literature* (1849–1856).

Your local library will be limited in its primary resources. Even major research libraries will be limited in some areas of the collection. Understandably, no library can collect the breadth of material available. However, you can discover what other libraries hold, as well as a way to borrow those materials. The database *Worldcat*, discussed in Chapter Three, is an excellent source for locating published primary source material at other institutions. Remember, *Worldcat* is not comprehensive, even for the libraries included; still, it is an invaluable tool to find published primary sources that will be useful for your research.

Your search techniques for primary sources in *Worldcat* will not differ much from those discussed in Chapter Three on finding books as secondary sources, and you will follow the same patterns described above for your local catalog. One of *Worldcat's* most helpful features is its ability to categorize your search results into types of materials, for example, books, manuscripts, audiovisuals, periodicals, and Internet sites.

Several other means of more comprehensive book indexing exist and can be quite useful. Bibliographic book catalogs, or bibliographies, contain references dating back to the late fifteenth century. Most of these bibliographies use the traditional catalog format of author, title, and subject. They are more generally available in print, although some libraries have access to online versions that allow for additional, more thorough searching. In all cases the online versions have improved upon the print versions, updating and correcting the contents and providing unique full text access. A selection of these follows.

Catalogs and Bibliographies for Books

English Short Title Catalog (ESTC) (1475–1800). http://www.rlg.org/en/
page.php? Page ID5 179 (accessed March 29, 2006) This catalog provides a bibliographic description of works printed in any language in England or its dependencies or printed in English anywhere in the world. The print version is often referred to as "Pollard and Redgrave" or "Wing," but is also known as *Short-Title Catalogue of Books Printed in England, Scotland, & Ireland and of English Books Printed Abroad, 1475–1640*. 2nd rev. & enl ed. A. W. Pollard and G. R. Redgrave, comps. London: Bibliographical Society, 1976–1991; and Short-Title Catalogue of Books Printed in England, Scotland, Ireland, Wales, and British, America, and of English Books Printed in Other Countries, 1641–1700. 2nd ed rev & enl. Donald Wing, comp. New York: Index Committee of the Modern Language Association of America, 1972–. The catalog also refers to a set of microfilm that contains the complete text of the book referred to in this index. Many libraries will loan the microfilm.

Early English Books (EEBO) (1475–1700). http://eebo.chadwyck.com/home (accessed March 29, 2006). Covering a smaller time period than the ESTC, the EEBO provides access to the full-text electronic edition of the books listed in its pages.

American Bibliography: A Chronological Dictionary of All Books, Pamphlets and Periodical Publications Printed in the United States of America from the Genesis of Printing in 1639 Down to and Including the Year 1800. Chicago: Privately Printed for the Author by Blakely Press, 1903–1959. (called "Evans," also available online through subscription called "Early American Imprints," http://www.readex.com/scholarl/eai_digi.html accessed March 29, 2006).

Bibliotheca Americana: A Dictionary of Books Relating to America, from Its Discovery to the Present Time New York: Sabin, 1868–1936 29 vols. (called Sabin).

SEARCH TIPS

1. Search for primary source books in your home catalog. (Use the general search tips for books as primary sources.)
2. Search for books in *Worldcat*.
3. Use bibliographies and footnotes of other secondary sources on your subject to find other primary source books.

Magazines and Journals as Primary Sources

Magazines, journals, and newspapers were the primary means by which social, cultural, political, and intellectual information traveled prior to the advent of radio and television. Magazines and journals grew in prominence and frequency in Western society starting in the eighteenth century and acted as a medium for political debate as well as entertainment. Magazines serialized novels, printed poetry, reported gossip, discussed local news, debated politics, and called upon individuals to rally around political movements. They can also tell you what knowledge was available to common people, for example, what was commonly known about diseases and their causes and treatments, as well as about nations and peoples around the world. Journals contributed to the transfer of scientific and philosophical ideas. Journals were and indeed continue to be published by learned societies and groups as a means of exchanging knowledge among intellectuals and practitioners. Journals also allow these societies to communicate their beliefs and scientific findings to their members and initiate professional debate. Through journals you can understand, among other things, the development of psychoanalysis, the discovery and evolution of germ theories, and treatments, both valid and invalid, of diseases. Magazines and journals are fruitful sources of primary material and usually easily obtainable.

Two searching techniques can be used for locating magazines and journals. Since older publications often are not indexed or are self-indexed (providing an annual index in the last issue of the year or the first issue of the next year within the publication), you must first know of a magazine's or journal's existence to be able to find its index. You can use a catalog, such as your library's online catalog or *Worldcat*, to look for a journal title by subject. For instance, if your research topic is "abolitionism," you could search under the subject heading "Antislavery Movements" and limit the results by using the subject subheading of "Periodicals" or using material type "Serials." You will likely have to learn about the existence of magazines and journals in this manner and then read them issue by issue for relevant material. Many times, no index to individual articles within the periodical will exist. Then, you must be a smart researcher and know a bit about your topic from your secondary sources. Often, you can pin down a period of activity that relates to your topic in order to limit the number of issues you would need to read.

For more popular magazines and journals that were published during or after the nineteenth century in the United States and Great Britain, good bibliographic and subject indexing does exist. Listed below are the major indexes, which most libraries will have, either in paper or online. Always remember that these indexes were created at the specific time these periodicals were published and, as a result, use the terminology of that time. Some of the online periodical indexes have attempted to rectify this archaic, and sometimes offensive, language with more modern terminology.

Indexes for Magazines and Journals as Primary Sources

This list details the basic sources available in most libraries. A more extensive list of less common indexes appears at the end of this chapter.

Poole's Index to Periodical Literature rev. ed. William Frederick Poole.
  Gloucester, MA: P. Smith, 1963 (1802–1907). (commonly called
  Poole's Index). Also available through online subscription, *19th Century Masterfile*™ http://poolesplus.odyssi.com/19centWelcome.htm
  (accessed March 28, 2006). *Poole's Index* is a bare-bones index to
  nineteenth-century periodical literature of the United States and Britain.
  As both of these countries had empires and colonial holdings, the information, however biased, does cover other world regions. *Poole's* in print
  can be difficult to read but is worth the perseverance because of its
  breadth. Reading the instructions at the beginning of volume one will
  help you navigate and decipher this complicated reference work. Some
  libraries subscribe to the enhanced online version of *Poole's*, which is
  called *19th Century Masterfile*. The online version is only slightly easier
  to use than the print version but includes some other smaller indexes to
  magazines of the same era, which are not included in *Poole's* in print.
  19th Century Masterfile also includes other primary indexes, such as selected years of the *New York Times*, the *Times* (London), some coverage
  of the *British Parliamentary Papers,* and *U.S.Congressional Publications.*

Readers' Guide to Periodical Literature. Minneapolis: H. W. Wilson, 1890–. Online title Readers' Guide Retrospective (1890–1982). http://hwwilsonweb.com (accessed March 28, 2006). *Reader's Guide to Periodical Literature* has been a staple for libraries and researchers since before 1900. Indexing both popular and scholarly journals, the print and online versions provide bibliographic citations to the articles. The online version compensates for differences in historical terminology, so searching under "polio" also retrieves articles on "infantile paralysis," the 1930s term.

American Periodical Series (APS). UMI/Proquest. Available microfilm. Divided into three periods (1740–1800, 1800–1850, and 1850–1900), the APS collected and microfilmed over 1,100 magazines. An online version has selected some of the periodicals and digitized their contents (see http://www.proquest.com/products/pt-product-APSOnline.shtml).

SEARCH TIPS

1. Use one of the general indexes (*Poole's* or *Readers' Guide to Periodical Literature*) to do a subject search through many journals or magazines. (See a longer bibliography of indexes at the end of the chapter.)

2. Use *Worldcat* or your local catalog to find titles of journals and magazines on your specific topic by doing a keyword or subject search and then limiting your results by using the subject word "Periodicals."

Newspapers as Primary Sources

Newspapers have a different purpose from magazines and journals and provide different types of primary source evidence. They tie communities together, report events, and provide political commentary. They allow individuals within communities to share information, sell products, and announce births, deaths, and other life events. In the past, they often reported the arrival of commercial goods in ports and cities or the activities of the royal courts. Newspapers did not and still do not always report the facts of a particular event, but they are nonetheless an excellent primary source for discovering public opinion and the issues and activities that surround particular events. The two longest published and farthest-reaching newspapers in the world are the *New York Times* and the *Times* (London). However, almost every town throughout the world, whether large or small, has at least one newspaper. You can use one of the directories listed below to locate the title and date of origin of a newspaper for a particular city, town, county, or country. Sometimes a local library or historical society will have an in-house index to the newspapers in the area it serves. At times, those indexes will include other local historical publications (magazines, journals, and other published histories).

SEARCH TIPS
1. Look for your topic in one of the major newspaper indexes listed in the following section.
2. Look for the title of a newspaper in a particular city or country by using one of the directories or bibliographies listed below.
3. Look at the bibliography of your secondary works.
4. Use *Worldcat* or your catalog to look up newspapers by city.

Indexes for Newspapers

New York Times Index. New York: Bowker and New York Times Company, 1851–. As the United States grew as a world economic power with New York City at its center, the *New York Times* reported the significant national and international events that shaped the world. Most libraries will have the print index referenced above. Several companies offer indexes and full-text access. *Paratext* (19th Century Masterfile) and *ProQuest* (*New York Times Historical*) offer different dates and forms of the *New York Times* either as an index or as full text.

Times Index /Palmer's Index to the Times. Sheperton, UK: Palmer/London: Times Publishing Co., 1785–. The *Times* grew from a small "sheet" designed to "register the times" to the official newspaper of the capital city and its nation's government. The United Kingdom was a major world power from the seventeenth to the mid-twentieth centuries. Consequently, the *Times* reported stories that were of concern to all of its colonies and territories, including the story of a new nation in the New World, now better known as the United States of America. The print index changed titles a number of times and is sometimes also called *Palmer's Index to the Times* as well as *Official Index to the Times*. *Chadwyck-Healy* and *Paratext* also provide some online indexing and some full-text access to the *Times*.

Proquest Historical Newspapers. Subscription to the online versions of the *New York Times, Wall Street Journal, Boston Globe, Atlanta Constitution, Hartford Courant, Christian Science Monitor, Los Angeles Times*,

Chicago Tribune, and *Washington Post*. For details, see http://www
.chadwyck.com/products-pq/hnp/default.shtml (accessed March 29, 2006).
British Library Online Newspaper Archive, http://www.uk.olivesoftware.com/
(accessed March 29, 2006). Searching in selected years of nineteenth-
and twentieth-century British newspapers. Years were selected by significance of the historical events that occurred, so coverage of years is
not complete.

How to Read a Bibliographic Entry in a Printed Newspaper Index

Reading an entry in a newspaper index can be complicated. While the information varies from index to index, the entry usually contains the date (month
and day only, the year is listed on the outside of the volume), the page number and section (a number, a letter, and/or a Roman numeral), and column
number (sometimes a number, sometimes a letter, counting over from the
left side of the page). Sometimes the entries are listed by the headline; more
often the entry is a paraphrased summary of the scope of the article. Usually,
the articles are listed under a subject heading in chronological order. Broad
subject headings will encompass common types of information, for instance,
"Motion Picture Reviews," "Book Reviews," "Shipping News," "Murders,"
"Deaths," etc. In most cases, you will not find information listed under a title
of the book or movie or the name of the ship. In the case of the *New York
Times Index*, a reference is printed only once, so you may be referred to another subject in the same volume. For instance, in Figure 6.1 the subject
heading "Hindenburg (Airship)" suggests another subject heading, "Aeronautics–Commercial Service–Ocean." While coverage of the story began on
May 7 (1937), looking down the list of descriptions of articles, you find major coverage with "witnesses describe fire. . . . "This is a summary of a series of articles on May 8, 1937, on pages 2–4 in the front section of the paper, as well as another major article published on May 8 on page 18, located
in column 1, listed as "(18:1)."

Bibliographies to Locate Historical Newspaper Titles

These indexes will help you locate the titles of newspapers, the dates they
were published, and if and when they ceased publication, changed title, or
were absorbed by a competitor.

Newspaper Indexes: A Location and Subject Guide. Anita Cheed Milner.
Metuchen, NJ: Scarecrow Press, 1977–1983. 3 vols. Guide to locations
of indexes, both published and unpublished, of newspapers held in the
United States (but not necessarily limited to American newspapers).

1024 THE NEW YORK TIMES INDEX *Year 1937*

HINDENBURG, Paul von Beneckendorff und von (1847-1934)
Por, Ja 31, IV, 5:1
Book, Hindenburg the Wooden Titan, banned, F 4, 7:2
Por, Ap 4, IV, 2:3
1927 war guilt s assailed by Gen Ludendorff in book, Ag 23, 4:3

HINDENBURG (Airship)
See also Aeronautics—Commercial Service—Ocean
Destroyed by fire and explosions while landing at Lakehurst, N J; 33 reptd killed or missing; notables aboard; Capts Pruss, comdr, and E Lehmann, former comdr, injured; comment; German reaction; illus, My 7, 1:3-8; rept on mail carried; return passenger list; survivors and missing; ship's history; disaster 1st on passenger line, My 7, pp 18-21; U S Commerce Dept and German investigating comms apptd; experts discuss causes of fire; repts of sabotage denied; death list at 33, including Lehmann; F T Birchall on German reaction, My 8, 1:5-8; witnesses describe fire; illus; repts on survivors' condition; list of casualties; comments; ship insured; originally built for helium; films of disaster released; some of mail salvaged; Eckener to aid inquiry; repts threatening lrs, My 8, pp 2-4; ed, My 8, 18:1; disaster occurred on day before 22d anniversary of Lusitania sinking, My 8, 21:3; U S Navy appts investigating bd; death list at 35; Prof O Stern on hydrogen combustion as cause, My 9, 1:6-8; German survivors return by ss, My 9, 4:3;

Figure 6.1. Excerpt from the printed version of the 1937 *New York Times Index* providing references to the Hindenburg airship disaster. *©1937 by the New York Times Co. Reprinted with permission.*

United States Newspaper Program: National Union List. Dublin, OH: OCLC, also available http://www.neh.gov/projects/usnp.html (accessed January 1, 2006). Complicated but comprehensive list of newspapers held in United States and its territories. Subject, title, geographic, and audience index. The website provides links to each of the states, some of which may have online indexes or bibliographies to their newspapers.

Center for Research Libraries (CRL) Foreign Newspaper Collection, http://www.crl.edu/content.asp?l1 5 5&l25 23&l35 44&l45 27 (accessed January 1, 2006). Index to the titles of CRL's extensive foreign newspaper collection. Searchable by title, place (city and country), language, years held. You may use the index but will be unable to get the papers from CRL unless you are a member.

Willings Press Guide. London: Willings Service. 1928 Annual. Directory of newspapers in Great Britain and worldwide.

British Newspaper Library Catalogue, http://www.bl.uk/catalogues/newspapers.welcome.asp (accessed March 29, 2006). Listing of United Kingdom newspapers since 1801.

Newspapers in Microform: Foreign Countries: 1948–1983. Washington, DC: Library of Congress, 1983. Gives worldwide holdings of foreign newspapers available in microfilm or microfiche.

Gale Directory of Publications and Broadcast Media. Detroit: Gale. 1869 Annual. [title varies] Provides addresses and dates of inception of current newspapers, by city. Many papers have been around a long time, and this directory is mostly useful for those papers that have been continuously published since the nineteenth century.

Modern Sources of News

Television News Archive (Vanderbilt University), http://tvnews.vanderbilt .edu/ (accessed January 1, 2006). Since 1968, Vanderbilt has been recording network news (ABC, CBS, NBC, some CNN) and making the newscasts available to researchers. Use its "TV News" search to find news programs. Copyright restrictions will not permit you to use these clips on a website. Check to see if your library has a subscription.

LexisNexis Academic: News, http://www.lexisnexis.com (accessed January 1, 2006). Subscription service. In the "News" section, a transcripts database provides transcripts for such news outlets as the major networks, public radio, and television, as well as *Burrelle's Transcript Service* and some foreign news services. Dates of coverage vary by source in the database but are concentrated in the last 30 years.

Benn's Media Directory. Tonbridge, UK: Benn Business Information Services. 1846-Annual. [title varies] Directory of television and cable stations worldwide. Provides contact information for paper/media outlets.

World News Connection, http://wnc.fedworld.gov/ (accessed January 1, 2006). *World News Connection*, a fee-based service, provides translations of newspaper articles, conference proceedings, television and radio broadcasts, periodicals, and some technical reports from other countries. It is the continuation of the Foreign Broadcast Information Service (FBIS) begun in 1941. The older translations, titled "Daily Report," were issued to U.S. government depository libraries in various forms (print, microfilm).[4] While *World News Connection* is issued today as a depository item in CD-ROM format, access is restricted due to copyright rules. If you think this would be a useful resource, check with your librarian. A useful website explains FBIS's evolution (see http:// www.library.osu.edu/sites/reference/resources/fbis.htm).

Unpublished Sources and Manuscripts

It might be said that manuscripts and other unpublished sources are the most exciting finds for the historian. Looking at a document in the handwriting of someone who lived hundreds of years ago is exciting. Imagine that you were researching Jane Addams, founder of Hull-House, the Chicago settlement house established in 1889 as a social agency for immigrant women and children and the working poor. Addams worked tirelessly for daycare, established after-school activities for girls, and taught English classes. Finding a letter in Addams' own handwriting in which she lobbied both the Illinois state government and the federal government for aid for these women and children connects you to her thoughts and to the issues of the day. Diaries, correspondence, household and business account books, surveys, court and parish records, and land books are all unique primary sources that can illuminate historical periods.

There are several ways to begin looking for locations of manuscripts. Always start with what you know. If you are searching for the papers of an individual, look at some of the standard biographical sources listed in Chapter Two on reference materials. Many biographies and biographical dictionaries will list where an individual's papers are held and if those papers have been published. Use what you know about the person's life and correspond with libraries and historical societies in the region in which the person lived to see if they hold any papers relevant to the individual's life. If not, they will probably be able to give you some leads. If you are looking for manuscripts that relate to an event, a similar strategy applies. Look for the papers of famous individuals involved. Correspond with the libraries and archives in the area. In addition, check *Worldcat*. If you are doing a general search for manuscripts on a topic, you may want to try the indexes listed below. One quick note about manuscripts and other primary source material on the Internet: increasingly, archives are putting *portions* of their collections on the Internet for researchers, and although the quality of these sites continues to improve, you must be sure that these sites are legitimate and accurate. Chapter Seven provides more details.

Well-organized manuscript collections are categorized in folders and boxes with a finding aid to help the library staff and researchers navigate their way through the collection. The term "finding aid" refers to various unpublished indexes that archivists and librarians create to more easily access documents in manuscript collections. Sometimes finding aids are simply a chronological listing of the boxes with a general description of the material contained in them. In other cases, a list might identify every item in the collection, down to the fishing lure enclosed in someone's letter. Unfortunately, there will be many instances when no finding aid exists. Some archives and repositories have put their finding aids online. Called EADs (encoded archival description finding aids), they describe and list the contents of the archival collection. One very useful example is the Library of Congress' EAD page (http://www.loc.gov/

rr/ead/eadhome.html). It is unlikely that your local historical society or archive will have EADs, however. If you are trying to determine whether an archive has material that will be useful in your research, more often than not you will have to write to the archivist with a specific request.

Catalogs, Bibliographies, Directories, and Indexes for Manuscripts

Subject Collections: A Guide to Special Book Collections and Subject Emphases as Reported by University, College, Public, and Special Libraries and Museums in the United States and Canada. 7th ed. New York: Bowker, 1993. Subject, author, and title bibliography of major manuscript collections held in libraries and archives across the United States.

National Union Catalog of Manuscript Collections Collective Catalog of Manuscripts and Related Textual Material Held in Archives in the United States. (NUCMC), Washington DC: Library of Congress, 1959–1993 (in print and through *Worldcat* thereafter). Begun in 1959 as a print index and later placed online, first through *RLG database* (1985) and then *Worldcat* (1993), NUCMUC contains a wealth of references to manuscripts throughout any time in history. Prior to 1986, you must use the printed catalog. For a more detailed discussion, see http:// www.loc.gov/coll/nucmc/.

Women's History Sources. Andrea Hinding, ed. New York: R. R. Bowker, 1979. Index to women's manuscripts in U.S. repositories.

Archives USA, http://archives.chadwyck.com/ (accessed January 2, 2006). Requires subscription. Current directory of over 5,480 repositories and over 132,300 collections of primary source material across the United States. Sponsored by Chadwyck-Healy, a large publisher of primary source microfilm and microfiche.

Guide to Federal Records in the National Archives of the United States. Robert B. Matchette, et al., comps. Washington, DC: National Archives and Records Administration, 1995, http://www.archives.gov/research _room/federal_records_guide/ (accessed March 29, 2006). Discusses what is available in each record group at the archives. Some examples of what the federal archives saves and provides access to are records and documents from the Indian Claims Commission, War Production Board, Civil War Pension, Rural Electrification Service, Forest Service, and other administrative offices of government.

National Archives and Records Administration, http://www.archives.gov/ (accessed January 1, 2006). The National Archives is the major documentary preservation agency of the United States. Included in this site are indexes to their collections as well as actual digitized collections. Enter the "Research Room" and browse. Use *ARC* (http://arcweb.archives.gov/arc/basic_search.jsp) to do some searching.

The European Library, http://www.theeuropeanlibrary.org/portal/index.htm (accessed January 1, 2006). Unified catalog of major European national libraries. Includes their digital collections as well.

Worldcat, Online, available through subscription, http://newfirstsearch.oclc.org/. Many archives and libraries catalog their collections in *Worldcat*.

Historical Manuscripts Commission, http://www.archon.nationalarchives.gov.uk/archon/ (accessed January 1, 2006). Online reference for British manuscripts. It provides access to locations of collections and archives. See also *Archives HUB*.

Archives HUB, http://www.archiveshub.ac.uk/ (accessed January 1, 2006). Online index that connects UK universities' archives into one catalog.

Other national libraries and archives of note (there are many other sites like these, see the Directories to Archive Repositories section below to find others):

- *National Library of France*, http://www.archivesdefrance.culture.gouv.fr/ (accessed January 10, 2006).

- *Bibliothèque Nationale de France*, http://www.bnf.fr/ (accessed January 10, 2006).

- *Biblioteca Nazionale Centrale "Vittorio Emanuele II,"* http://www.bncrm.librari.beniculturali.it/ (accessed January 10, 2006).

- *Russian Federation National Library*, http://www.nlr.ru/eng/ (accessed January 10, 2006).

- *National Library of China*, http://www.nlc.gov.cn/ (accessed January 10, 2006).

Directories to Archive Repositories

When you need to locate a library, archive, or historical society, use one or more of the directories below. In general, the books are more comprehensive than the Internet sites. However, neither is comprehensive, so looking in different sources may be necessary.

Directory of History Departments, Historical Organizations and Historians. Washington, DC: American Historical Association, 1975-Annual. See also

http://bibpurl.oclc.org/web/45 or http://www.historians.org/pubs/directory/
index.cfm. Directory that includes addresses of historical associations in the
United States and Canada. Often includes websites and e-mail addresses.

Europa World of Learning. London: Allen and Unwin, 1947-Annual. Directory of learned societies worldwide, including archives, libraries,
and museums.

UNESCO Archives Portal, http://portal.unesco.org/webworld/portal
_archives. Online directory of archives. Use the map to select by coun-
try or the menu to select by type.

European Archival Network, http://www.european-archival.net/ (accessed
January 1, 2006). Fairly comprehensive listing of European archives.
Includes links to archive home page. Aimed at historians.

Repositories of Primary Sources, http://www.uidaho.edu/special-collections/
Other.Repositories.html (accessed January 1, 2006). Worldwide listing
of archives and historical societies with primary source material. Organization is geographic.

National Libraries of the World, http://www.ifla.org/VI/2/p2/
national-libraries.htm (accessed January 1, 2006). Country listing of
national libraries, which are often the holders of the major manuscripts,
government documents, and other unpublished documents from that
country. Includes web addresses.

Ready, 'Net, Go! Archival Internet Resources, http://www.tulane.edu/~lmiller/
ArchivesResources.html (accessed January 1, 2006). Index to archive
sites as well as list of tools of archivists and archival search engines.

British Archives: A Guide to Archive Resources in the United Kingdom.
4th ed. New York: Palgrave, 2002. Listing by city of archives and special libraries and their holdings.

SEARCH TIPS

1. Look at the bibliography in an entry in a biographical encyclopedia to find the location of an individual's papers.
2. Locate a library or archive in the place where your person lived
   or an event occurred and correspond with that library. Use one
   of the directories above to find the contact information.
3. Search *Worldcat* and your local library's catalog. Some manuscripts may have been put into microformat and may be available outside of the archive.
4. Check the Internet. (See Chapter Seven for specific search
   techniques.)

Documents from Governments and Other Official Bodies

Finding official publications of governments and other governing bodies can be challenging. Every government operates differently, has changed its operation over time, and has preserved different records depending upon its administrative needs. As mentioned throughout this chapter, having a general understanding of the secondary literature is always useful before searching for the primary sources. Find an encyclopedia article that will explain the structure of the government for the time period that interests you. Know the name of the governmental agency or ministry and in which department it resided or how it fits in the government's structure. Begin by doing a keyword search in your library's catalog and in *Worldcat*, understanding that some libraries do not put government documents in their online catalogs. Check with your librarian to be sure. Once you have determined your department's or agency's official name, search for that name as an author. The United States has many avenues to search for government documents. Several indexes are listed below. For a substantial listing of indexes and sources, use the Sears and Moody book in the Directories/Bibliographies section below.

Finding documents from governments of other nations can be especially tricky if you have a limited knowledge of those nations. Nations with long democratic and parliamentary traditions, such as many of the European nations, have huge numbers of records, documenting government procedures, laws, and the like. Many developing nations that have had monarchies, dictatorships, and forms of government not open to their citizens have kept fewer documents and have made (and continue to make) fewer government documents available. Many of these nations might have been colonies before independence, so governmental records would be included not only in that colonial power's government documents but also in its language and from its viewpoint. An example is Great Britain's Foreign Office, which administered many of its colonies and thus kept records on such places as India and Canada. Sometimes, oppressive regimes have sealed or hidden records. Finding reliable and accurate Soviet government documentation of Stalin's purges in the Soviet Union, during which more than twenty million people perished, has proven challenging. Only in 1998 did President Boris Yeltsin order secret state documents concerning Stalin declassified. Much material from the Soviet regime remains difficult, if not impossible, to access, even for experienced scholars.

Other government documents are those records produced by quasi-governmental organizations. The United Nations is the prime example of such an organization, as are the European Union and the World Bank. They all have or had a representational organizational structure that creates legislation that is theoretically binding to its members. In addition, there are reports, studies, and statistical publications created and issued for a general public to read. These sources are especially useful for topics in the post-1945 era and as a means of discerning a wider world viewpoint. The same search techniques apply for these organizations as for government documents.

The process of using your online catalog and *Worldcat* is much the same as looking for information in the United States. Also, the *Guide to Official Publications of Foreign Governments* (listed below), while intended for contemporary use, will assist in identifying when governments began producing selected publications, such as journals of assembly proceedings and statistical publications.

Indexes and Bibliographies of Government Documents

Note that this is a very abridged selection of indexes to U.S. government publications. There are too many to list here. For a complete listing with an excellent explanation, see Sears, Jean, and Marilyn K. Moody. *Using Government Information Sources: Electronic and Print.* 3d ed. Phoenix: Oryx Press, 2001.

Monthly Catalog of United States Government Publications. Washington, DC: GPO, 1895–. Provides bibliographic citations to government documents produced by U.S. government agencies (i.e., not Congress, the president, or the judiciary).

CIS U.S. Serial Set Index 1817–1969. Washington, DC: Congressional Information Service, dates vary. The Serial Set includes selected House and Senate reports and documents, including documents submitted by government agencies to Congress. Indexes are divided into parts, by years. Parts of this index and or the material included in the serial set may be included in other indexes available at your library. Consult your librarian. Also available online for a subscription fee.

British Parliamentary Papers, http://www.bopcris.ac.uk/18c/ (accessed September 6, 2005). Project to make available copies of papers from the eighteenth century (1688–1800). Still in progress.

Great Britain, Parliament, House of Commons. *Journals of the House of Commons.* London: Various Printers 1503–.

Great Britain, Parliament, House of Lords. *Journals of the House of Lords.* London: Various Printers 1503–. Journals are the official record of the proceedings of the two legislative bodies of Great Britain. There are numerous indexes to these that have been commercially published as well as annual indexes to each session. Check with your library to see in what format they own these and who is the publisher.

Great Britain, Parliament. *British Sessional Papers*. London: Various Printers. Bills, reports, and papers presented to Parliament. Check with your library to see in what format they own these and who is the publisher.

LexisNexis Congressional, http://web.lexisnexis.com/congcomp (accessed January 1, 2006). Fee-based database, *LexisNexis* includes congressional hearings, public laws, and other congressional publications, dating back to 1789. Includes the U.S. Serial Set.

United Nations, http://www.un.org; *United Nations System of Organizations*, http://www.unsystem.org/ (accessed January 1, 2006). The first site is the official website of the United Nations and has records of the general assembly and some of its commissions. The second site provides an alphabetical list with links to websites of U.N. agencies that are often hard to find. In both cases, the documents associated with the sites are relatively recent, late twentieth century to the present.

Directories/Bibliographies for Governments/Guides to Government Publications

Using Government Information Sources: Electronic and Print, Jean L. Sears and Marilyn K. Moody. 3d ed. Phoenix: Oryx Press, 2001. Heavily oriented to publications in the United States but also includes a chapter on foreign countries. Discusses current and historical publications. Offers concrete search strategies.

Guide to Official Publications of Foreign Governments. 2d ed. Bethesda, MD: CIS/American Library Association, 1997. Under each country is listed the types of government publications they produce, statistical yearbooks, court decisions, annual budgets, and census materials, for example.

Public Records and Genealogical Sources

Public records contribute to our knowledge of people's everyday lives and values. Census records, wills/probate court records, tax records, cemetery records, municipal health records, and church records (baptisms, marriages), among others, all provide information about communities and the people who lived and worked in them.[5] They vary in availability by country and throughout time. Written records were created and maintained when governments and, in some cases, the Catholic Church felt the need to count individuals, to record property, to tax, and to adjudicate disputes between its inhabitants or when businesses needed to keep track of their transactions. It can be challenging to figure out what the branches of government that administer these records are called in different countries. For example, the Exchequer, the treasury, is the main governmental office in Great Britain that collected taxes. Before you begin to look for public records, it will serve you well to look thoroughly at the primary sources listed in your secondary works' notes. This will give you a clue as to the terminology and the types of sources for which you will be looking. Follow up on those footnotes in your library and by looking in *Worldcat* to see if some of these primary sources may be available on microformat or in some other format besides the original document in the archive.

Searching for public records is not always easy. If you know what you are looking for, your library's catalog and *Worldcat* are good starting points. Search by the government or the office of the government as an author, for example, "United States. Congress. House," "Great Britain. Parliament. House of Lords," "League of Nations," or "France. Parlement." If you are not exactly sure of the records you are looking for, you might browse through the guides to public records listed below. Major collections have been issued in large multivolume sets or in microformat. You can determine their availability by looking in *Worldcat*, although in this complicated sphere, asking a librarian for assistance would be a good idea.

SEARCH TIPS

1. Search your catalog, *Worldcat*, or other online catalogs using the name of the office or the department of government as an author.
2. Use the footnotes in your secondary sources to lead you to government departments or agencies.
3. Use one of the guides below to locate the records that exist for your country of interest.

Guides to Public Records

Librarian's Guide to Public Records: The Complete State, County, and Courthouse Locator. Michael L. Sankey and Carl R. Ernst, eds. Tempe, AZ: BRB Publications, 1997. Provides access to over 11,500 major federal (U.S.), state, and county public record locations. Each court, county, and recorder's office lists the specific records it houses.

The WPA Historical Records Survey. A Guide to the Unpublished Inventories, Indexes, and Transcripts. Loretta A. Hefner, comp. Chicago: Society of American Archivists, 1980. From 1935 to 1942, the Works Project Administration (WPA) took a state-by-state inventory of all available public records. This guide updates those records' locations and other supplemental inventory projects since the ending of the WPA's survey.

Vitalrecords.com, http://www.vitalrec.com/links1.html (accessed January 2, 2006). Aimed at genealogists, this source provides links to many state and local pages, which include directions for requesting information as well as summaries of holdings of each state or locality.

Cyndi's List, http://www.cyndislist.com/ (accessed January 2, 2006). Comprehensive, worldwide list of genealogical sources in print and online. Will provide links to other countries' resources, including locations of local records.

Business Records

All corporations keep records. What is publicly available beyond what is mandated by law is at the discretion of the corporation. Contemporary business archives are a relatively new development in archival preservation and are maintained primarily for the use of the corporation. If a company is still in existence, you will need to make direct contact to inquire about the availability of its records. Be explicit about what you want and how you will use the information. Companies are often more forthcoming with information when they understand that your request is for a student paper and not for a competitor's marketing report. If the company is no longer in existence, you will need to check with the local historical society or public library to see if the records are in their collections. Sometimes, however, company records do not exist. In this case, look for supporting documentation such as labor union publications, newspaper articles, and advertisements to fill some of the gaps.

SEARCH TIPS

1. Use one of the directories below to determine if the corporation is still in existence and has a library.
2. Search in *Worldcat* for the corporation as an author.
3. Contact the local historical society or public library.
4. Look for supporting primary source information such as labor union materials and newspaper and magazine articles.

Directories

The directories below do not specifically list individual collections within business archives. However, they will lead you to the depositories and libraries of corporations that hold those records. You will have to contact the organizations, libraries, or corporations directly with your research query.

Directory of Corporate Archives in the United States and Canada, http://www.hunterinformation.com/corporat.htm (accessed September 6, 2005). Contains description of the collections, gives contact information, and indicates if the archive is open to the public.

American Library Directory. New York: R. R. Bowker. 1912-Annual. [title varies] Directory that provides contact information by state and county for libraries of all types including public, academic, and corporate.

World Guide to Special Libraries. 7th ed. Willemina van der Meer and Helmut Opitz, eds. Munich: K. G. Sauer, 2005. Directory to locate libraries that would have archival or corporate materials in countries other than the United States.

Directory of History Departments, Historical Organizations and Historians. Washington, DC: American Historical Association, 1975-Annual. See also http://bibpurl.oclc.org/web/45 or http://www.historians.org/pubs/directory/index.cfm (accessed September 5, 2005). Directory that includes addresses of historical associations in the United States and Canada. Often includes websites and e-mail addresses. Defunct companies' archives may be deposited at a local historical society.

Oral History

Oral history is a somewhat recent addition to the historian's repertoire of primary sources. Hearing the voices or reading the words of individuals who experienced the common and uncommon events of history enlivens the historical narrative. For example, the words of Japanese Americans who lived in internment camps provide a fuller picture of the American homefront during World War II. Oral histories can be found both as audio files (various methods of audio recording such as cassette tapes, reel-to-reel tapes, or streaming audio on the Internet) and as transcripts (typed testimony of the interviewee). Remember that you can gather and create your own primary source material by collecting your own oral histories. Countless books offer instruction on the technique. Your professor can offer assistance on the technique of collecting oral testimony as well. Two guides that are useful are Valerie Raleigh Yow. *Recording Oral History: A Guide for the*

Humanities and Social Sciences and Donald A. Ritchie. *Doing Oral History: A Practical Guide.*[6] When using oral history, be aware of the problems of fallible memory and the inadvertent influence that the interviewer may have on the interviewee.

Indexing of oral testimonies has been spotty at best until the advent of the Internet and streaming audio, which allows sounds to be broadcast to your desktop. In the past, large oral history projects, such as the Works Project Administration's (WPA) 1930s interviews with former American slaves, have been the most accessible to researchers, mainly through transcripts. Now, however, a much wider range of oral history material is available. Begin by using your online catalog and *Worldcat*. Do a very broad keyword search. For instance, if your topic is the "WPA slave narratives," described above, begin by doing a keyword search with the words "slaves" or "slavery" (or as you learned earlier in this book, truncate the word and search under "slave*"). Then limit (remember, all databases have the ability to narrow a search by adding extra criteria) by using the subject words "personal narratives." Another strategy would be to do a search using both the phrase "oral history" and the name of your topic in its broadest terms. For example, you can do a keyword search for "african american" (with truncation) and "oral history."

Many local historical societies and special interest groups collect oral histories of their members, and the Internet has become a useful resource for making these local oral history projects available. Doing an Internet search using the name of your topic and the phrase "oral history" can be fruitful. Carefully check the legitimacy of a web-based source. Look for the producer and that individual's purpose. For more on evaluating Internet sites, see Chapter Seven.

SEARCH TIPS
   1. Use the words "personal narratives" or "oral history" when searching in your catalog or in *Worldcat*.
   2. Use the guides in the following section to locate large oral history repositories and printed resources.
   3. Search the Internet (see Chapter Seven on Internet searching).

Guides to Oral History Repositories

Directory of Oral History Collections. Allen Smith. Phoenix. Oryx Press, 1988. General listing by library of collections probably still on cassette

tape. Because of the date of the publication, contact the libraries to verify the existence of the materials and their condition before visiting.
The Oral History Collection of Columbia University. Elizabeth B. Mason and Louis M. Starr, eds. New York: Oral History Research Office, 1979, http://www.columbia.edu/cu/lweb/indiv/oral/offsite.html (accessed March 30, 2006). Columbia is one of the pioneers in oral history and has amassed a large collection of interviews of famous or significant individuals. Some of the transcripts of written interviews are available on microform. Columbia also provides a set of links to other online oral history programs.
UCLA Oral History Program: Catalog of the Collection. 3d ed. Teresa Barnett, comp. Los Angeles: Oral History Program, Dept. of Special Collections, University of California, Los Angeles, 1999. Large collection of oral histories. Similar in scope to Columbia but a more recent program.
Oral History Index: An International Directory of Oral History Interviews. Westport, CT: Meckler, 1990. Index to holdings worldwide. Again, because of the date, you would need to contact the libraries before a visit.
Oral History Collections. Alan M. Meckler and Ruth McMullin, eds. New York: Bowker, 1975. Name and subject index to U.S. and foreign oral history centers. Because of the date, check with the archive to see if the collection and the archive still exist.
Oral History Collections and Centers Online, http://www.h-net.org/~oralhist/centers.html (accessed January 2, 2006). Maintained by *H-Net*. Some of the centers may have transcripts or streaming audio recordings of oral histories online.
Oral History Association's List of Centers and Collections, http://dickinson.edu/organizations/oha/org_cc.html (accessed January 2, 2006). List with links to centers. Some of the centers may have transcripts or streaming audio recordings of oral histories online.
Australia's Oral Histories, http://www.nla.gov.au/ohdir/about.html (accessed January 2, 2006). Large, searchable database of Australian oral histories.

Media and Audiovisual

Finding radio and television programs and motion pictures can be even more challenging than locating ancient manuscripts. Much of the early media was considered ephemeral. Even though we have records that it existed, no one thought it was important enough to save. What remains is now tightly controlled in private collections or the archives of the production companies and studios that originally created them or purchased their parent companies. Sometimes scripts of early radio and television programs do exist even though the broadcasts themselves were not saved. Access to motion pictures is somewhat better. With home video and now DVD, many classic movies are easily accessible. Copyright restrictions must be followed when using clips for a scholarly website. See Chapter Nine on incorporating images and moving pictures into your research.

History before 1400: Ancient and Medieval Cultures and Those with Substantial Oral and Material Culture Traditions

Many factors make finding accessible primary resources prior to the fifteenth century challenging. The documentation of some cultures' histories relies more heavily on material culture, such as pottery, or oral stories that have been passed down through generations of storytellers. The ancient and medieval European worlds used terms like "rolls," "royal skins," "daybooks," "formularies," and "charters," which are more reflective of their physical form and function (skins were written on skins, rolls are lists) than indicative of content. So, as a researcher in these eras and cultures, you must know something about the type of primary source and its form.

The availability of written sources prior to the twelfth century varies according to place and culture. Much of what has been handed down to present-day scholars exists as copies of originals. If the original still does exist, few researchers are ever allowed to view it. Copies are seldom exactly true to the original document and could have been altered inadvertently because of copying or dictating errors or purposely by scribes who objected to their content. Undoubtedly, you will be working with facsimiles and reprints. Even modern printers make mistakes, and authoritative editions make textual changes to account for language and translation conflicts. In addition, these sources are often translated from their original language, usually Latin, Greek, Hebrew, or older versions of English, French, or other vernacular languages. Translation is a skill practiced by a scholar who knows the language and understands the culture of the speakers and writers of the language. Part of translation is also conveying the meaning of the words, as well as the literal equivalent of the text.

What has survived to be studied also depends upon the medium on which it was recorded. At certain times, paper did not exist or was expensive, so documents were written on clay, papyrus, leather, and other less durable materials. Some cultures' records survived because climatic conditions were conducive to their preservation. For instance, sand and a dry Middle Eastern climate preserved many Egyptian papyrus records. In other cases, cultures purposely destroyed records and documents during war and conquest. During and immediately after the French Revolution, many medieval French documents were destroyed because of their association with the monarchy. Sometimes information is preserved by accident, such as when clay potsherds used as "scrap" were thrown into a fire and accidentally fired and hardened.

The sheer increase in quantity of production and survival of documents as well as artifacts speaks to the prosperity and literacy of a population. Certainly, if more documents are produced and survive, there must have been more people to read and save them at some point. A shift from oral memory to documentary evidence indicates that documents and literacy became more common.[7]

For various reasons, some cultures have stronger oral traditions than written ones. This does not mean these societies were not literate but that they functioned governmentally and socially more efficiently with a spoken record of their past and their laws than with a written record. Just as classical cultures had the *Iliad* and medieval cultures had traveling bards, African cultures have griots who pass local history and folklore down through the generations. Linguistically, you can follow cultural influences to see how words and phrases have evolved.

Material culture, the buildings, tools, and artifacts left behind by humans, can be especially useful in learning about cultures that leave scant written records. Archaeologists dig up former sites where people lived and try to recreate past communities and the lives of those who lived in them. For instance, historians use archaeological reports of Mayan and Incan ruins to understand these ancient societies. Environmentally, you can study how crops, plants, and animals migrate and spread and how trade and conquest by other nations bring new foods and diseases into a culture.

As students of ancient and medieval cultures, you must rely on a multitude of types of primary sources and, in many cases, become a "jack of all trades" when it comes to analysis and interpretation.

Ancient History

When looking for primary resources for ancient civilizations, thinking about the types of information that a civilization would produce will be helpful. For instance, ancient Egypt, Greece, Rome, and many of the civilizations of the Near East were highly bureaucratic and recorded laws, day-to-day governmental activities (in the forms "royal skins" of Persian kings or day-books of Roman officials), finances of the operation of the kingdom, finances of the income and personal property of the ruler (land surveys, deeds, and tax records), and private business contracts.[8] While these types of primary source records are not that different from those discussed throughout this chapter, locating such records, many of which no longer exist in their original form, presents a special research challenge.

Thinking of your ancient history sources in the following groups will help you search for the appropriate source for your project.[9] Literary works, such as histories, epic poems, plays, speeches, and some private letters of individuals, have survived by various means but, again, rarely in their original manuscript form. You will be working with authoritative translations by eminent scholars of important ancient texts by Homer, Herodotus, and Thucydides, for example, and such texts as the Christian Bible or the Torah.

Unique to ancient history, especially studies of Greece and Rome, is *epigraphy*, words inscribed on stone or metal. These inscribed objects could be displayed publicly, heralding the outcome of a great battle or the memory of an individual; hidden in a tomb for only its occupant to see; or placed on coins. Not meant to be preserved, clay tablets and potsherds were used as early "scribbling pads" and accidentally heated in the fire and preserved. Ancient Greece and Rome even had graffiti. Epigraphs are found in a multiplicity of languages throughout the Mediterranean, even as far east as Romania and as far south as the Persian Gulf.[10] *Numismatics*, or the study of coins, is also important to ancient Greek and Roman historians. Looking at the circulation of coins provides clues to commerce and how people traveled. Debasement of the metal indicates the political health of the empire. Themes and inscriptions (names and images) on the coins can be interpreted alongside other primary sources. Another specialized area of study for ancient historians is *papyrology*, the study of ancient documents written on papyrus. However, papyrology by its nature is restrictive because only certain cultures in Middle and Upper Egypt and parts of the Near East had the climate to preserve the material. These documents can be both public and private accounting records as well as letters. Archaeological evidence is also another key component to primary evidence in ancient societies, especially Greece and Rome. Studying the artifacts that individuals left behind tells us about their lives. Archaeological reports discuss the size and location of towns as well as the decoration of clay pots, wall murals and mosaics, structures of houses, garbage heaps, and layouts of cities.

SEARCH TIPS

1. Think about the types of sources that might be useful for you to study, look up that term as a subject in your library's online catalog (e.g., "Numismatics" or "Inscriptions"), and then look at the subdivisions by country or region. You can also look by subject, "Coins, Roman" or "Inscriptions, Latin" (or whatever language you are looking for).

2. In your library's online catalog, search for the culture or country as a subject and limit by words in subject "Sources" or "Antiquities." For example, "Roman Law" as a subject and then limit by words in subject "Sources." Remember, there may be intervening words between these two subject words, for instance, "Roman Law–History–Sources."

3. Another subject term to use is "Excavations, Archaeology" and limit to the country or region by words in the subject.

Selected Ancient History Primary Sources

Ancient History Sourcebook, http://www.fordham.edu/halsall/ancient/ asbook.html (accessed January 1, 2006).

Loeb Classical Library. Translated texts of classical authors. See the publisher's website for the complete list of titles (http://www.hup.harvard .edu/loeb/index.html). Your library will probably have most of these. If not, you should be able to order them through interlibrary loan.

Individual authors (e.g., Herodotus, Livy)

Orientis Graeci Inscriptiones Selectae: Supplementum Sylloges Inscriptionum graecarum. Wilhelmus Dittenberger, ed. Hildesheim: G. Olms, 1960.

Inscriptiones Graecae ad res Romanas Pertinentes. R. Cagnat, ed. Paris: E. Leroux, 1906–1927.

Inscriptiones Latinae Selectae. Hermannus Dessau, ed. Berolini: Apud Weidmannos, 1954–1955.

Corpus Inscriptionum Latinarum. Berolini: Apud G. Reimerum, 1869–1963.

Bibliotheca Scriptorum Graecorum et Romanorum Teubneriana. Leipzig: Teubneri, 1866–.

Perseus Digital Library, http://www.perseus.tufts.edu/ (accessed January 2, 2006).

Motif—Index of Folk Literature: A Classification of Narrative Elements in Folktales, Ballads, Myths, Fables, Mediaeval Romances, Exempla,

Fabliaux, Jest-books, and Local Legends. rev. and enl. ed. Stith Thompson. Bloomington: Indiana University Press, 1955–58. Also available online through subscription, *Motif—Index of Folk Literature*, http:/www .library.nix.com (accessed March 29, 2006).

For more suggestions, see *Sources for Ancient History.* Michael Crawford, ed. Cambridge: Cambridge University Press, 1983.

Medieval European History

Medieval history has its own language and specialties, which makes the search for primary sources different compared to some of the other topics described in this chapter. The greatest number and variety of sources are available from the twelfth century forward. Prior to that, there are significant numbers of sources available, but coverage is geographically and chronologically scattered.[11] Historian R. C. van Caenegem divides medieval sources into two types, narrative and nonnarrative. Narrative sources include annals, chronicles, histories, tracts, letters, and genealogies. Because medieval European society saw God associated with all aspects of life, common sources of history are ecclesiastical histories that attempted to explain how the Christian God affected historical events. Chronicles, ecclesiastical in origin, compiled facts and commemorated events. Annals were yearbooks of happenings. Genealogies, often part of chronicles, trace the histories of papacies, bishoprics, abbeys, kingdoms, princedoms, and their leaders. Letters were a form of public conversation, used as teaching tools or pieces of propaganda. Examples of nonnarrative sources are charters, laws and legislation, writs and mandates, chancery registers and rolls, formularies, land surveys, rolls of persons, and account books, all materials that documented property or regulated behavior. Charters are deeds or proof of ownership of land or goods. Court records are both from secular cities and ecclesiastical courts. Writs and mandates are documents that the rulers, local authorities or papal authorities used to inform the public of regulations, orders, or facts. Chancery registers or rolls list (and sometimes abstract or include the complete text of) charters or documents that were dispatched abroad. Sometimes these documents were grouped by concern or subject. Formularies were frequently used form letters and documents. Surveys of local lands, as well as of counties and crown holdings, were put into registers so that local lords, municipalities, and the king knew what was owed to them by their tenants as well as what they owned and where the crown's money came from (tolls, taxes, fishing rights, etc.). One of the most famous of these surveys is the Domesday Book, a one-year (1086) snapshot, county-by-county survey of England, recording by household names each estate and its value, yield in taxes, and production. Records for individuals exist also in rolls registers of deaths, births, funerals, and marriages, although not until late in the medieval period and frequently not in a continuous chronology so that you can study a significant time period. Some examples of records of individuals include parish registers, registers of freedmen, and rolls of deaths in religious communities.

Just as for ancient societies, literature is very important to the interpretation of medieval society. Few books were widely available yet. Individuals and libraries attached to churches and the newly founded universities had both learned works such as summas (something like a collection of someone's works) as well as copies of the pagan (Greek and Roman) classics. Liturgical books, such as holy scriptures, missals, prayer books, and books of hours, were also popular and prized.

Many of these sources have been published or printed in modern texts and collections. Britain was one of the best, most meticulously documented medieval societies, but many other sources exist for continental Europe. Many of these texts have been reprinted in a series by learned societies. Your key to finding these sources is to use many of the kinds of books (rolls, registers) in the above paragraph or one of the finding aids listed in the bibliography below or available online. To search for rolls, registers, annals, charters, writs, and mandates as keywords in your library's catalog or online could be useful. Language could be a barrier since until about the twelfth century most documents were written in Latin. After that, the vernacular or spoken languages gained in popularity, but they will be an older form of the modern language you are used to. Many times, translations into English or into a modern form of the original language are provided.

SEARCH TIPS

1. In a keyword search, in your library's catalog, use one of the terms that describes what you are looking for ("writ," "charter," etc.) and combine it with place, ruler, topic, or office (e.g., the name of a court).
2. You may wish to limit your results by publication date or to limit the time the content covers.
3. You can also use the word "sources" in the subject heading to indicate primary sources.

Bibliographic Guides to the Study of Medieval History

Medieval Studies: A Bibliographic Guide. New York: Garland, 1983.
Contains a list of primary sources and major secondary works. The
categories are quite extensive (e.g., "National Laws," "Art," and
"Folklore") and cover more geographic areas and cultures than just
Europe.

Guide to the Sources of Medieval History. R. C. van Caenegem. Amsterdam: Elsevier/North-Holland, 1978. Content includes sections
on the sources of medieval history as well as listing libraries and
archives.

From Memory to Written Record: England 1066–1307. M. T. Clanchy,
2d ed. Oxford: Blackwell, 1993. Highlights the explosion of documents in British history. Wealth of references to the types and titles
of sources.

The Labryinth, http://labyrinth.georgetown.edu/ (accessed January 2, 2006).
Digitized selection of primary documents with reference materials.

Medieval History Sourcebook, http://www.fordham.edu/halsall/sbook.html
(accessed January 1, 2006). Digitized selection of primary documents.

What Every Medievalist Should Know. James Marchand. http://www.the-orb
.net/wemsk/wemskmenu.html (accessed January 2, 2006). Guide to research. Contained in *ORB: The Online Reference Book for Medieval
Studies.*

Using Bibliographies to Locate Primary Sources

In some cases, you may find a comprehensive bibliography on your country
or time period that highlights the major primary resources relevant to your
research. While this bibliography will not list every resource available, published or unpublished, it will usually suggest the principal groups and the
records they produced. For instance, such bibliographies will provide a survey of documents produced by the governing bodies, common literary texts,
famous personal accounts, diaries and correspondence, statistical collections, and records of statesmen. A list of seminal bibliographies follows, including some websites. Many of the multivolume histories listed in Chapter
Two will also have extensive bibliographies that will lead you to seminal
primary sources. Looking through these lists may lead you to other resources. However, the topics of the bibliographies are too broad and may
not be the place to begin your research if your topic is not well defined. You
may find too many sources that will be too focused for your topic.

Bibliographies Containing References to Primary Sources

The American Historical Association's Guide to Historical Literature. Mary Beth Norton, ed. 3d ed. New York: Oxford University Press, 1995. 2 vols.

Sources for Ancient History. Michael Crawford, ed. New York: Cambridge University Press, 1983.

Latin America: A Guide to the Historical Literature. Charles C. Griffin, ed. Austin: University of Texas Press, 1971.

Africa, Asia, and South America Since 1800: A Bibliographical Guide. A. J. H. Latham, comp. Manchester: Manchester University Press, 1995.

Chinese History: A Manual. Rev. and enl. ed. Endymion Wilkinson. Cambridge, MA: Harvard University Asia Center for the Harvard-Yenching Institute, 2000.

Medieval Studies: A Bibliographic Guide. New York: Garland, 1983. Contains a list of primary sources and major secondary works. The categories are quite extensive (e.g., "National Laws," "Art," and "Folklore") and cover more geographic areas and cultures than just European ones.

Guide to the Sources of Medieval History. R. C. van Caenegem. Amsterdam: Elsevier/North-Holland, 1978. Content includes sections on sources for medieval history as well as libraries and archives.

From Memory to Written Record: England 1066–1307. M. T. Clanchy, 2d ed. Oxford, UK: Blackwell, 1993. Highlights the explosion of documents in British history. Wealth of references to the types and titles of sources.

A Bibliography of British History, 1914–1989. Keith Robbins, comp. and ed. Oxford: Clarendon, 1996.

A Bibliography of English History to 1485. E. B. Graves, comp. Oxford: Clarendon, 1975.

Bibliography of British History: Tudor Period, 1485–1603. Conyers Read, comp. 2d ed. Totowa, NJ: Rowman and Littlefield, 1978.

Bibliography of British History: Stuart History, 1603–1714. G. D. Davies and M. F. Keeler, comps. 2d ed. Oxford: Clarendon, 1970.

Bibliography of British History: The Eighteenth Century, 1714–1789. S. Pargellis and D. J. Medley, comps. Oxford: Clarendon, 1951.

Bibliography of British History, 1789–1851. L. M. Brown and I. R. Christie, comps. Oxford: Clarendon, 1977.

Bibliography of British History, 1851–1914. H. J. Hanham, comp. Oxford: Clarendon, 1976.

WWW–Virtual Library History Index, http://vlib.iue.it/history/index.html (accessed January 2, 2006). Massive directory of sites focused on history and covering all eras and countries imaginable. Look for the sections on archival materials under each country or time period.

Stanford University Library Guides, http://library.stanford.edu/depts/hasrg/
index.html (accessed March 28, 2006). Many of these guides have an
extensive list of primary sources.

Yale University Library Subject Guides, http://www.library.yale.edu/guides/.
(accessed March 28, 2006). Many of these guides have an extensive list
of primary sources.

Evaluation

Once you have located your primary sources, you must examine their inter-
relatedness. Much like a detective or a crime scene investigator, you must
read and review your evidence carefully, looking for obvious omissions as
well as clues the past has left you. The following questions will be helpful
in determining the usefulness of a source:[12]

1. Who produced this source? Clearly identify the author and find out as
    much as you can about that individual in the secondary literature and
    biography and encyclopedia resources.

2. What was the purpose of the primary source?

3. Who was the intended audience?

4. Is something or someone missing? Did the author intend to omit some-
    thing or someone on purpose? Why? Do the facts seem incomplete or too
    complete? Are the conclusions too logical or illogical? Would the indi-
    vidual creating this primary source really have access to all of this infor-
    mation? Should she or he have been able to include more information?

5. What is the perspective of the author and how might this affect the con-
    tents of the source?

6. How does the document reflect the time in which it was written? What
    other sources or materials might support or refute this evidence? Com-
    pare different primary sources from the same period. What voices are
    missing? Does it reflect a particular gender, racial, ethnic, regional, reli-
    gious, or political perspective?

7. Is something implicit that would be clear to the original audience but
    might be hidden from the modern researcher? Is there a set of values,
    assumptions, or biases that the audience would have had that the mod-
    ern researcher does not?

8. What other sources or materials might support or refute this evidence?

9. Is the document believable? That is, could it have been created in the
    time in which it appears to have been created?

Case Study ▪ Finding Primary Sources: Tobacco through the Ages

Now that you have an idea about the variety and types of primary sources available, putting them all together is the challenge. Below is an example that will help you think about primary sources and their role as the foundation for your research.

Tobacco use was, and still is, a controversial economic and social issue in virtually all societies. You can find information about its commercial, social, and medical influence in almost every century throughout the history of its use by Europeans. Some of the potential sources are as follows:

1. *Published sources for mass consumption.* Looking in your catalog as well as resources such as *Early English Books* using "tobacco" as a subject and limiting the results by date of publication will produce all sorts of discussions on tobacco's influence. Prior to 1800, you might find a book by Giles Everard entitled *Panacea, or, The Universal Medicine: Being a Discovery of the Wonderfull Vertues of Tobacco Taken in a Pipe, with its Operation and Use Both in Physick and Chirurgery* (London: Printed for S. Miller 1659). After 1800, when smoking was often regarded as a vice, you would find a book entitled *Smoke Not: An Essay, by Miss E.S.C., to whom a prize has been awarded by a committee of the British Anti-Tobacco Society* (Richmond: Macfarlane & Fergusson, 1861). Using *Poole's Index* or *Readers' Guide to Periodical Literature* (or their online counterparts, if available at your institution) or a newspaper index, such as the *New York Times Index* or the *Times (London) Index*, and looking up "tobacco" would also be revealing. You could read "The Dangers and Delights of Tobacco," in *St. Pauls: A Monthly Magazine* in 1868–69, or an editorial from the *New York Times* in 1866 discussing Baron Bramwell's suggestion that tobacco was necessary for English children.

2. *Manuscripts.* Using one of the manuscript indexes above or *Worldcat*, and doing a keyword search, and looking at the results in the archival materials section, you would find materials like the John B. Hutson papers (1933-1957). Hutson was the assistant to the secretary-general of the United Nations and undersecretary of agriculture. These papers include scrapbooks, speeches, articles, and letters centering on Hutson's involvement in the tobacco industry.

3. *Government documents.* Using your local catalog or some of the bibliographic sources above, such as the *Monthly Catalog*, you might find a report, "Smoking and Health; Report of the Advisory Committee to the

Surgeon General of the Public Health Service," by the U.S. surgeon general's Advisory Committee on Smoking and Health, issued in 1964.

4. *Public records.* Public records for tobacco can be extremely varied, depending on the time and geographic location. You could look for local revenues of taxes placed on tobacco. You could find market prices for tobacco. Health records of populations and aggregate statistics might be available but not for individual smokers. In each of these instances, the records would be located at a local historical society, library, or the city or state's department of health. Use the guides listed previously to locate the contact information for these institutions and ask them if such information exits. Doing a keyword search on *Worldcat* for "tobacco" and your state or locale might also prove fruitful.

5. *Business records.* Using some of the directories listed, you could look for the archives of Philip Morris/Altria Group or another of the major tobacco companies still in existence. Because of recent controversies, your access to the archives would probably be restricted.

6. *Oral testimony.* Searching one of the directories provided above or looking in *Worldcat* (searching for keywords "tobacco" and "oral history"), you would find a reference to the Southern Folklife Collection at the University of North Carolina at Chapel Hill and a manuscript collection entitled "Collection 1941–1946; 1987," which is a series of interviews with Anglo-American musicians who grew up on tobacco farms or were involved in the tobacco business.

7. *Media and advertising.* Search the sources provided in the media section in Chapter Nine to see what might be available. Do not forget that some advertisements might be in print sources. Check with your librarian. See Chapter Seven on using the Internet.

FOR FURTHER READING

American Memory Learning Page: What Are Primary Sources? http://memory.loc .gov/learn/lessons/psources/source.html (accessed March 29, 2006).

Brundage, Anthony. *Going to the Sources: A Guide to Historical Research and Writing.* 3d ed. Wheeling, IL: Harlan Davidson, 2002.

D'Aniello, Charles A., ed. *Teaching Bibliographic Skills in History: A Sourcebook for Historians and Librarians.* Westport, CT: Greenwood Press, 1993.

Fisher, Steven, ed. *Archival Information: How to Find It, How to Use It.* Westport, CT: Greenwood Press, 2004.

Lusker, Marilyn. *Research Projects for College Students: What to Write Across the Curriculum.* New York: Greenwood Press, 1988.

Using Primary Sources on the Web, http://www.lib.washington.edu/subject/History/RUSA/ (accessed January 1, 2006).

Yale University Guide to Primary Sources, http://www.library.yale.edu/instruction/primsource.html (accessed January 1, 2006).

Bibliography of Advanced Indexes to Published Primary Sources

Below are titles of specialized journal indexes that span much of the twentieth century and, in some cases, some of the nineteenth. The main title is the current or latest title. Listed underneath are the previous titles.

Alternative Press Index 1969–.
    Index to the radical press of the 1970s. Find out what antiwar, labor, and women's publications were discussing.
L'Année philologique; bibliographie critique et analytique de l'antiquité gréco-latine, 1924–.
    Multilingual index to articles concerning classical culture. Good for ancient history.
Art Index, 1929–.
    Index to articles about art, including art history, folk art, sculpture, architecture, painting, and anything art-related.
Biological Abstracts, 1926–.
    History of biology and scientific development.
    ▪ *Abstracts of Bacteriology*, 1917–1921.
    ▪ *Botanical Abstracts*, 1918–1926.
Biological and Agricultural Index, 1964–.
    Agricultural/farming developments.
    ▪ *Agricultural Index*, 1916–1964.
Chemical Abstracts/Chem Abstracts, 1907–.
    History of chemistry and related industries.
    ▪ *Review of American Chemical Research*, 1905–1906.
Combined Retrospective Index to Book Reviews in Scholarly Journals, 1886–1974.
    Index to book reviews.
Education Index, 1929–.
    History of education and educational theory.
Essay and General Literature Index, 1900–.
    Indexes essays in books.
Index Islamicus, 1906–.
    Index to the study of the Islamic world.

Index Medicus, 1879–.
  Index to articles on all aspects of medicine. (Online version, *Medline* 1966– and *Old Medline* 1953–1965.)
Industrial Arts Index, 1912–1957.
  Index to publications in the trades, business, technical sciences, etc. Later split into the two titles below.
  ▪ *Business Periodicals Index*, 1958–.
  ▪ *Applied Science and Technology Index*, 1958–.
International Index to Periodicals, 1901–1965.
  Index to scholarly journal articles. Parallel index to *Readers' Guide to Periodical Literature*, which indexes popular articles. Split into the indexes below.
  ▪ *Social Sciences and Humanities Index*, 1965–1974
    • *Social Sciences Index*, 1974–.
    • *Humanities Index*, 1974–.
PAIS International/Public Affairs Information Service, 1990–.
  Index to articles in public administration and the operation of governments.
  ▪ *PAIS Bulletin*, 1986–1990.
  ▪ *Bulletin of the Public Affairs Information Service Bulletin*, 1915–1986.
Psychological Abstracts, 1927–.
  History of the study of psychology.
Wellesley Index to Victorian Periodicals, 1824–1900. Walter E. Houghton, ed.
  Toronto: University of Toronto Press, Routledge, Kegan Paul.
  Major nineteenth-century British periodicals, with listing of table of contents, issue by issue.

NOTES

1. Howell and Prevenier have a nice discussion about the evolution of archives from private collections to this current organizational division. Martha Howell and Walter Prevenier, *From Reliable Sources: An Introduction to Historical Methods* (Ithaca, NY: Cornell University Press, 2001), 34–42.
2. Nicholas Culpeper, *A Directory for Midwives: or, A Guide for Women, in their Conception. Bearing; and Suckling their Children* . . . (London: printed, and are to be sold by most booksellers in London and Westminster, 1693).
3. James C. Dobbins, *Letters of the Nun Eshinni: Images of Pure Land Buddhism in Medieval Japan* (Honolulu: University of Hawaii Press, 2004).
4. A depository library is a library designated by the U.S. government to receive all or nearly all (as specified by the library) U.S. publications automatically when they are published. Every state and each congressional district has one full depository library. The system began in 1813.
5. Church records present a particular problem. In some eras and some regions, a church, usually the Catholic Church, was the administrative, governing body,

while in other eras and regions, it was simply an organization with a great deal of influence in society and politics.

6. Valerie Raleigh Yow. *Recording Oral History: A Guide for the Humanities and Social Sciences* 2d. Walnut Creek: CA. AltaMira Press, 2005; Donald A. Ritchie. *Doing Oral History: A Practical Guide.* 2d. Oxford: Oxford University Press, 2003.

7. M. T. Clanchy, *From Memory to Written Record: England 1066–1307* (Oxford: Blackwell, 1993).

8. Ernst Posner, *Archives in the Ancient World.* (Cambridge, MA: Harvard University Press, 1972), 3–4.

9. Michael Crawford, ed., *Sources for Ancient History* (Cambridge: Cambridge University Press, 1983).

10. Emilio Gabba, "Literature," in *Sources for Ancient History*, Michael Crawford, ed. (Cambridge: Cambridge University Press, 1983), 1–80.

11. R. C. Van Caenegem, with the collaboration of F. L. Ganshof, *Guide to the Sources of Medieval History.* Amsterdam: Elsevier/North-Holland 1978), 15.

12. Some of these questions came from Marilyn Luzker, "The Undergraduate Researcher and Primary Sources," in *Research Projects for College Students: What to Write Across the Curriculum (*New York: Greenwood Press, 1988), 43. An in-depth discussion of evaluating primary sources can be found in Howell and Prevenier*, From Reliable Sources*, 62–68. For evaluating primary sources on the Internet, see *Using Primary Sources on the Internet* (Instruction and Research Services Committee of the Reference and User Service Association, History Section, American Library Association), http://www.lib.washington.edu/ subject/History/RUSA/ (accessed January 1, 2006).

7

History and
the Internet

WHAT YOU WILL LEARN IN THIS CHAPTER:

- when the Internet is appropriate for history research
- how to perform efficient searches using a search directory, search engine, or meta-search engine
- how to evaluate your search results
- how historians use the Internet to communicate

The Internet and Research

The Internet offers a new resource to add to the others already discussed. Many novice researchers, however, treat it as a virtual library, equivalent to the collection of monographs, journals, and primary sources discussed in the previous chapters. A website can integrate a collection of primary sources, documents, images, and maps, for instance, that a single researcher has collected as well as connect these sources with interpretive materials such as explanatory essays or reference-like texts such as encyclopedias and glossaries. A powerful tool, the Internet can allow greater communication between teacher and learner, regardless of the purpose of the website. For instance, a site on the Song Dynasty in China (http://afe.easia.columbia.edu/song/) examines the economic and social history of twelfth-century China as seen through a scroll painting. The site contains images with explanatory text and a bibliography of further readings. Yet, while sites such as this are amazing research tools, the Internet does not have the organization (precise, controlled subject headings) of an online catalog or index, nor does it employ the review process that many publishers of journals and monographs use to assure quality publications. Scholars and nonscholars alike take advantage of the freedom of the Internet, posting websites of varying quality. Because of this you can waste a lot of time searching for websites and finding nothing of value. As a researcher, you must learn to efficiently search for and evaluate websites, just as you do all the other sources you gather. When used appropriately and in conjunction with monographs and journals, information from websites can enhance your research. Understanding what the Internet is and how it functions will allow you to use it appropriately.

Thinking about the types of common Internet sites will help you decide which are most valuable for certain aspects of historical research. Websites fall into the following categories, and many are combinations of these categories (an example of a historical site in each category is listed in parentheses):

- collections of primary sources (*Internet History Sourcebooks*, http://www.fordham.edu/halsall/)
- papers and projects (*History Matters: Student Projects on the Web*, http://historymatters.gmu.edu/browse/studhist/)
- webliographies (*Latin American Network of Information Center*, http://lanic.utexas.edu/)
- collections of an organization's documents, policies, and activities (*The American Historical Association*, http://www.historians.org/)
- blogs or personal reflections on topics (History News Network's list of blogs, http://hnn.us/departments/86.html)
- connections to listservs for scholarly discussions (*H-Net Humanities and Social Sciences Online*, http://www.h-net.org/)
- reference or encyclopedia sites (*Ecole Initiative: Creating a Hypertext Encyclopedia of Early Church History*, http://www2.evansville.edu/ecoleweb/), an exhibit of artifacts and interpretations on a subject (*Turning the Pages* [British Library] http://www.bl.uk/collections/treasures/digitisation4.html) and current scholarly research and analysis (*History Cooperative's Online Proceedings* [for a fee], http://historycooperative.press.uiuc.edu/proceedings/)

When Is the Internet Appropriate for Historical Research?

Again, if used correctly and critically, the Internet can be a valuable source for your historical research. Knowing when it is useful and when books and journal articles are more appropriate is the key to being a good and accurate historian. Historian Carl Smith in his oft-quoted, groundbreaking article "Can You Do Serious History on the Web?" answers in the affirmative.[1] He defines serious history "to mean original work that is responsibly based on primary sources, is intelligently informed by relevant scholarship, and makes a clear argument or group of arguments." If a website meets these criteria, it contains serious history. So what kinds of serious history can be found on the web?

- *Primary sources.* Many historical societies, museums, and archives are beginning to digitize *parts* of their collections and place them online. Sometimes universities, other research agencies, or individual faculty members create a collection of out-of-copyright or primary materials on a subject. For example, *The Labyrinth* (http://www.labyrinth .georgetown.edu) categorizes both primary and secondary materials about medieval life and culture. Another goldmine of primary sources is the *Internet History Source Books* maintained by historian Paul Halsall and a host of volunteer editors (http://www.fordham.edu/halsall/). This collection of sites contains links to primarily print texts from ancient history to the present day. The Internet is especially useful for modern historical primary source material such as video clips and oral interviews. Websites such as *History and Politics Out Loud* (http:// www.hpol.org/) at Northwestern University contain audio versions of political speeches and include transcripts online. Other primary source materials are the Cambodian Genocide Project (http://www .yale.edu/cgp/) and the Paris Siege and Commune (http://www.library .northwestern.edu/spec/siege/).

- *Bibliographies/webliographies.* Collections of references to secondary source materials, such as journal articles, books, and some websites, are widely available. Individuals, organizations, or research institutes interested in a particular subject often will compile lists of key references, allowing you to build on someone else's research. If you are lucky, such resources will include an internal search engine or some sort of topical arrangement to facilitate your search. If you are very lucky, you may find some links to full-text articles that have no copyright restrictions. For an example, see *Africabib* (http://www.africabib.org), a site that, among other components, contains three major searchable bibliographic databases: *Bibliography of Africana Periodical Literature Database, African Women's Bibliographic Database, and Women Travelers, Explorers, and Missionaries to Africa 1763–2003*, compiled by Davis Bullwinkle, director of the Institute for Economic Advancement Research Library at the University of Arkansas-Little Rock.

- *Organizations' and governments' documents.* Many organizations have begun to link their current documents to an online page. Numerous projects are creating collections of digitized historical documents. For example, *Eurodocs* (http://library.byu.edu/~rdh/eurodocs/), while not a site by a government, organizes full-text historic European countries' and territories' documents by country. It was established and is maintained by the Western European Studies Section of the Association of College and Research Libraries. The *United Nations* (http://www.un .org) makes a large portion of its official documents from the last 10 years available through its website. For example, you can find International Court of Justice proceedings against Yugoslavia for genocide in Bosnia, Herzegovina, and Croatia as well as Economic and Social Council programs on health. Seldom will you find documents older than the past decade or two placed online by an organization or government, although some notable exceptions exist. The African National Congress has a growing collection of documents (http://www .anc.org.za/). *American Memory* (http://memory.loc.gov/ammem/) has an online collection of the proceedings of the U.S. Congress from 1774 through 1875.[2]

- *Specialized reference sources.* The Internet's use of hyperlinks makes it an ideal vehicle for reference sources, such as definitions and longer articles of explanation on topics that can be too specialized to be published in book form or that can be enhanced by multimedia. For an example, see the *Encyclopedia of Cleveland History* (http://ech.cwru .edu/). In this encyclopedia, you will find images and historical information about Cleveland, Ohio. Remember to be careful of out-of-date resources. Until recently, the edition of *Roget's Thesaurus* that Bartelby.com supplied was published in 1901.

- *Cutting-edge secondary source research.* Historians usually engage one another to work out theories they have devised based on their research, and some of this discussion takes place on forums on the Internet. At the *Center for History and the New Media* (http://chnm.gmu .edu/), selected essays are posted by the authors to promote discussion among historians about doing digital history. The site also contains a number of primary source collections as well. In the same way, some of the chatter on the *H-Net* series of listserv groups cites cutting-edge research. What the Internet will not provide, generally, is access to published, refereed journal articles or books. While there are exceptions, usually access to such materials requires a paid subscription by your library. An exception is *Google Scholar*, a separate section of the search engine *Google* which does provide links to some full-text academic journals (see Chapter Four for a discussion). There are also some academic journals that do publish freely online and will not be indexed in a periodical index. As discussed above, the search engines will not search in a fee-restricted database or in an online journal. For a list of online history journals, some free, some subscription, see http://www.history-journals.de/articles/index.html and http://www.doaj.org.

- *Communication.* Many scholars belong to a listserv, and some read blogs or create their own blogs. With a listserv, you subscribe to a list on which you can ask, view, and reply to questions about topics around a central theme, for instance, early modern history. Blogs are public, personal diaries in which anyone can participate. Finally, *RSS (Really Simple Syndication)* allows you to receive notifications, much like a personal newsletter, of new postings in selected blogs. More about this below.

- *Syllabi.* Sometimes online course syllabi can be useful in research. Professors create specialized guides for their students to use in a course. Be very careful to evaluate your source. Make sure that the person writing the document has some authority and is not a student completing an assignment. Be careful using websites by other students. Some will be of excellent quality, while others may be poorly constructed and researched. It is difficult to judge quality if you do not yet know much about the subject you are studying. Be cautious using syllabi and the documents linked to them as sources. See the online American History survey *History Matters* (http://historymatters.gmu.edu/) and *World History Matters* (http://chnm.gmu.edu/worldhistorysources/) for examples of an online course and the integration of multimedia into the basic American civilization course. Also see the section of this site titled "Syllabus Central," which provides links to other syllabi that may have web pages with explanatory material useful for your research.

Using the Internet: The Basics

To access the World Wide Web and all of those wonderful sites mentioned, you will use a piece of software called a browser. *Internet Explorer, Netscape, Mozilla, Foxfire,* and *Safari* are just a few. If you have problems reading a website, it could be that the webmaster did a poor job in creating the site and it can only be read by the particular browser for which that site was created. Be careful not to confuse browsers with a database or with the search engines, or the search directories, discussed below.

How Do I Access Websites on the Internet?

Most of us have a favorite search engine that we use, such as *Google*, and we simply type some words in its search box and hope for the best. You can waste a great deal of time "surfing" on the Internet, looking for useable information, finding very little, and getting lost on interesting but unrelated websites. Before you become mired in your Internet search, you need to be sure that the time you spend will be worth the effort when you find results. Performing efficient searches in the right places, just as you learned in using online catalogs and indexes, will improve your time-investment-to-results ratio. Using effective search strategies in search directories, search engines, and meta-search engines will produce useful results from quality websites. Each of these three Internet tools has different uses for specific kinds of research.

Search Directories

A search directory is a very large but limited collection of links categorized by knowledgeable people. Purposely selective and not comprehensive, the collection of links implies quality by any one link's inclusion. Search directories are useful when you have a very broad subject that you are unable to focus into a research topic. Because they are organized by subject categories, you can do a keyword search *within* the directory, discover a subject category, and browse through that category, still within the directory. You have already practiced this same technique in an online catalog by doing a keyword search and then searching by the subject headings attached to the catalog record. But you still must use your evaluation skills. Not all websites, even though they have been selected for a directory, will necessarily be of good quality or meet *your* research standards. Follow the evaluation guidelines later in this chapter and think about your research needs as you search for online sources.

SEARCH TIPS
1. Choose a search directory.
2. Using the search box, do a keyword search within the directory.
3. When the results appear, use the subject headings/subject categories attached to one of the results to browse for other similar websites in the directory.

General Search Directories

Librarians' Internet Index, http://lii.org (accessed January 1, 2006). Very selective but extensive list of about 30,0001 quality sites. Not all are history-related, but this is a good place to start looking.

BUBL Link, http://bubl.ac.uk/ (accessed January 1, 2006). A directory, similar to the *Librarians' Internet Index* but somewhat smaller in scope, with about 11,0001 highly selected sources. However, because of its British origin, it contains many more British and European sources that may not be listed in some of these other directories.

MERLOT (Multimedia Educational Resource for Learning and Online Teaching), http://www.merlot.org (accessed January 1, 2006). Provides ratings and descriptions of websites that are more academic in nature and usually designed to supplement teaching. Includes links to assignments created by professors and teachers.

Voice of the Shuttle, http://vos.ucsb.edu/ (accessed January 1, 2006). Scholarly directory established in 1994 at the University of California, Santa Barbara. Long lists to search through but useful.

Open Directory, http://dmoz.org (accessed January 1, 2006). Billed as the "most comprehensive human-edited directory of the Web," *Open Directory* has the usual categories. It also has a number of links to directories in other languages.

INFOMINE, http://infomine.ucr.edu (accessed January 1, 2006). Directory created by librarians from a number of university libraries for students and faculty using the Internet for research. The search interface is a bit different from most, looking much like an online catalog with options to search in author, title, subject, description, and full text.

The Internet Scout Report, http://scout.wisc.edu/ (accessed January 1, 2006). A searchable, weekly newsletter of recommended Internet sites. Lengthy reviews. Not a directory in the true sense of the word but a good place to begin looking.

Yahoo, http://www.yahoo.com (accessed January 1, 2006). The original directory. It is vast, though not approaching the size of a search engine. When it comes to scholarship, there are good finds as well as lots of junk in *Yahoo*. This directory is not as selective as the previously listed ones, but its organization is good. Use your evaluation skills carefully.

General History Search Directories, Webliographies, and Print Bibliographies

WWW-VL History Central Catalog, http://vlib.iue.it/history/index.html (accessed January 1, 2006). Part of the *World Wide Web Virtual Library*, a massive directory of sites focused on history and covering all eras and countries imaginable. There is no search feature included, so you must browse through the categories. Some marginal sites are included in this site's attempt to be comprehensive. Still, a gem.

Best of History Websites, http://www.besthistorysites.net/ (accessed January 1, 2006). Selective collection of sites for students and teachers of all levels and all areas of history.

History Guide, http://www.historyguide.de (accessed January 1, 2006). Very comprehensive. German site but multilingual with scholarly websites. European focus.

Humbul Humanities Hub, http://www.humbul.ac.uk/ (accessed January 1, 2006). Large directory of websites with good coverage for Europe and Canada. Best to perform a keyword search as the subject categories are by type (i.e., primary sources), and then contain long alphabetical lists of websites.

Stanford University Library Guides, http://library.stanford.edu/depts/hasrg/index.html (accessed March 29, 2006).

Yale University Library Subject Guides, http://www.library.yale.edu/guides/ (accessed January 1, 2006).

Trinkle, Dennis A., and Scott A. Merriman, eds. *The History Highway 3.0: A Guide to Internet Resources.* 3d ed. Armonk, NY: M. E. Sharpe, 2002. Huge print bibliography of websites organized by country and general subject. However, because a printed book can be dated and websites disappear, some links might be out of date.

Trinkle, Dennis A., and Scott A. Merriman, eds. *The European History Highway: A Guide to Internet Resources.* Armonk, NY: M. E. Sharpe, 2002. Print bibliography of websites focused on Europe, including the former Soviet republics. Some duplication in the "general" section with the *History Highway 3.0* above.

Trinkle, Dennis A., and Scott A. Merriman, eds. *The World History Highway: A Guide to Internet Resources.* Armonk, NY: M. E. Sharpe, 2002. Print bibliography of websites focused on world history. Some duplication in the "general" section with the *History Highway 3.0* above.

Search Engines

Search directories, while incredibly useful for a topic that is not well developed, cover only a small portion of the available Internet resources. Search engines attempt to index a larger portion of the Internet. Scouring the Internet for websites and remembering their locations, a *bot* or *spider* (essentially a piece of software) crawls into servers, the machines that house web pages, and stores and catalogs the locations of those web pages, returning regularly (every month or so) to update its information.[3] This means that if a page disappears before the spider or bot returns to make updates, you will find a *dead link,* a nonworking connection to the web page that previously existed. (There is no serious archiving of web pages at present. So, unlike print documents of the past, little of the Internet historical record is being preserved. One attempt is the *Internet Archive or Wayback Machine*, http://www.archive.org/.)[4]

When you perform a search, the search engine posts the results, matching the keywords and web pages with uniform resource locators (URLs) related to your search request. In this process, there is no human intervention. The search as well as the posted and ranked results are the result of a mechanical process. Traditionally, search engines searched only through HTML (or web) pages.[5] Now, at least several search engines also compile locations of pdf documents (.pdf), excel files (.xls), adobe postscript (.ps), Microsoft *Word* files (.doc), *PowerPoint* files (.ppt), and rich text files (.rtf). This makes more of the invisible or deep web material (discussed below) available.

Because of its immense inventory of websites and lack of subject control, a search engine requires a good search strategy. Your Boolean logic skills will be useful in constructing a productive search in a search engine. As a search engine is just another database, the same search concepts apply. When you enter your keyword search in the search box, most search engines assume you want both words to appear in the web page, but not as a phrase. This is the Boolean concept of "and." (Always check the "search tips" section that each search engine provides for the peculiarities of that search engine.) For instance, a search for "Dust Bowl California" could get you a website advertising a maid service located in California, if they claim to dust your ceramic bowls carefully! A more precise search would be " *"Dust Bowl" California"*. The quotation marks indicate you want to do a phrase search for the words "dust bowl" and that the word "California" should be included. One result would be *Dust Bowl Refugees in California* (http://www.sfmuseum.org/hist8/ok.html), a website maintained by the Museum of the City of San Francisco. Other search techniques include the use of the word "or" ("California or San Francisco") or of search boxes to restrict your terms to the same sentence or title. (These extra search boxes are usually located in the "advanced search" section.) Some search engines also allow you to restrict your searches to a particular domain. Restricting your search to .edu is sometimes useful, if you think academic websites will provide more authoritative information (as opposed to .com or .org). Sometimes a .org website will give you an organization's unique view, for instance, that of the Institute for Historical Review (http://www.ihr.org/), which denies the Holocaust.[6] (A .org is not necessarily nonprofit as originally intended in the domain extension monikers. It is given for any organization and often for any group that does not fit into any of the other domain categories.) Each search

Box 7.1 How to Read a URL

Your browser "reads" a URL (uniform resource locator) or the address of a website, which is the location of the computer where the web page you want resides. Knowing how to read a URL is essential to understanding where you are on the Internet. See Figure 7.1 for an example of a URL.

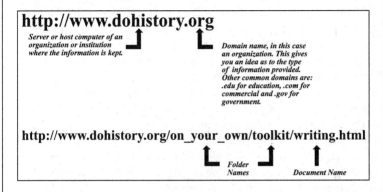

Figure 7.1. The parts of a URL (uniform resource locator). By stripping each of the file names, separated by a forward slash (/), you can discover the origin or hosting computer.

Using the diary of Martha Ballard, an eighteenth-century midwife, this website illustrates how the past can be pieced together using fragments of evidence. The first URL takes you to the main website, an organization called "dohistory" that provides materials to study Martha Ballard's diary. The second URL above leads you to a guide on deciphering eighteenth-century handwriting. By reading the URL itself, you will see the name, or host, of the website you are visiting, the kind of site (domain) it is (.com, edu, .org, etc.), and which particular part of the file you are looking for. You can actually use your knowledge about a URL's structure to evaluate a website. Even though you know nothing about the content of the website, by peeling off the file names back to www.dohistory.org, you know that an organization, in this case the Center for History and the New Media Film Study Center at Harvard University cited at the bottom of the page, has made this website available on the Internet. That should prompt you to ask questions about the purpose and intent of the organization and the influence that might have on the content of the site.

engine has features in its advanced search that are unique to that search engine. Again, look at the help files linked on the main page of the search engine and decide which tips will be useful for your particular research project.

An algorithm, which varies by search engine, ranks your results. *Google*, for instance, has a sophisticated ranking system that combines the number of times a page is linked on other web pages as well as the number of occurrences of your query words and their location in the web page. (For the technical explanation, see the *Google* help pages.) So, if a web page is linked often to other websites, it will be ranked higher in *Google's* results list. Web designers have tried to influence rankings by having a large number of websites link a phrase, usually a derogatory phrase, to a website. This practice, called "Google bombing," has recently been used to link George W. Bush's biography to the phrase "miserable failure." Other targets of this malicious practice include Bill Gates and Fox News columnist Cal Thomas, who was marked as "ignorant asshole" because in his column he called the Dutch "murderers" for allowing euthanasia on certain newborns.[7] Regardless of your view of these individuals and issues, this is a way to manipulate *Google* search results. Other search engines have their own ranking techniques. In some cases, a search engine charges fees to website producers to have their website appear higher in a results list.

Each search engine listed below and the numerous others that you may encounter has different devices and techniques for searching and creating the database. Remember to read their search help files to determine their unique features. Because each search engine's spider or bot collects and indexes sites differently, use more than one search engine. The same search strategy in different search engines will yield different results.

SEARCH TIPS

1. Use Boolean search techniques such as 1 (for "and") and "term." (put your phrase in quotation marks. Check the "help" section for your search engine to see how to indicate Boolean connectors, such as "and". Many search engines assume that you want all of the words included in your search.
2. Use the advanced search features and limit by domain, such as .edu, .gov, or .org.
3. Be as concrete and specific with your search terms as you can. General searches often produce voluminous results that are even more vague than your search and will waste your time.
4. Use more than one search engine.

General Search Engines[8]

Google, http://www.google.com (accessed March 26, 2006).
AllTheWeb, http://www.alltheweb.com (accessed March 26, 2006).
Teoma, http://www.teoma.com (accessed March 26, 2006). Since the
  demise of Argus Clearinghouse, Teoma is now indexing meta-sites,
  those large sites with many links and complicated subject organizations.
AltaVista, http://www.altavista.com (accessed March 26, 2006).

Search Engines for History

No *true* search engines exist specifically for history. Others will cite search engines for historical resources, but technically they are really collections of websites and/or directories with a search engine that searches within that directory.

Meta-Search Engines

The concept of meta-search engines can be a bit daunting and frankly engages in overkill when it comes to academic Internet research. Because meta-search engines search many search engines and directories simultaneously, if your topic is not well defined or unique, they create an overwhelming amount of redundant information and are therefore not recommended for your academic research. However, you may want to try *Vivisimo*, which groups your results and suggests subcategories of websites. It is probably the most useful meta-search engine below.

Selected General Meta-Search Engines

Vivisimo, http://vivisimo.com/ (accessed March 26, 2006).
Webcrawler, http://www.webcrawler.com/ (accessed March 26, 2006).
Dogpile, http://www.dogpile.com/ (accessed March 26, 2006).
Metacrawler, http://www.metacrawler.com/ (accessed March 26, 2006).

SEARCH TIPS
Use the same research techniques with meta-search engines as with search engines.

What Am I Missing? The Deep Web or Invisible Web

Because of the technology that search engines use to crawl the web, there are places and types of information that they may not be able to find. Referred to as the "deep web" or "invisible web," this portion of the Internet is inaccessible by most of the common search engines, which generally search only that portion of the web written in hypertext language or files with .html or .htm on the end of their URL. A graphic illustration of what you are missing is available at http://www.brightplanet.com/technology/deepweb.asp. While a search engine may find the existence of a project or a website, it is unable to search within a database. An obvious example is the website eBay, which offers personally owned items for sale. If someone wishes to sell his or her ancestor's Civil War surgical instruments, searching for "surgical instruments 'civil war' " generally does not find the eBay auction listing. A more scholarly example is the *Cambodian Genocide Program* at Yale University (http://www.yale.edu/cgp/), which is a site that contains three databases: a bibliographic section, a biographic database, and a photographic database. These databases attempt to provide access to Pol Pot's security police archives, which document a portion of the 1.7 million Cambodians who were killed in the genocide between the years 1975 and 1979. *Google* will list the URLs for the databases themselves, but it will not be able to search within their contents, for instance, to find an individual's name. Another example of a hidden database to which common search engines might not go is Northwestern University's collection of photographs on the Siege and Commune of Paris, 1870–1871.[9] Doing a search for "siege Paris" would find the web page. However, if you were looking for a photograph of the Chateau de Meudon, contained in the database, searching for "chateau meudon" might not find the photographs contained in this site. As technology changes, the ability to search within these kinds of databases may also change.

A database such as *DOAJ: Directory of Open Access Journals* (http://doaj.org) contains full-text articles of open-access journals, academic journals that are subscription-free. A search engine is unable to search in the contents of these journals. You will have to know about the *DOAJ* site and use its internal search engine. Likewise, fee-based periodical databases, such as *Historical Abstracts* or *America: History and Life*, or a database of online scholarly full-text journals, such as *JSTOR*, will not allow search engines to index their sites. This is one reason you will not find journal articles from subscription-based journals *freely* available on the Internet. Not only can the bots and spiders not get to the journals' servers but also the particular journals control what is published and how and to whom it is delivered. Remember, usually if you want refereed journal articles, you must go to a periodical index, such as *Historical Abstracts* or *America: History and Life*. Not all information is free.

Other types of information not accessed by some search engines include files that are in (.pdf) form, images (.jpg, .gif), audio files (.wav, .mp3, .ra, .au, aiff,), movies, (.mov, .mpg), *PowerPoint* files (.ppt), and Microsoft *Word* documents (.doc). Some search engines have sections that allow searching for images, audio files, and movies. Below are websites that compile other websites (called "webliographies") generally inaccessible by many search engines.

General Sites for Searching the deep or invisible web

Profusion, http://www.profusion.com/index.htm (accessed March 26, 2006). Directory of over 10,000 databases, archives, and search engines that are not accessible by the usual search engines. Created by Intelliseek, a corporation in the business technology field. Sources remain useful.

Complete Planet, http://www.completeplanet.com/ (accessed March 26, 2006). Searchable access to databases contained in its site.

Direct Search, http://www.freepint.com/gary/direct.htm (accessed March 26, 2006). Compiled by librarian Gary Price, one of the authors of the *Invisible Web* book and website. Has an even larger website with lists of other databases and other sites inaccessible by traditional search engines.

Special Search Techniques: Finding Primary Sources on the Internet

The Internet has made primary sources available to many more scholars and others who would previously have been unable to view and use them. A wide range of primary source material exists on the Internet. These sources range from simple scanned images or a collection of oral histories from a local historical society (e.g., *Shema, Arizona Jewish Historical Society*, http://www .asu.edu/lib/archives/shema/shema.htm) to an elaborate museum exhibit (e.g., *Colonial Williamsburg*, http://www.history.org/history) or a collection of an individual's papers (e.g., *Thomas Jefferson's Papers,* http://memory.loc.gov/ ammem/collections/jefferson_papers). The Internet can also provide a group's documents (e.g., *European Union*, http://europa.eu.int/) or a selection of primary sources from a given time period (e.g., *Civil Rights in Mississippi Digital Archive*, http://www.lib.usm.edu/~spcol/crda/; *The American Museum Congo Expedition, 1919–1915*, http://diglib1.amnh.org/) or region/country (e.g., *American Memory*, http://memory.loc.gov/ammem/amhome.html;

Gallica [France], http://gallica.bnf.fr/). All of these sites are invaluable to a researcher. There are, however, some issues to consider with primary sources found on the Internet. Unlike a collection in an archive but similar to a printed collection, when you view a collection online, you have no idea what might be omitted by those who have created and compiled it. Digitizing an online collection is costly both in human time and in computer (server) space, so items may be left out. When working with a box of individual manuscripts, you select the important documents for your research and ignore other documents. You can look at all of the original markings on the documents. However, the well-meaning individuals doing the scanning may clean up a scanned image for readability and destroy the historical integrity of the original, including some peripheral marks, which may offer clues to its significance. High-quality collections should offer the original scanned image along with an electronically enhanced image. Collections may include guides that explain that what is online is only a selection from a larger collection and give more information about the whole collection.

Searching for Primary Sources

Searching for primary sources on the Internet can be as challenging as searching for primary sources in print because the Internet has no subject headings. First, browse one of the academic search directories listed above to find a specialized website that might include primary sources among its contents. Next, use several of the search engines to find a website that contains your primary source material. As already noted, search engines gather information from the web differently, so your results may differ from search engine to search engine. When searching in a search engine, use the most specific and concrete terms you can. For instance, do not enter broad search words that are really concepts, such as "imperialism." Rather, you should search for something like "(britain or british or england) and (india or empire)." Alternatively, you could do an image search or search for files that have an extension of .jpg or .gif. If you are looking for the Treaty of Greenville, a treaty between the United States and the Northwest Indian Confederation that ceded large portions of what are now known as Ohio, Indiana, Illinois, and Michigan to the United States, then type in the title of that treaty. If you are looking for a specific form of primary source, an oral history for instance, incorporate that term into your search. The Internet will often use more common language, unlike an online catalog, previously discussed, which uses controlled vocabulary, or standard subject terms. You may be able to guess at the searching terminology on the Internet, but unlike in the online catalog and other indexes, there is no guarantee others are using the same words.

SEARCH TIPS
1. Use specific and concrete search terms.
2. Use the advanced search features to search for images or to exclude words.
3. Type in specific titles of documents and speeches.

Historians Communicating: Using *H-Net* for Information

Other very important Internet tools for the historian are listservs or discussion lists and blogs. Until now, the casual but public conversations of professionals went largely unrecorded. *H-Net* (http://www.h-net.org/) contains a series of discussion lists where specialists query, respond to, and debate issues in the humanities. For example, on the *H-Slavery* list in March 2005, a scholar had a question concerning a ca. 1800 account of the West African slave trade that discussed the fuller tribe, referred to white slavers as "Baccaranas," and called slave ships "monstrous birds." The scholar wanted to know what others on the list knew about these references. Respondents suggested that "Fulani" were called "Foulah" and located on the Upper Guinea Coast. Another suggested that "Baccaranas" was really a reference to buccaneers. Another suggested that this term could have ties to an African or European language, citing possibilities from Portuguese, Spanish, and local languages, an example being "barracoon," a term for a slave pen to hold persons at the coast until sold onto a ship.[10] This virtual discussion opened up numerous avenues for further research and drew upon a number of different experts. Undoubtedly a discussion list for whatever area of history you are researching exists. Representing both the cutting edge of research and topics that continue to be of central concern to scholars, these lists will often include information that is impossible to find elsewhere. All of the lists at *H-Net* are searchable, so if you want to see what has been discussed on your topic, you can select a list and search within it. If you are serious about becoming a historian, you should join a list in your area of interest and follow its discussions. This is where you will make professional contacts as well as see trends in the discipline. If you are struggling with an advanced history project and have already talked with your professor and your local librarian, you may wish to post, or perhaps ask your professor or teacher to post, a query to the appropriate list. Most of the conversants on these lists would expect you to ask an advanced question after having done some research on your own.

In recent years, blogs have had influence over historical and political ideas and discourse. A blog, the word formed by the union of the words "web" and "log," is, in the words of historian Ralph Luker, "a commonplace journal maintained on the Internet, where it is accessible to other readers. . . . Blogs take a variety of forms from daily personal journals to occasional essays." [11] This form of communication offers a new avenue, other than the forms above, for historians to engage in historical discussion. For example, Sharon Howard, a British PhD student, on her website *Early Modern Resources* (http://earlymodernweb.org.uk/), runs the *Early Modern Notes Weblog* (http://www.earlymodernweb.org.uk/emn/). Her weblog discusses such topics as eighteenth-century reactionaries, sources for research funding, and early modern "blood sports"/ball games. Blogs and listservs, e-mail-distributed among a list of individuals to create an online discussion around a focused topic, are informal means of historical discussion. The website *History News Network* maintains a list of historical blogs called *Cliopatria* (http://hnn.us/blogs/2.html).[12]

Evaluation of Websites

No matter where your information originates on the web, you must be careful about its quality. The process of evaluating websites is not entirely different from the process of evaluating print secondary sources discussed in Chapter Five. You must still consider the author's/creator's credentials and the accuracy of the information. In addition, you must consider the readability of the site and its currency, as well as certain navigation issues. Below is a basic checklist that will help you evaluate Internet material. There are numerous variations on these criteria. Your library may even have a set they recommend.

General Websites

Listed below are generally accepted criteria that are based on two excellent guides developed by Esther Grassian, a librarian at UCLA.[13]

- *Authority*. Who produced the website and what do they know? Is this someone who has studied in the field? Is this person or organization the logical one to be creating a website about this topic? Look for a biography of the author and that author's credentials on the site. Check the domain (.edu, .com) that the website comes from. Is the website trying to sell you something? Is there a conflict of interest?

- Example:

  Institute For Historical Review (IHR), http://www.ihr.org. Organization that argues with the documentation of the Holocaust, among other issues. Many historians question the authority of the authors of the articles published by the IHR and its publications and website. Authors often lack advanced historical credentials like a PhD or practice in a related field or are journalists or not practioners of history at all. Many historians also argue that the primary sources used by the IHR to make claims, such as that the gas chambers never existed in the concentration camps or that there was no Nazi-organized attempt to exterminate the European Jews, are weak and used in a biased manner.

- *Audience.* For whom was the site created? If it was for Mrs. Smith's fourth-grade social studies class, the information may be too basic. If it was created for a general audience, it may not be academic enough to use in a scholarly research paper. This is the equivalent of using the *World Book Encyclopedia* for your research, a fine encyclopedia when you are in grade school but unacceptable for college-level research.

- *Accuracy and content.* Does the information appear accurate based on your research? Make comparisons with other web pages, journal articles, and books. Watch for inaccuracies with dates and other material. How is this website unique compared to other websites and print resources you have examined or read? In comparing other sources, can you detect controversy by looking at differences in the facts and analyses presented? Do you detect bias? Has the website been created by a person or an organization that has a viewpoint that might bias data? Is the collection and arrangement of the information sloppy? Look for inaccuracies if documents have been transcribed or retyped.

- Example:

  Compare *Martin Luther King Jr.—A True Historical Examination* (http://www.martinlutherking.org) to *The King Center* (http://www .thekingcenter.org). The first site is created and maintained by someone who is sympathetic to the white supremacist movement. Not providing any individual author information but sponsored by Stormfront, a "white pride" organization, the site not only focuses on the controversial issues of Martin Luther King's life, such as plagiarism in his writings, but also includes tangential issues such as rap lyrics, Kwanzaa, and Jews and the civil rights movement. Heavily cited is a book by David Duke, who is closely affiliated with the Ku Klux Klan. In contrast, *The King Center*, the recognized authority site, seeks to present and preserve King's papers and scholarly writings and to publicize programs about his legacy.

- *Currency.* When was the website last revised? Old information can be false, inaccurate, and, in some cases, harmful. Websites unrevised for over 2 years probably are not very useful for scholarly research.

- *Navigability and structure.* Do the links work well, or are most of them dead? Is the site logically organized? If you cannot find your resources, does it matter what the site contains? Websites lend themselves to the integration of "chunks" or distinct paragraphs of text coupled with illustrative photographs, documents, and links to other websites. This method of conveying information is a different process from a printed book or journal article. Does the website use the web/hypertext format well?

Rely on your own gut instinct as well. If the website appears too good to be true and you cannot find an authoritative author or producer, then it probably is not as good as it seems. Another way to help you decide the quality of a website is to evaluate the web pages that list it as a link. In the *Google* or *AltaVista* search box, you can type "link:" in the search box and then copy the address of the web page in which you are interested. The results will have links to that particular page. Remember that a popular page does not always mean quality; it could be the universal example of a bad page.

Evaluating Sites Concerned with Primary Sources[14]

The Public History Resource Center offers additional criteria for websites that include primary sources.

- *Quality of scans of documents and images.* Has the integrity of the original image been preserved? Are there mechanisms such as enlarging to enhance the image for better examination? Has the document been transcribed to assist you in reading the handwriting?

- *Searchability.* Is the text of the documents searchable? Is there also a subject search? As historical concepts are hard to find through a keyword search, a directory or subject listing for a website is useful.

- *Bibliography or webliography.* Is a list of materials for further research, both print and web-based, included?

- *Interpretive or descriptive materials.* Are there added materials that help you understand the collection? Since you cannot see the original "box" of materials, how will you get a sense of the whole collection? Is the interpretation by someone who is an authority?

The Internet can be a valuable resource for your historical research. However, just as with any other research tool, you must know how to use it critically and effectively, as the *Institute For Historical Review* and the *MartinLutherKing.org* sites illustrate.

Case Study ▪ Using the Internet: Japanese Americans and Internment Camps

You have selected your general topic of Japanese Americans and their incarceration in camps in the United States during World War II. While you develop a thesis statement with your professor, you can begin searching on the web.

1. Use a search *directory* to begin your search. Often, you will find the best information without having to search through pages of irrelevant information that a search engine can bring up. For instance, if you go to the *Librarians' Internet Index* (http://lii.org) and enter the search terms "Japanese internment," you will find about 16 websites. Not all are relevant, but the following are very useful:

- *Suffering Under a Great Injustice: Ansel Adams's Photographs of Japanese American Internment at Manzanar*, http://memory.loc.gov/ammem/aamhtml/aamhome.html.

- *Japanese American Relocation Digital Archives*, http://jarda.cdlib.org/.

2. Use one or two of the search engines listed to find other resources to add to your list above. Using *Google*, you could, in this case, use the basic search and type in the keyword box "japanese american internment camps." As you know search engines search through many thousands more sites than a search directory organizes, you would want to be more specific with your search criteria as you have no subject categories to browse once your search is complete. Historically, American soldiers were also "interned" as

prisoners in Japan, so your results may reflect a completely different topic if you are not careful. Some possible useful results follow:

- *Japanese American Exhibit and Access Project*, http://www.lib .washington.edu/exhibits/harmony/.
- *Children of the Camps*, http://www.pbs.org/childofcamp/.

If you felt you wanted more images, you could do an advanced *Google* search and limit your results to files that had .jpg or .gif extensions.

3. Check the sites for the deep web listings of databases. In this case, no likely database appears, as of the writing of this book.

4. Make sure you evaluate your sources. Use the criteria above.

FOR FURTHER READING

American Social History Project, Center for Media and Learning and the Center for History and New Media. *History Matters*, http://historymatters.gmu.edu/ (accessed January 10, 2006).
    Online history textbook for American history. Has many links to projects, readings, and assignments, as well as other websites.
Center for History and the New Media. *World History Matters*, http://chnm.gmu .edu/whm/ (accessed January 10, 2006).
    Online History textbook for world history. Has many links to projects, readings, and assignments, as well as other websites.
Center for Teaching History with Technology, http://thwt.org/ (accessed March 29, 2006).
    List of sites that include teaching techniques for K–12.
Craver, Kathleen W. *Using Internet Primary Sources to Teach Critical Thinking Skills in History*. Westport, CT: Greenwood Press, 1999.
    Assignments with study questions for upper-division secondary school students and college-level students.
Drobnicki, John A., and Richard Asaro. "Historical Fabrications on the Internet: Recognition, Evaluation, and Use in Bibliographic Instruction." *In Evolution in Reference and Information Services: The Impact of the Internet*. ed. Di Su. Binghamton, NY: Hayworth Press, 2001.
Reagan, Patrick A. *History and the Internet: A Guide*. Boston: McGraw-Hill, 2002.
    Barebones guide to Internet sites and searching.
Trinkle, Dennis A., and Scott A. Merriman, eds. *The European History Highway: A Guide to Internet Resources*. Armonk, NY: M. E. Sharpe, 2002.

Bibliography of websites focused on Europe, including the former Soviet republics. Some duplication in the "general" section with the *History Highway* below.

Trinkle, Dennis A., and Scott A. Merriman, eds. *The History Highway 3.0: A Guide to Internet Resources.* 3d ed. Armonk, NY: M. E. Sharpe, 2002. Huge bibliography of websites organized by country and general subject.

Trinkle, Dennis A., ed. *Writing, Teaching and Researching History in the Electronic Age: Historians and Computers.* Armonk, NY: M. E. Sharpe, 1998. Series of essays that include using computers in the classrooms to teach history, as well as examples of nontraditional history projects.

NOTES

1. Carl Smith, "Can You do Serious History on the Web? " *AHA Perspectives*, (Feb 1998), http://www.historians.org/perspectives/issues/1998/9802/ 9802COM.CFM and http://chnm.gmu.edu/resources/essays/serioushistory.php (accessed January 1, 2006).
2. Library of Congress, *A Century of Lawmaking for a New Nation: U.S. Congressional Documents and Debates, 1774–1875*, http://memory.loc.gov/ ammem/amlaw/lawhome.html (accessed January 1, 2006).
3. Ran Hock, "A New Era of Search Engines: Not Just Web Pages Anymore," *Online* 26 (Sept/Oct 2002): 20–27.
4. For some of the initiatives, see *Web Archiving Bibliography*, from the Austrian Online Archive, http://www.ifs.tuwien.ac.at/~aola/links/WebArchiving.html (accessed January 1, 2006).
5. HTML is the scripting language used to create the traditional web page.
6. *Institute for Historical Review*, http://www.ihr.org/ (accessed January 1, 2006). Not to be confused with the very reputable British *Institute of Historical Research*, http://history.ac.uk (accessed January 1, 2006).
7. "Google Bomb," *Wikipedia*, http://en.wikipedia.org/wiki/Google_bomb and "Google Bomb" *Links and Law: Information about Legal Aspects of Search Engines, Linking, and Framing*, http://www.linksandlaw.com/technicalbackground -google-bombing.htm (both accessed January 1, 2006).
8. For an interesting comparison of search engines, see Greg Notess' web page http://searchengineshowdown.com/. See also http://searchenginewatch.com (both accessed January 1, 2006).
9. Charles Deering McCormick Library of Special Collections, Northwestern University Library. *The Siege and Commune of Paris, 1870–1871*, http://www .library.northwestern.edu/spec/siege/ (accessed May 18, 2006).
10. Eric Gardner, "Fuller Tribe, Baccaranas and Monstrous Birds," *H-Slavery*, March 23, 2005, http://www.h-net.org/~slavery/; Rachel G. Malcolm-Woods, "Fuller Tribe, Baccaranas and Monstrous Birds" *H-Slavery*, March 23, 2005,

http://www.h-net.org/~slavery/; Christopher Lowe, "Fuller Tribe, Baccaranas and Monstrous Birds," *H-Slavery*, March 23, 2005, http://www.h-net.org/~slavery/; Jacqueline Knoerr, "Fuller Tribe, Baccaranas and Monstrous Birds." *H-Slavery*, March 23, 2005, http://www.h-net.org/~slavery/ (all accessed September 10, 2005).

11. Ralph E. Luker, "Were There Blog Enough and Time," *Perspectives* (May 2005), http:www.historians.org/Perspectives/Issues/2005/0505//tec1.cfm (accessed May 23, 2005).

12. Ibid.

13. Esther Grassian, *Thinking Critically and World Wide Web Resources*, http://www.library.ucla.edu/libraries/college/help/critical/index.htm and *Thinking Critically about Discipline-Based World Wide Web Resources*, http://www.library.ucla.edu/libraries/college/help/critical/discipline.htm (both accessed January 5, 2006); see also *Evaluating Web Pages: Techniques to Apply and Questions to Ask* (U.C. Berkeley Library), http://www.lib.berkeley.edu/TeachingLib/Guides/Internet/Evaluate.html (accessed January 1, 2006). For an alternative approach, see Marc Meola, "Chucking the Checklist: A Contextual Approach to Teaching Undergraduates Web-Site Evaluation," *portal: Libraries and the Academy* 4 (July 2003): 331–344.

14. Debra DeRuyver, Jennifer Evans, James Melzer, and Emma Wilmer, *Evaluating Web Sites* (Public History Resource Center Rating System, April 30, 2000), http://www.publichistory.org/evaluation/index2.html (accessed January 1, 2006).

8

Maps: From Simple to Geographic Information Systems

WHAT YOU WILL LEARN IN THIS CHAPTER:

- the historical uses of maps
- how to understand the components of modern maps
- how to read and evaluate a map
- how to find maps and atlases for your research
- how Geographic Information Systems work and how to plan a small historical map

---

Maps as Representations of Our World

Our lives are filled with geographical references, conveying a sense of place and space. It is hard to imagine life without the visual representation and accuracy of the maps we use to navigate city streets, mark land plot ownership, and watch weather patterns. Historically, maps were not always so representational of a spot on the globe. Prior to ca. 1450 and the Age of Discovery, large area and world maps tended to express worldview philosophies, indicative of the religious and spiritual beliefs of the mapmakers and their nations. Local maps of villages and cities did often reflect actual on-the-ground features but were not drawn with accurate measurements or "to scale." Driven by exploration and trade, *cartographers*, or drawers of maps, were compelled to create more accurate navigational maps.[1] Not until after World War II did the maps and atlases commonly used to express sociocultural trends begin to appear in textbooks and in many newspapers and magazines. Contemporary maps and atlases, such as Collins' *Atlas of Twentieth*

Century History, contain maps on desertification, sea pollution, and incidences of acquired immunodeficiency syndrome (AIDS) worldwide.[2] Maps and atlases also compare and illustrate data such as gross domestic product, life expectancy, and water quality. More recently, technology has enabled individuals other than cartographers to create maps and to incorporate data that allow for in-depth study of geographic patterns. Studying history through the use of visual material, including maps, can dramatically change certain long-held historical beliefs. For instance, the maps associated with the *Salem Witch Trials Documentary Archive* (http://etext.lib.virginia.edu/salem/witchcraft/) reveal that the concentration of accusations of witches was greater in Andover than in Salem, Massachusetts. This new way of compiling and examining data geographically has changed the traditional focus of witchcraft from Salem to Andover.[3]

This chapter presents a short history of the evolution of maps and atlases to help you to knowledgeably incorporate this primary source into your research. Then, the components of a map, "reading" and evaluating a map, and finding maps are covered. Finally, you may decide you want to make your own, using Geographic Information Systems (GIS) software. Some tips on using this software and organizing a map will be offered.

A Short History of Maps and Cartography

Geographers define a map as a "geographic representation drawn to scale and usually on a flat surface, of features, for example, geographical, geological, or geopolitical, of an area of the Earth or of any other celestial body."[4] Yet, Chinese philosophy saw the world in concentric rings drawn around a globe. Babylonians drew the world as flat plains connected by stairs. Neither of these maps of the world was based on observation of the physical environment of the earth or the sky.[5] The Age of Discovery, fueled by trade and colonization, made world and large regional navigational maps necessary. These maps contained greater detail, included physical features, and encompassed larger areas and regions. In early maps, the hallmarks that are valued in modern maps, such as scale and legend, were seldom present. Maps have been drawn on clay tablets, parchment, and animal skin, as well as paper.

In 1595, the first publication using the term "atlas" in the title originated with a collection of European maps from the cartographer Gerhardus Mercator (1512–1594) (aka Gerhard de Kremer).[6] Several types of historical atlases exist. In fact, the term "atlas" covers the more traditional collection of maps as well as something that looks and reads much more like a book or encyclopedia in that it contains more explanatory and analytical text than a map. Other atlases assemble a collection of color-coded maps that display information including the changes of territory over time, the spread of a particular disease, or the measure of economic stability in a certain period. Some provide a significant amount of textual explanation, while others are simply maps. Technically, an atlas could also take the form of a website, one example being *Images of Early Maps on the Web*.[7] In this chapter, "map" will refer to the many forms in which maps are created, including atlases.

Maps for Navigation and Commercial Use

Much of what has been discussed above refers to maps as commercial or navigational primary sources. Each of these necessary functions changed the map from a more philosophical expression to a more practical object. As navigational and commercial tools, maps highlighted the best trade routes for goods, (the Silk Road, for example, the caravan trade route that connected Mediterranean Europe and the Middle East and China [Asia]); charted the sea coasts of North and South America for explorers as early as the 1500s; and provided road highway routes for vacationers in the post-World War II U.S. vacation boom.

Maps as Political Tools

Maps can be used as political tools to purposely or inadvertently indicate control over a particular territory, country, or peoples. English monarch Elizabeth I commissioned Christopher Saxton to perform a topographic survey of England and Wales, resulting in a large, decorative, printed atlas entitled *Atlas of England and Wales* (1579). The atlas unified England in a book of maps just as Elizabeth ruled a unified England. It was a symbol of her controlling power.[8] Artwork on the map identifies Elizabeth as the patron of geography and astronomy.[9] However, it was not until later, in the nineteenth century, that the genre of nationalistic atlases produced other maps. Beginning in the 1920s and 1930s, colonies of European nations gained their freedom, and some began producing atlases as one method of declaring independence.[10] Prior to independence, in the seventeenth to the nineteenth centuries, many peoples on the continents of Africa and Asia were colonized by the United States and western European nations, creating disputed claims over territory. Mapmakers of neutral nations were often faced with trying to decide whom to label as colonial rulers or occupiers.[11] In other cases, disagreement between two nations caused different names to be given to the same land features. The name for the body of water between Japan and Korea has been in dispute for many centuries, with Korean maps labeling it the "East Sea" and Japanese maps the "Sea of Japan." Historically, cartographers have also labeled it the "Sea of Korea" or the "Oriental Sea." Nations may also have political agendas that lead them to exclude or even distort certain aspects of their countries.

In a twentieth-century example of unintentional cultural dominance, geographer Robert Rundstrom reports on a health project using GIS to map Zuni Indians' residences in their small towns and villages (*pueblos*) to enhance health-care delivery. These residences have no house numbers, nor do the pueblos have street names. The data collectors ended up using mostly English names to identify locations, with a few Zuni words if they could be rendered into English and were "not too humorous."[12] This is an example of assimilation by map, even if the intentions of the mapmakers were to improve the delivery of health care to the Zuni.

Maps as Propaganda

Maps can also be used to create a skewed opinion or present a desired version of reality. In the 1920s and 1930s, many English-language textbooks used Ellsworth Huntington's (1876–1947) map of "The Distribution of Civilization," which was blatantly imperialistic and racist and differentiated the "civilized" nations from the "backward" nations. In 1939 and 1940, Nazi cartographers portrayed Germany as surrounded by hostile neighbors, to gain sympathy and sway support from a still neutral American public.[13] In the twentieth century, *The Nuclear War Atlas* attempted to illustrate the horrors of the effects of a nuclear war by showing the numbers of anticipated deaths and in what areas those deaths would occur. In none of these cases are the data on these maps so much "wrong" as they are so subjective that even when scientifically based, as in the *Nuclear War Atlas*, they have a specific message to convey that sometimes obscures other facts.[14] Understanding purpose is especially important in understanding how maps can be used in your research. Chapter Five provides tips on how to identify and evaluate propaganda.

Maps Marking Territory

Maps have also been used to indicate personal and public territory. Roman landowners as well as medieval landlords paid mapmakers to draw the extent of their estates. Hardly the epitome of modern mapmaking replete with precision or scale, such a map symbolized the landowner's reach of authority as well as served the purpose of a record for collecting taxes owed by those living and farming on these lands on behalf of the landowner.[15] These maps not only marked who lived where but also indicated crop yields, size of livestock herds, and forests for hunting. To register land ownership for taxation purposes and redistribution, governments, churches, and other official bodies used this kind of mapping, called *cadastral*. For example, in ancient Egypt, the Nile River flooded annually and land ownership boundaries had to be reestablished. In post-World War II Europe, such maps were used to redistribute land confiscated by the Nazis.[16]

Maps in War

Poorly made maps have wrought havoc in military maneuvers. In *How to Lie with Maps,* Mark Monmonier provides excellent examples of the problems of poor maps. During the U.S. Civil War, part of General George B. McClellan's inability to reach Richmond, Virginia, and take control of the Confederate capitol in 1862 was due to inaccurate topographic maps that did not indicate obstacles, such as hills, which hindered Union troop movements. In the 1983 invasion of Grenada, U.S. troops relied on outdated and inaccurate British topographic and tourist maps, which led to both the bombing of a mental hospital, not indicated on the map, and an air strike that killed U.S. troops because the field commanders and the bombers had different maps and grids.[17] As a ploy to protect their country from enemies during the Cold War, Soviet cartographers intentionally moved, distorted, or omitted cities and natural features, such as rivers or coastlines, on maps.[18]

Components of Modern Maps

Understanding the basic parts of a modern map, one that pays great attention to physical detail and accuracy, will help you to evaluate the evidence it provides. Maps have certain features, some of which are generally common to all well-designed maps. Legend, scale, and direction are essential to understanding the markings and their spatial relationships on a map. The other features addressed below are commonly, but not universally, found on maps.

- *Legend.* The legend defines the features and symbols of the map. It tells you what the colors and symbols mean and may include measurements. It is often located near one of the corners of the map (see Fig. 8.1).

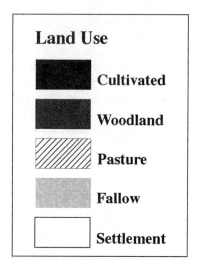

Figure 8.1. Example of a map legend which defines the symbols on a map.

- *Scale.* The scale describes the relationship between the paper map space and the actual physical space on the earth. This is reflected in two ways, by a bar which allows for physical measurement, with a ruler, and by a ratio scale such as 1:100,000, where 1 centimeter on the map reflects 1 kilometer on the face of the earth. Maps are sometimes referred to as "large-scale" or "small-scale." Large-scale maps show greater detail because they cover a smaller area. But, for example, Native American maps do not have scale. Digital delivery of maps makes scale problematic. Scale is often useless on the Internet because the size of computer screens as well as type size vary and thus prevent measurement with a ruler. Imprecise drawing of scale is one reason that using historical maps with modern maps in GIS is difficult (see Fig. 8.2).

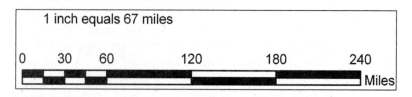

Figure 8.2. Example of scale with verbal scale. The scale, the ruler-like line, graphically defines the relationship (area) on the paper to the real, physical world. Above the line is a verbal scale which describes this relationship in words.

- *Coordinates.* Every place on earth has a location that crosses latitude and longitude. Obviously, city streets and cross streets lie in the same latitudinal and longitudinal plane; thus, a city street map would not have this feature, nor do many older maps.
- *Direction.* Compass points, or at least a direction marker indicating north, should appear on the map.
- *Elevation.* Wavy lines, called *isolines*, denote how high or low land is as well as landforms above and below sea level. These are prevalent on topographical maps.

Of these features, the legend is the most crucial to your research and to understanding the map. The legend tells you, for instance, that gray arrows on a U.S. Civil War map might mark the movement of Confederate troops at the Battle of Gettysburg. Looking next for some directional marker, you would see if they moved north or south across the field of battle. A legend might also tell you that a skull-and-crossbones icon on a map illustrates the spread of the plague in fourteenth-century Europe.

Finding Maps

Map Resources

Many general and very specific collections of historical atlases and maps are available both in print and on the Internet. Below are examples of atlases and maps available in print and on selected websites. All have copyright restrictions. (See Chapter Nine for a discussion on copyright.) For maps, there is a copyright-free solution with a series called *Maps on File* and *Historical Maps on File*, which provides outline maps onto which you can draw your own features. The result is fairly low-tech but will provide you with a custom map, without having to learn geographic information software like ArcGIS. Another copyright-free solution is, of course, creating your own maps from scratch.

To find other maps, use the following search tips in your library's catalog or in *Worldcat*.

SEARCH TIPS
1. Do a broad subject search on a country, continent, or region.
2. Limit the results by words in the subject maps or words in the title atlas.

Selected Historical Atlases

Atlas of American History. 2d rev. ed. New York: Scribner, 1984. Black-and-white maps arranged chronologically. Indexed. Supplements the *Dictionary of American History*.

Historical Atlas. 9th ed. rev. William R. Shepherd. New York: Barnes & Noble, 1980. Standard historical atlas that covers 1450 B.C.E. to 1980. Includes color maps and index.

Times History of the World. 5th ed. Geoffrey Barraclough, ed. London: Times, 1999. The *Times* atlas is a standard, high-quality world atlas with a European view of world history.

Atlas of World History. Jeremy Black, ed. New York: Dorling Kindersley, 2000. Richly illustrated atlas of world history.

Routledge Atlas of Russian History. Martin Gilbert. 3d ed. New York: Routledge, 2002. Black-and-white line-drawing maps with boxes to explain significance of maps and their markings. This is an example of a number of historical atlases Routledge has published by Martin Gilbert. Search in a catalog for Gilbert as an author or *Routledge Atlas* by title to see a fuller listing.

Perry Castañeda Map Collection, http://www.lib.utexas.edu/maps/map _sites/hist_sites.html (accessed January 1, 2006). From the University of Texas at Austin's collection of maps. Historical section organized by continent, country, or region.

David Rumsey Map Collection, http://www.davidrumsey.com (accessed January 1, 2006). Vast collection of historical maps from private collector, David Rumsey. With the use of GIS, some maps are three-dimensional.

Map Collections: American Memory, http://memory.loc.gov/ammem/ gmdhtml/gmdhome.html (accessed January 1, 2006). From the Library of Congress' collections. A wide variety of maps, mostly concentrated on the United States but includes some from other countries.

Maps For Students, http://www.unc.edu/awmc/mapsforstudents.html (accessed March 29, 2006). Maps of the ancient world.

Historical Maps on File. New York: Facts on File, 1984– Updated periodically. Maps of events and places of historical significance. Designed to be photocopied and altered.

Outline Maps, Houghton Mifflin Online, http://www.eduplace.com/ss/maps/ (accessed March 29, 2006). For educational purposes (pdf files).

Examples of Sites with Interactive or Online Historical Maps

Africa Maps, http://library.stanford.edu/depts/ssrg/africa/map.html (accessed March 29, 2006). Listing of maps, in various formats.

Afriterra, http://www.afriterra.org/ (accessed March 29, 2006). Nonprofit organization to preserve rare African maps. Small but growing online collection.

Alabama Historical Map Archive, http://alabamamaps.ua.edu/historicalmaps/ (accessed March 29, 2006). Digital images of maps from a number of Alabama institutions, although coverage is worldwide.

American Memory: Map Collections 1500–2004, http://memory.loc.gov/ ammem/gmdhtml/gmdhome.html (accessed January 1, 2006). Maps of cities, battles, landscape, conservation. Coverage is worldwide.

Blaeu Atlas, http://www.library.ucla.edu/yrl/reference/maps/blaeu/ (accessed January 1, 2006). Seventeenth-century atlas of Europe.

China Historical GIS, http://www.fas.harvard.edu/~chgis/ (accessed March 29, 2006). Historic maps and sketches of Chinese land throughout history.

Cyndi's List of Maps, http://www.cyndislist.com/maps.htm (accessed January 1, 2006). Part of a genealogical list, good for local maps.

David Rumsey Map Collection, http://www.davidrumsey.com (accessed January 1, 2006). Vast collection of historical maps from private collector David Rumsey. With the use of GIS, some maps are three-dimensional.

Electronic Cultural Atlas Initiative, http://www.ecai.org/ (accessed January 1, 2006). Links to online atlas projects. Worldwide in coverage, all time periods.

Great Britain Historical GIS Project, http://www.gbhgis.org/gbhgis/ (accessed March 29, 2006). Collection of digital information about Great Britain, useful for creating electronic maps.

Hargrett Rare Map Library, http://www.libs.uga.edu/darchive/hargrett/ maps/maps.html (accessed March 29, 2006). Primarily United States historical maps.

Historic Cities, http://historic-cities.huji.ac.il/ (accessed January 1, 2006). Maps of cities of the world throughout history, as well as future renderings taken from books, documents, and other similar sources.

Historic Maps in K–12 Classrooms, http://www3.newberry.org/k12maps/ (accessed January 1, 2006). American history maps for teaching from the Newberry Library.

Historical Atlas of the Twentieth Century, http://users.erols.com/mwhite28/ 20centry.htm (accessed January 1, 2006).

Historical Text Archive: Maps, http://historicaltextarchive.com/links.php ?op5 viewslink&sid5 0&cid5 10 (accessed January 1, 2006). Links to other collections.

James Ford Bell Historical Maps, http://bell.lib.umn.edu/hist/ (accessed January 1, 2006). From the University of Minnesota, worldwide coverage.

Mapping History: Darkwing Atlas Project, http://www.uoregon.edu/~atlas/ (accessed January 1, 2006). Interactive maps to highlight issues in American and European history.

Maps of Scotland, http://www.nls.uk/digitallibrary/map/early/index.html (accessed January 1, 2006). Covers 1560–1929.

Oddens Maps, http://oddens.geog.uu.nl/index.php (accessed January 1, 2006). Extensive set of links to other collections, both historical and current. Established and maintained by Roelof Oddens, the curator of the map library at Universiteit Utrecht. Good world coverage.

Perry Castañeda Map Collection, http://www.lib.utexas.edu/maps/map_sites/hist_sites.html (accessed January 1, 2006). From the University of Texas at Austin's collection of maps. Historical section organized by continent, country, or region.

Salem Witch Trials Historical Maps, http://jefferson.village.virginia.edu/salem/maps.html (accessed January 1, 2006).

Sanborn Fire Insurance Maps. Teaneck, NJ: Chadwyck-Healy/ProQuest, http://sanborn.umi.com/ (accessed January 1, 2006). Maps of U.S. cities and towns with buildings and their uses marked. Used by fire insurance companies. The *ProQuest* database is fee-based. Check with your library to see if you have access. Some individual states have been providing free online access to selected maps of cities in their own states. For example, Utah, http://www.lib.utah.edu/digital/sanborn/browse.html, and Virginia, http://fisher.lib.virginia.edu/collections/maps/sanborn/. In addition, many libraries have print and microfilm copies.

TimeMap (University of Sydney), http://www.timemap.net/ (accessed January 1, 2006). Allows you to build a map using HTML.

Gazetteers

Another geographical tool useful for locating places on a map are *gazetteers*, or dictionaries of places. Places include cities, states, administrative divisions, and natural features. Gazetteers provide facts about a place (such as population) and include coordinates (such as longitude and latitude) to locate that place on a map. They are especially useful for those places that have disappeared or are difficult to locate because they are so small.

Selected Gazetteers

Columbia Gazetteer of the World. Saul B. Cohen, ed. New York: Columbia University Press, 1998. Provides population, exact location, and very brief description of cities, states, countries, areas, territories, etc.

Place Name Changes 1900–1991. Adrian Room. Metuchen, NJ: Scarecrow Press, 1993. Name changes in all countries, especially post World War II and the post-Soviet era. Refers to new name of place.

Getty Thesaurus of Geographic Names, http://www.getty.edu/research/ conducting_research/vocabularies/tgn/ (accessed January 1, 2006). Place names related to history, archaeology, and art.

How to Read a Map

Reading between the latitude and longitude, or between the lines as it were, when interpreting a map is a bit more complex. Remember, by their nature maps are a distortion of reality or a representation of the perception of reality. They represent a three-dimensional object, the earth, on a flat surface. Often, what is at the center of a map is what the cartographer has chosen as the focus of attention. This will give you a clue as to the purpose of a particular map. It is just as important to identify what has been left off of a map as it is to analyze what has been included.[19] For example, Martin Gilbert, in his map "The Intifada, February 1992" from *The Atlas of the Arab-Israeli Conflict,* includes a box of information with statistics indicating that Palestinians were killed by Israeli and Palestinian troops.[20] However, Gilbert makes no mention of the Israeli-backed occupation of Lebanon, even though he makes mention of the border. He also includes the West Bank as a part of Israel, when Palestinians consider this area independent territory. Gilbert is not intentionally trying to deceive, and his atlases are excellent and instructive; but like any other author, he has a perspective from which he is presenting his information.[21]

While some modern-day cartographers and others who create atlases may have unintentional biases, mapmakers in the past have had both overt and covert agendas in their creation of maps and atlases. Be sure to "read" and evaluate your map.

Questions to Ask When Reading a Map[22]

1. What is at the center of the map? The culture of the mapmaker tends to be at the center of the map. This is evident in maps of the Indians of North America as well as in medieval Islamic maps.

2. What is in the margins? More than just artwork, decoration in the margins of maps can be signs of a monarch's power (what he or she has dominion over), examples of the local flora or fauna, or symbols of the local

religion or mythology. More modern maps might include points of interest that no longer exist.

3. Who was the map made for and why? Every map has a purpose and an audience. This would explain why certain features are included on a map and some are excluded.

4. What is missing from the map? Not only does this help you to date the map, but it hints at the quality of the map as well as the possibility that the cartographer is intentionally trying to deceive his or her audience. What is absent from a map can create just as interesting a study as what is on it.

5. What is the perspective of the mapmaker/cartographer? Understanding this perspective is just as crucial as understanding the perspective of the author of a text. Aside from cultural influences, the cartographer also has a purpose for creating the map and perspective from which he or she analyzes the contents.

6. Was the map part of a collection of single-sheet series maps, a printed atlas, or another printed work, such as a book or magazine? In the latter two cases, might it have been meant as a visual companion to a verbal description, which could affect what is included on the map? In the former case, a single legend may exist on one of the sheets that may fit together to form a larger map.

7. How was it made? By professional survey? What is the quality of the drawing and engraving or printing? This is particularly crucial if your map was created before the advent of modern mapmaking tools and common survey practices.

Planning Your Own Map: Simple to Complex

You may decide that you have collected some interesting and unique facts and data and that you want to illustrate your results by designing your own map. With the development of desktop GIS software, you can create a fairly simple map in a short amount of time. However, before beginning a project, you need to understand that GIS is not simply the computerization of colored pencil drawings on an outline map. Instead, it is a new way of visually and analytically thinking about your historical research. Although simple maps can be created with the software, you need to think about whether or not GIS is the proper tool for your needs because it can be challenging to use.

Simply put, GIS allows you to take layers of data that have a spatial relationship and stack them together on a map. The following is a more complex definition from geographer Anne Kelly Knowles:

> [GIS] digitally links locations and their attributes so that they can be displayed in maps and analyzed, whether by their geographical characteristics such as location, proximity, density, and dispersal, or by their attributes, such as social, economic, and physical characteristics.[23]

In their article "Using GIS for Spatial and Temporal Analyses in Print Culture Studies,"[24] library historians Bertrum H. MacDonald and Fiona A. Black graphically show how the layers of variables of book culture can be compiled and explained geographically in a city. In this case, they consider the variables of book production and locations of bookstores and libraries with migration patterns, demographic information, and transportation routes. These data on a map would show the relationship of the availability of text (bookstores, libraries, and publishers) to readers (migration, transportation, and demographics such as population) (Fig. 8.3).

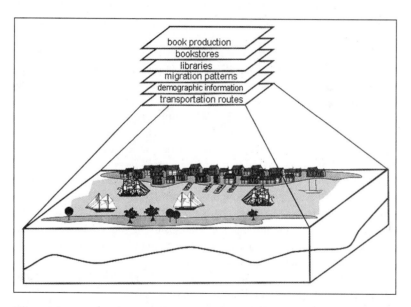

Figure 8.3. A graphic representation of the way GIS layers data or variables. MacDonald and Black's suggested ways in which GIS could be applied to understand a fuller picture of literacy rates and the availability of the printed word (through libraries and booksellers).[25] ©*Elsevier and reprinted with permission Elsevier, MacDonald and Black.*

By layering data, much in the same way one might layer transparencies of maps, although in much greater complexity, GIS allows the discovery of new spatial relationships. If you change the arrangement of your data, it is possible to arrive at different conclusions, as in the case of the Salem witch trials discussed earlier in the chapter. Through animation, GIS also has more complex features that will allow you to reflect change over time. You should consult your professor or librarian if you wish to reflect this kind of complex geographic relationship of ideas.

In preparation for creating your own map, first consider a few issues. Planning out what you want your map to include and what features it will illuminate is the most important step. Much like planning a website or preparing to do a bibliographic database search, you must decide on your major topics and components. What are you trying to compare and correlate? Can your ideas be reflected in data (a statistical table), or are they more conceptual (more bookstores mean a more literate population, as in the example above)? Why are these ideas reflected better visually, on a map, rather than in a chart, bar graph, or textual description? Will you need more than one map to reflect your data? Cramming too much information onto one map will dilute your analysis because no one will be able to see your correlations.

To set up the contents of your map, think in terms of themes and attributes (sometimes called "features"). For example, if you are trying to map troop movements during a battle, a theme could be something as simple as roads with attributes such as name, width, length, type (gravel or dirt), location (east, west), control (French or British), number of troops transported, and so forth. When you combine your data for roads, trenches, and field movements for a specific geographic area, you have a database. You may also want to think in layers. In the past, complex maps were created by laying a series of transparencies over a basic outline map. This is one way to reflect change over time. The most common piece of software used for creating maps, ArcGIS, has the ability to create tables and layers as well as to link these to maps. Thinking through the relationship of your data and the components of the map prior to beginning your map project will help you produce a meaningful map.

You might think that overlaying a historical map onto a modern map to demonstrate change over time would suit your purposes. Beware: superimposing a historical map onto a present-day map is sometimes impossible. Prior to aerial photography, map scales were imprecise.[26] For instance, placing an eighteenth-century map of London on a modern map of London will probably not work to illustrate change because the scales would not match, due to the earlier cartographer's imprecise measurements. If you do decide to use an older map, it is recommended that you scan the map at a higher resolution.[27] Then you can perform a process known as *georectifying*, which assigns real-world coordinates to the historical map. In addition, if you decide to build a map using historical data that is preformatted for a GIS project, websites are available that will provide that computerized data for you to insert in your map program. In both of these examples, you are getting into complicated mapping exercises and should probably seek assistance from your library, professor, or someone in your geography department. The provider of the ArcGIS software also has a tutorial page (http://www.gis.com/).

FOR FURTHER READING

History of Maps and Cartography

Black, Jeremy. *Maps and History: Constructing Images of the Past.* New Haven, CT: Yale University Press, 1997.
  Thorough history of the development and use of maps but not focusing on the science of cartography. More of a social history of maps.
Black, Jeremy. *Maps and Politics.* Chicago: University of Chicago Press, 1997.
  Similar to *Maps and History*, this volume takes a more contemporary focus and examines the uses of maps in twentieth-century world politics.
Goffart, Walter A. *Historical Atlases: The First Three Hundred Years 1570–1870.* Chicago: University of Chicago Press, 2003.
  Interesting history of the development of atlases and their cultural as well as practical value.
Harris, Nathaniel. *Mapping the World: Maps and Their History.* San Diego: Thunder Bay Press, 2002.
  Individual histories of significant maps, 2300 B.C.E. to 2001 C.E.
Knowles, Anne Kelly, ed. *Past Time, Past Place: GIS for History.* Redlands, CA: ESRI Press, 2002.
  Excellent introduction to the use of GIS in history. Includes case studies of actual online projects with lots of illustrations.
Monmonier, Mark S. *Bushmanders & Bullwinkles: How Politicians Manipulate Electronic Maps and Census Data to Win Elections.* Chicago: University of Chicago Press, 2001.
  Discussion of how politicians gerrymander maps to create political districts and how such mapping with GIS speaks to the notions of community, identity, and the construction of the American political body.

Monmonier, Mark S. *How to Lie with Maps.* 2d ed. Chicago: University of
Chicago Press, 1996.
Excellent discussion of how maps have been purposely or inadvertently used to
mislead and misconstrue information. Chapters include "Maps for Political Pro-
paganda," "Maps that Advertise," and "Blunders that Mislead."
Rumsey, David, and Edith M. Punt. *Cartographica Extraordinaire: The Historical
Map Transformed.* Redlands, CA: ESRI Press, 2004.
North and South America's change from wilderness to civilization.
Short, John Rennie. *The World Through Maps: A History of Cartography.* Buffalo,
NY: Firefly Books, 2003.
Broad, heavily illustrated history of mapmaking.

Maps and General Geography Texts

Campbell, John. *Map Use and Analysis.* 4th ed. Boston: McGraw-Hill, 2001.
Excellent, in-depth primer on map terminology and construction.
Dorling, Daniel, and David Fairbairn. *Mapping: Ways of Representing the World.*
London: Longman, 1997.
Textbook that integrates the history of maps with the newer trends in mapmaking.
Kaiser, Ward L., and Denis Wood. *Seeing Through Maps: The Power of Images to
Shape Our World View.* Amherst, MA: ODT Inc, 2001.
Simpler discussion of maps, including how to read a map.
Tufte, Edward R. *The Visual Display of Quantitative Information.* 2d ed. Cheshire,
CT: Graphics Press, 2001.
Discussion of graphs, including maps and their evolution in the display of data.

Geographic Information Systems

Software

ArcGIS, http://www.esri.com/software/arcgis (accessed January 1, 2006).
Website for the producer of the leading GIS software. Site contains tutorials
and guides for using the software.
Shareware and Freeware for GIS, http://www.inweh.unu.edu/unuinweh/giscategories/
share.htm (accessed January 1, 2006).
Listing of free software for GIS.

Guides and Resources

Audet, Richard, and Gail Ludwig. *GIS in Schools.* Redlands, CA: ESRI Press, 2000.
Using GIS in K–12 setting.
Davis, David E. *GIS for Everyone: Exploring Your Neighborhood and Your World
with a Geographic Information System.* 3d ed. Redlands, CA: ESRI Press, 2003.
Simple introduction to GIS for beginners. Includes free software.

ESRI Website, http://www.esri.com (accessed January 1, 2006).
The full range of GIS software provided by ESRI.

GIS.com: Your Guide to GIS, http://www.gis.com (accessed January 1, 2006).
Beginner's guide to GIS including training modules. Provided by ESRI.

Gregory, Ian N. *A Place in History: A Guide to Using GIS in Historical Research.*
Oxford: Oxbow Books and History Data Service, 2003.
Step-by-step guide to planning a history project using GIS techniques, including software package.

Geographic Network Explorer, http://www.geographynetwork.com/ (accessed January 1, 2006).
Searchable database of data useable for GIS applications as well as static maps. Better for more contemporary topics than historical.

NOTES

1. Daniel Dorling and David Fairbairn, *Mapping: Ways of Representing the World* (London: Longman, 1997), 6–7.
2. Jeremy Black, *Maps and History: Constructing Images of the Past* (New Haven: Yale University Press, 1997), 204, 240.
3. Benjamin Ray and University of Virginia, *Salem Witch Trials: Documentary Archive and Transcription Project: Regional Accusations Map*, http://jefferson .village.virginia.edu/salem/maps/ (accessed January 1, 2006).
4. "Map," *Encyclopædia Britannica*, http://search.eb.com/eb/article?eu5119044 (accessed January 1, 2006). For an interesting discussion concerning the definition of the word map since 1649 to the present, see J. H. Andrews, *What Was a Map? Lexicographers Reply*, *Cartographica* 33 (Winter 1996): 1–11.
5. Dorling and Fairbairn, *Mapping*, 9.
6. Ibid. 52.
7. *Images of Early Maps on the Web: WWW-VL: History*, http://www.maphistory .info/webimages.html (accessed January 1, 2006).
8. Mark Monmonier, *How to Lie with Maps*, 2d ed. (Chicago: University of Chicago Press, 1996), 88–89.
9. Mark Monmonier, "The Rise of the National Atlas," *Cartographica* 31 (Spring 1994): 2.
10. For a history of the national atlas, see Monmonier, "The Rise of the National Atlas," 1–15. See also Monique Pelletier. "Cartography and Power in France During the Seventeenth and Eighteenth Centuries," *Cartographica* 35 (Autumn/Winter 1998): 41–53.
11. Monmonier, *How to Lie with Maps*, 90.
12. Robert A. Rundstrom, "The Role of Ethics, Mapping, and the Meaning of Place in Relations Between Indians and Whites in the United States," *Cartographica* 30 (Spring 1993): 21–28.

13. Dorling and Fairbairn, *Mapping*, 138–139, for more on Huntington, see David N. Livingstone, *The Geographical Tradition: Episodes in the History of a Contested Enterprise* (Oxford: Blackwell, 1992), especially the chapter "A 'Sternly Practical' Pursuit: Geography, Race and Empire."

14. Dorling and Fairbairn, *Mapping*, 154; William Bunge, *Nuclear War Atlas* (New York: Blackwell, 1988).

15. Dorling and Fairbairn, *Mapping* , 82–83.

16. Ibid., 84–85.

17. Monmonier, *How to Lie with Maps*, 45–47.

18. Ibid., 117–118.

19. Ward L. Kaiser, *Seeing Through Maps: the Power of Images to Shape Our World View* (Amherst, MA: ODT, 2001), 4–5.

20. Martin Gilbert, "The Intifada, February 1992," in *Atlas of the Arab–Israeli Conflict*, 6th ed. London: Oxford University Press, 1993).

21. Black, *Maps*, 217, fig. 46. Black suggests that Gilbert's Zionist beliefs caused him to represent certain controversial issues in a certain way, " . . . but mention of the Lebanon–Israeli border was made without reference to the Israeli-backed occupation of part of southern Lebanon, the use of Judea and Samaria was questionable and the West Bank was presented as part of Israel." The map is identical in the 7th edition, *The Routledge Atlas of the Arab–Israeli Conflict* (New York: Routledge, 2002).

22. For a fuller explanation of some of these points, see J. B. Harley, "The Evaluation of Early Maps: Towards a Methodology," *Imago Mundi* 22 (1968): 62–74; J. B. Hartley, "Deconstructing the Map," in *Human Geography: An Essential Anthology*. John Agnew, David N. Livingstone, and Alisdair Rogers, eds. (Oxford: Blackwell, 1996), 422–443.

23. Anne Kelly Knowles, *Past Time, Past Place: GIS for History* (Redlands, CA: ESRI Press, 2002), xiv.

24. Bertrum H. MacDonald and Fiona A. Black, "Using GIS for Spatial and Temporal Analyses in Print Culture Studies," *Social Science History* 24 (Fall 2000): 505–536.

25. Ibid., 510.

26. David Rumsey and Meredith Williams, "Historical Maps in GIS," in Knowles, *Past Time, Past Place*, 4–5.

27. Ibid., 5.

9

Beyond the Written Word: Finding, Evaluating, and Using Images, Motion Pictures, and Audio

---

WHAT YOU WILL LEARN IN THIS CHAPTER:

- how to use and interpret different types of media (visual media, motion pictures, and audio)
- how to search online catalogs, special media collections, and the Internet to find media
- how to incorporate media into your paper or website

The Role of Media in Historical Research: Media as Historical Evidence

The previous chapter focused on maps as a primary source and their development from print to a multidimensional, Geographic Information Systems project. Another set of primary sources that deserves more in-depth analysis is visual media and audio resources. Different from the written word as primary evidence, these categories of media require different searching and evaluation techniques from those already discussed. A quick overview of the purpose of each type of image and its evolution will assist you in using visual media as primary source evidence in your research. Audio materials are different in certain ways from visual media and will be discussed separately.

Images Throughout History

Images have been reflective of humankind's culture since the first cave drawing in prehistoric times.[1] Whether symbolic of the hunt or of a noble's position in life or documentary proof of war crimes, they offer a wide variety of visual evidence and through different mediums of expression. Images often reflect the social norms and public opinion of the time in which they were taken or created as a reaction to those norms. Images, both moving and still, as well as other types of multimedia highlight political rhetoric, chart economic trends, provide glimpses of daily life and its material trappings, and show the imagination and intellectual ideas of a society.[2] Seeing President Teddy Roosevelt give a speech or listening to an African American discuss his or her life under slavery can focus and even alter our feelings and assessments of current and historical issues and events.[3] Printed materials such as books, magazines, and newspapers have always incorporated images, ranging from illuminated Bibles to lithographs and, later, photographs in magazines and newspapers. People displayed first painted portraits and then photographs of their loved ones on the mantle in the parlor. Images add a dimension to historical discussion that words or text alone cannot convey. We will divide a quick study of images and their use into the categories of photographs, artwork (primarily paintings but also including sketches and nonphotographic illustrations in printed material), and motion pictures. However, there are a number of other types of images that this chapter will not deal with or will deal with only peripherally, such as murals, graffiti, scientific illustration, advertising art, and political cartoons, which can be treated in a manner similar to artwork or photography.

Photography: Real Life Captured?

A photograph can metaphorically highlight the idyllic family, the delinquency of youth, or the romanticism of war. It may be, though, that no photograph is a true reflection of a time past. Additionally, photographs have value, for instance, as commercial products to sell newspapers or magazines or as evidence of the worth of an investment. Photographs were used to document the westward U.S. land survey, not only for scientific purposes but also to inform and persuade the U.S. Congress that the money allocated to purchase the territory was well spent. What photographers choose to "record," where they stand to take the shots, and what they decide to include in the shot are all part of their viewpoint, or perspective. Photographers who sought to document social conditions, such as Jacob Riis in the slums of 1870s New York City and Dorothea Lange and Walker Evans during the Great Depression in the 1930s, had their own visual idea of poverty and sought to have their photographs convey their social messages.[4] This idea of viewpoint is particularly evident in political cartoons and propaganda posters, of course, but it is present in all images. Carefully examining your visual evidence before you incorporate it into your paper or website is important. Below are some more detailed examples of how perspective, public opinion, and the social norms of an era have affected the meaning of photographs and images.

News photography, or photojournalism, is a relatively recent field. Prior to the 1940s, the reporter who was responsible for writing the story also took the photos. Until the end of World War II, news photographs were considered sensational.[5] Recording the atrocities in concentration camps at the close of the war brought new focus to the use of photography as documentary evidence, by both amateurs and professionally trained photographers, giving photojournalism respectability in news reporting.[6]

War photography had always been treated with a different sort of fascination. During the U.S. Civil War, there was a public demand for tragic, patriotic images of the war, leading photographers like Alexander Gardner to stage a photograph at the Battle of Gettysburg for such a dramatic effect. In his book *Gettysburg: A Journey in Time*, historian William A. Frassanito chronicles pictorial evidence of Gardner moving what is probably a Confederate infantryman's body into a sharpshooter's position at Devil's Den for a more picturesque shot. *American Memory*, a virtual library of primary source materials at the Library of Congress, explores this issue with this photograph in their online exhibit, "Does the Camera Ever Lie? The Case of the Moved Body."[7]

Photographs can give us a limited and sometimes false image of the social context of an era or the broader notion of what life was like for a whole population. For instance, *Life* magazine in the 1950s often presented photographs of the perfect, white, suburban middle-class family but ignored the civil rights issues brewing throughout the United States.[8] Images were selected for inclusion in the magazine both because they reflected the interests of the magazine's readers and because the editors needed to sell magazines by appealing to their audience's political and philosophical viewpoint and image. Certain images may offend an audience and cause a drop in sales. Yet images, photographs, and paintings used in a different way can give an accurate glimpse into everyday life. For instance, the old town of Warsaw, Poland, nearly completely destroyed by bombings in World War II, was reconstructed based on historical prints and paintings. A similar process was used for a restoration project at St. Paul's Cathedral in London.[9] Advertisements in magazines and on radio and television can reflect idealized views of cutting-edge culture since not everyone may have been able to afford the newest fashions of the day. Remember, advertising may not be entirely reflective of society as a whole, especially since its goal is to influence consumer buying and fashion trends.

Questions to Evaluate Photographs/Still Images[10]

Because of all of these issues, there are many factors when incorporating a photographic/still image in your research. Asking the following questions will help you to understand the image creator's intent, what you need to learn about the society in which the image was captured, and how to integrate the image into your analysis.

1. What is the social and historical context for this image?

2. What might have happened before and after this image was created?

3. What is outside the frame of the image? What has been left out? What should be in the image that is missing?

4. What gender, race, and class issues are reflected here? How has the photographer addressed or not addressed these issues?

5. What relationships or connections do the people have to the objects?

6. How did the photographer set up the photograph? Can you tell that the photographer made choices about the angle, lighting, and focus (foreground, background) that might influence how you perceive—and how the photograph's contemporaries may have perceived—the image's meaning and effect? Be careful not to label or stereotype people or objects as this may lead you to erroneous conclusions.

7. Does the photograph or image ignore issues and details contemporary to its depiction or present them in a certain way that may lead you to a certain view about the image?

Analyzing the image in Fig. 9.1, "Behind the Teller's Window at Oxford National Bank 1916," you can learn about women in the workforce in 1916. In this case, the female teller seems to be treated as an equal, using the same machinery as the men as well as having the same contact with bank patrons. Perhaps it is significant that the photographer snapped the photograph with the woman at the center of the frame. Was he (assuming the photographer was a man) trying to draw attention to her because he knew her or because her position in the bank was unusual? The image also leads to a discussion about a financial and commercial operation in a small town and its mechanization.

Figure 9.1. "Behind the Teller's Window at Oxford National Bank 1916," Frank Snyder Collection of Photographs, Miami University Libraries. *Used with permission of Miami University Libraries.*

Art as Visual Media: Painting and Drawing

Art historians analyze works of art in a way that is unique to their discipline. Art has many features beyond the content and historical significance, such as physical features (line, color, texture), composition (the organization of the piece), and style (traits that associate the piece with others like it). While you may also be concerned with these features, you will be looking primarily at the artwork's association to real life and how it reflects the social and intellectual philosophy, as well as the material culture, of the time. How an artist paints a landscape or a portrait conveys a particular understanding and opinion of the political, social, and intellectual climate of the era and place in which both artist and subject lived. Painting and art in general have different themes of interpretation across cultures. Unlike photography, art style differs drastically by culture and time period, making it difficult to provide a synopsis of its historical uses and development. For instance, it is difficult to compare style and cultural meaning and to connect historical development between northern Song painting of the Song Dynasty (960–1279 C.E.) that expressed Neo-Confucian ideals and a nineteenth-century American Impressionist landscape painting.

By its nature, art intends to send its messages through symbolism and allegory. The artist has more control over a creation than a photographer over a photograph, so a separate list of evaluation criteria needs to be applied.

Questions to Evaluate Art

1. What is the context of this image? How was it meant to be displayed? Publicly? In a private home? On a wall? Is it a reproduction? Was it used for a purpose other than the way you see it now?[11] Remember, many buildings were designed to include art and art was often designed to be part of a structure, such as frescos in the villas of Pompeii.[12]

2. What cultural presuppositions do you bring from your time that the contemporary viewer would not have had? (For example, what do you know about science, politics, etc. that the viewer did not and, conversely, what did the viewer know that you do not understand?)[13]

3. Why was the art object created? Was it commissioned? Was it a portrait for a family? By a patron? Was there an expected perception? (For instance, was a painting created to show a pastoral view of the countryside or to make a nobleman look like a "manly man"?)

4. What iconography is used in the scene? Paintings often use objects to symbolize philosophies or ideals, for instance, a skull for the presence of death or scientific instruments for learned men. Roman coins used iconography to honor emperors.[14] Several dictionaries exist that would explain these symbols.[15]

5. What was the artist's philosophy or viewpoint when the piece of artwork was created? This is similar to the photographer setting up the photograph. The artist paints with an overt or covert philosophy in mind. Whether a modern-day Marxist sensitive to class issues or, prior to Marxist philosophy, sympathetic to the oppressed masses, the artist has a viewpoint. Just as history has "schools," art history has "methodologies."[16]

6. What is the artist's message? Look at what is central to the piece of art to discern what the artist wanted to tell you.[17]

7. What was the artist's source for the piece of artwork? Was the artist the eyewitness, creating from the event, looking at the landscape, or posing the individual? Or was the artist working from a newspaper description or from memory?[18]

8. Was the artwork intended as a therapeutic act to assist the creator in dealing with a traumatic event, for instance, sketches from the aftermath of the bombing of Hiroshima by someone in the city?

Motion Pictures and Television

Films and television present different challenges to the historian. Portrayals of the past in popular entertainment are never "pure" but are filtered through the social and cultural norms of the period in which they were created. Historians would never use popular media as primary evidence about the time portrayed, even though the creators want us to believe they are allowing us, the viewers, to experience authentic history. The HBO series *Deadwood*, which explores the "wild west" in the town of Deadwood, South Dakota, tells us as much about urban social life in the early twenty first century as it does about frontier life in the United States in the late 1870s, with its overt emphasis on sex, violence, and foul language.[19] This contemporary view of frontier life can be contrasted with PBS's reality TV show *Frontier House*, which immersed three different modern families in a homestead experience in Montana. *Deadwood* is popular television; *Frontier House* is reality TV, despite its attempts at authenticity. Neither program is the real nineteenth-century American frontier and should not be confused with primary sources. Another example of historical films as reflective of the times in which they were created rather than the period that they portray are Westerns of the 1950s. These movies' portrayals of Native Americans are more indicative of the rights of Native Americans and their treatment in the 1950s than true historical documentation of the settlement of the west.

Searching for Visual Media

Still images and images of artwork can come from a number of sources. You must remember that copyright is always a central issue for a website, an honors or masters thesis, or a PhD dissertation. In these cases, your result will be a published document, even if you have designed a website, and you will need to secure the creator's or publisher's permission to reproduce an image. You can search for and obtain images in several places:

- in a book
- from images you own or have created
- in an archive at your institution or historical society

- on the Internet through specially designed search engines
- on the Internet in special collections of images

Using your local online catalog, you can find printed resources, usually books, with photographs and other images contained in them. Do a search, just as you would for any information on your topic, but look through the catalog record for "il." or "illus." in the notes field. If a book consists mostly of images, the subject subheading "pictorial works" will be applied and, if applicable, a credit line will be given to the photographer or illustrator. So you could do a search for your topic and limit your search by words in the subject "pictorial works." Images in published books are definitely copyrighted.

SEARCH TIPS
1. Select keyword search.
2. Find a book or two in the list that is about your subject.
3. Look at the subject headings attached to those books and use the same subject headings to search in the catalog.
4. In the catalog record, look for the abbreviation "il." or "illus." to appear in the notes/description.
5. Or limit your search by words in the subject "pictorial works."

If you have photographs that you have personally taken, you usually can freely incorporate those images into your website or paper. Also, you may have photographs passed down through your family that are now in your possession. All you need to do is scan them and save them in the appropriate format. You must be cautious about using photographs of works of art, though, as most museums have restrictions on taking photographs of items in their collections. In this case, even if you have taken the photograph, you do not have the copyright. You also must obtain permission to use snapshots of individuals. If you did an oral history and included a photograph of the individual interviewed, you need permission to use his or her image.

You may also go to a local historical society and use its historical collections. Many have vertical files and other collections of photographs. Sometimes a reproduction fee is involved if you want something more than a photocopy. Some collections may be too fragile to copy.

Probably the most frequent and easiest method of finding still images is through search engines and websites of collected images on the Internet. Most of these images can be immediately downloaded and incorporated into your website or paper with little or no adjustment by the available software programs. You can search for historical images in two ways on the Internet, either through a site that organizes images or by using a search engine designed to look for images. Below is a list of *mostly* free sites, meaning that you may search the site without paying a subscription. Each site has its own restrictions about the use of its contents, and some will charge you fees for downloading actual images. Just because you have found it on the Internet, though, does not imply it is copyright-free. For large collections of images, the search tips below are useful. For smaller collections, browsing through categories designed by the website may be more fruitful.

Using a general search engine designed for images, whether or not solely historical, will yield the largest number of results. Look for a button or special section for image searching. The libraries at the State University of New York, Albany, have a nice guide to search engines that will lead you to other search engines that are useful for finding images (http://library .albany.edu/internet/choose.html). However, quantity of results may be a problem. A vague and imprecise search will often produce overwhelming numbers of results. To search for an image, you must use specific, concrete search terms. You are in essence looking for the graphic representation of an object, an image. If you are looking for images of African Americans in the military, think of specific instances of their participation in the American military and search terms such as "Tuskegee airmen" or "Buffalo soldiers." While you can search for images of the Cold War or the Iron Curtain, your results will be messy and you might miss better images because you are relying on someone to associate those words with an appropriate image. Instead, you must search for images that represent those concepts, such as the Berlin Wall.

SEARCH TIPS (WITHIN AN ONLINE COLLECTION)

1. Use one of the collections listed in the section below.
2. Search for an object. Make sure that the subject you search for would be in the collection you have selected. For instance, *American Memory* does have images from around the world, but the British Library is probably a better choice for British images. The *Acunet/AP PhotoArchive* has mostly mid-twentieth-century photos, so you would be unlikely to find many U.S. Civil War photographs in that collection.
3. Be as specific as you can. Check to see if there is a date/time period limit or sort to focus your search.

Collections of Historic Images

Collections Providing Free Images

American Memory, http://memory.loc.gov/ammem/ (accessed March 28, 2006). Collections of photographs and moving pictures mostly concerning the United States. Covers nineteenth to twenty first centuries.

Daguerreian Society, http://www.daguerre.org/ (accessed March 28, 2006). Contains a database of daguerreotypes provided by the society's membership.

New York Public Library Digital Collections, http://www.digitalgallery.nypl.org/nyp/digital (accessed March 28, 2006). Thumbnails of photographs from collections and exhibits. See also New York Public Library digital galleries.

Images Canada, http://www.imagescanada.ca/ (accessed March 28, 2006). Images, primarily photographs, from a number of cultural institutions throughout Canada, searchable in one single spot. You may use these images for noncommercial purposes for no fee.

British Library Images Online, http://www.imagesonline.bl.uk/britishlibrary/ (accessed March 28, 2006). Images from the British Library throughout British history. Searching is free. There is a cost for reproduction.

UNESCO Photobank, http://www.unesco.org/photobank/exec/index.htm (accessed March 28, 2006). Photos of UNESCO's activities. Search for particular historical landmarks.

Image Base (Fine Arts Museums of San Francisco), http://www.thinker.org/fam/about/imagebase/ (accessed March 28, 2006). From the collections of the fine arts museums of San Francisco. Non-commercial use is permitted. Sometimes the zoom will not work, so the images are hard to view.

International Center of Photography, http://www.icp.org/ (accessed March 28, 2006). Series of exhibitions.

Life Magazine Covers and Photo Essays, http://www.life.com/Life/lifeclassic.html (accessed March 28, 2006). Search or browse covers of Life magazine. Reproduction is limited.

Americana Museum of Photography, http://www.photography-museum.com/ (accessed March 28, 2006). Fascinating exhibits at this virtual museum on topics related to American history.

PBS's American Photography, http://www.pbs.org/ktca/americanphotography/ (accessed March 28, 2006). Exhibits of photography.

Harrapa, http://www.harappa.com/ (accessed March 28, 2006). Images of south Asia prior to 1947.

Digital Library for the Decorative Arts and Material Culture, http://digital
.library.wisc.edu/1711.dl/DLDecArts (accessed March 28, 2006). Documents and images about and of American material culture at the University of Wisconsin–Madison

Web Gallery of Art, http://www.wga.hu/ (accessed March 28, 2006).
Searchable database of European painting and sculpture, twelfth to
nineteenth centuries.

British Museum's Africa Collections, http://www.thebritishmuseum.ac.uk/
world/africa/africa.html (accessed March 28, 2006). Images from some
of the British Museum's collections.

Harvard Visual Image Search, http://via.harvard.edu:9080/via/deliver/
advancedsearch?_collection5 via (accessed March 28, 2006). Search
Harvard's union catalog called VIA of visual resources owned, held,
or licensed by Harvard. Catalog is accessible to the general public, but
access to some of the images may be restricted.

Africa Photo, http://www.africa-photo.com/ (accessed March 28, 2006).
See the historical section

Pictures Catalogue: National Library of Australia, http://www.nla.gov.au/
catalogue/pictures (accessed March 28, 2006). Searchable database of
photos of Australian life, including history.

PastPix, http://www.pastpix.com/ (accessed March 28, 2006). British
product of over 15,000 historical images for educational use. If you
register (at no cost), you will have full access to larger images.

Digital South Asia Library Images, http://dsal.uchicago.edu/images/
(accessed March 28, 2006). Group of four collections of photographs
mainly of India from the nineteenth century to the present.

Ad* Access, http://scriptorium.lib.duke.edu/adaccess/ (accessed March 28,
2006). Advertisements in U.S. and Canadian newspapers and magazines
from 1911 to 1955.

Political Cartoons and Cartoonists, http://www.boondocksnet.com/gallery/
pc_intro.html (accessed March 28, 2006). Nineteenth- and early twentieth-
century political cartoons.

*Collections Requiring a Library Subscription or Commercial Collections
Charging Fees (but Allowing Searching)*

Acunet/AP Photo Archive, http://photoarchive.ap.org/ (accessed March 28,
2006). A subscription-based product. Contains photographs, current
and historical, in the Associated Press' archive. Coverage is worldwide.
Includes an audio section. Check the online agreement for reproduction
rights.

ARTSTOR, http://www.artstor.org/ (accessed March 28, 2006). A subscription-based product. Contains images of all types of artwork: paintings, statues, architecture, material culture objects, and more. Coverage is worldwide and of all periods of history.

Time/Life Picture Collection, http://www.thepicturecollection.com/ (accessed March 28, 2006). Selected collection of photos from *Time/Life* photographers. If you wish to use most of these photographs, there will be a fee involved. You must register to use the database, although registration is free.

George Eastman House, http://www.eastmanhouse.org/ (accessed March 28, 2006). Click the Collections Online button. Search by a number of different ways, including photographer, subject, and type or style of photograph. Access is generally by menus. Reproduction Right discusses print and not web use. Contact the Eastman House for details.

GettyImages, http://www.gettyimages.com/ (accessed March 28, 2006). Collection of royalty-free as well as rights images, motion pictures, and other types of images. The Creative section contains archival photographs. Most photos, however, are from the twentieth century.

Corbis, http://pro.corbis.com/creative/appleaday (accessed March 28, 2006). Rights managed as well as free photos and illustrations. Duplicates some of the Getty collection.

National Geographic Images, https://www.ngsimages.com/ (accessed March 28, 2006). Similar to *GettyImages* and *Corbis* except includes some *National Geographic* images. Duplicates from the other databases can be found in this database.

SEARCH TIPS(FOR SEARCH ENGINES)

1. Select one of the specialized search engines listed below and click on the section that searches just for images.
2. If it has an advanced search section, select that.
3. Enter words that describe the *object* you seek. For instance, the name of a place or person or event such as "Mahatma Gandhi," "slaves," or "Buddhist temple." You would not want to enter a concept like "nonviolence" or "civil disobedience." However, "Gandhi" and "protests" will bring up examples of nonviolent civil disobedience.
4. If your search engine allows, you may want to limit your search to certain image formats (.jpg or .tif) or color/greyscale. These terms are explained later in the chapter.

Search Engines and Meta-Search Engines for Images and Indexes to Image Collections[20]

Google.com, http://images.google.com/ (accessed March 28, 2006).
AlltheWeb, http://www.alltheweb.com/ (accessed March 28, 2006).
Picsearch, http://www.picsearch.com/ (accessed March 28, 2006).
The State University of New York, Albany (SUNY), has a guide to other image search engines (http://library.albany.edu/internet/choose.html).
IMAGELIB and the Clearinghouse of Image Databases, http://clearinghouse .ltc.arizona.edu/search.asp (accessed March 28, 2006). Search through registry for collections of all types of images, photos, artwork, sheet music, etc.
Digital Library Federation: Public Access Collections, http://www.hti.umich .edu/cgi/b/bib/bib-idx?c5 dlfcoll (accessed March 28, 2006). Index to over 34 institutions and 600 collections. Not all are truly public-access.

Images on the Internet: Some Cautions

It is likely that the majority of your images will be acquired through searching on the Internet. Many organizations such as historical societies or libraries digitize and mount portions of their collections on the Internet to preserve them and to make them available to a wider audience. However, these images, as well as those you may find in published sources, present some issues that you must consider if you use them on your website or for your project.[21]

- *Images on the Internet can be altered—intentionally and/or accidentally.* To make an image clearer and cleaner, it may be sharpened, cropped, or changed in some way by the piece of software used to scan and mount it on the web. Individuals with the best intentions can wipe away valuable historical evidence. When you add images to your website, be careful not to alter their integrity. Do not edit out tears, watermarks, flaws, blemishes, or marks on the original image. These marks give the image authenticity and are part of the original historical record/artifact. Possibly someone contemporary with the image may have left notes and identifying markings, such as names of individuals or buildings, on the image that your cleaning would erase. Sometimes the image is intentionally altered to create the desired illusion. For instance, the website *The Commissar Vanishes* (http://www.newseum.org/ berlinwall/commissar_vanishes/) shows photographs Joseph Stalin and the Soviet government altered to provide a version of Russian society and politics that was not necessarily realistic. There are countless other examples of intentional deception on the web. Use the techniques to evaluate sources listed in Chapters Five (Evaluation) and Seven (Internet) to make sure you have an image that is representative of the evidence you wish to present.

- *Be aware that you are viewing only part of a collection.* Seldom are entire collections digitized because of the time and expense involved. Therefore, you cannot know how the image fits into the whole of the collection. If a photograph of the Taj Mahal was included with a letter to Aunt Sophie detailing niece Clara's grand tour of Asia in the 1850s, complete with letters describing Agra, India, and its inhabitants, you may not get the letter to Aunt Sophie in the digital collection, only the image. Thus, the image is isolated from its author's purpose and perspective. Also, you may not see all of the photos of a building that has undergone a number of renovations and, therefore, you might miss a crucial phase of its development.

- *Unknown selection criteria have been applied.* You have no idea why these images have been selected. If the images are part of an exhibit, they may have been selected by someone to exemplify an issue and therefore reflect someone's point of view.

- *The scanning process loses some of the information of the image.* When images are scanned and translated into *pixels*, the series of dots arranged in rows and columns that create the image, they lose some of their visual information. A scanned image is not as sharp and clear as the original; its tone is reduced and its color, changed. Images are often compressed to save space and to speed their transfer over the Internet, which further degrades the information. These factors are true of all digital information, not just images; but it is less of an issue for text-based documents because they are less complex than photographs.

- *Monitors and printers differ in their ability to display and print colors, including greyscale or shades of grey.* No matter how high the quality of scan you provide, the image will only be as good as the equipment used to display it. The image may be crisp and show incredible historic detail on your monitor but look quite ordinary on another viewer's monitor.

- *Some items are intended to be viewed from a distance.* Posters and paintings were meant to be hung on a wall and viewed from a distance and in person. Mounting them on a webpage may destroy their scale and sometimes their impact.

Scanning and Downloading Still Images

If you are going to add images to your website, regardless of their source, you will need a basic understanding of image types, image format, and image resolution. In creating and using digital images, you will encounter or create several types of file formats. Knowing their purposes and when to use them is essential.

Common Image Files

Images will have the following file extensions or formats at the end of the name of the file. Different formats are useful for different types of images.

- *.gif (Graphics Interchange Format).* Useful for line-art drawings and other black-and-white drawings. Even black-and-white photographs have shades of grey and are not reflected well in GIFs.

- *.jpg/.jpeg (Joint Photographic Experts Group).* Used for most photographs and artwork, both color and black and white, which does have shades of grey. JPGs are compressed files (files that are made smaller, thus easier to store), so some information is lost in their creation. All browsers (*Internet Explorer, Netscape, Mozilla, Firefox, Safari,* etc.) can recognize and display them. Generally, this is the format in which you will want to save your scanned images. JPG is the best format for printing.

- *.png (Portable Network Graphics).* PNG is a patent-free improvement to the GIF format. It is a format that is best used for line drawings. While it is a search limit option in some of the image search engines, not all browsers support it.

- *.tif/.tiff (Tagged Image File Format).* TIFF is an archival image format used for all types of images (color, black and white, and greyscale). Since the file is uncompressed, no information about the image is lost, making the file extremely large. Also, some browsers cannot read the file unless you use a special plug-in as the purpose is to preserve the image. Many libraries use this as the digital image from which they make JPG copies. If you are working on a collection for your institution, you need to discuss the specifications with the project manager, archivist, or librarian. For a class project, you will not have the server space to scan and save your images in TIFF format and keep JPG copies as well.

Now that you understand the types of images you may encounter or create, you will have to make some choices about downloading or scanning images.

Downloading Images

When you download images from the Internet, many of the choices discussed in the scanning section below will have been predetermined for you. You may not be able to change certain aspects of the image to meet the aesthetic requirements of your website. For instance, enlarging the image will cause a distortion and possibly result in an unclear and unusable image because its original scanned resolution was too low. To download an image from another website, place your mouse over the image and either right click (for a PC) or hold the mouse button down (on a MAC) and download the image to your hard drive or to your desktop. (*Never* link to an image on someone's webpage as it increases your page's loading time and, if the other webpage disappears or moves, your link is broken.) You will then be able to make adjustments to the downloaded image by using such software as *Adobe Photoshop* and place it in your website or paper. Rename the image file and record the bibliographic information such as the website address, title, and author. You will need to attribute your sources of images just as you do your other primary and secondary sources. In a website, it is customary to provide a link to the site of origin for your images. (In a paper, you will need to supply a footnote.) For many sites, this link is their requirement for permission.

Scanning Images

If you decide to do your own scanning, you need to understand the color and physical construction of digital images.[22] The scanning and image manipulation software you are using will require you to make decisions about the image type, resolution, and format. We have already discussed the formats above (.jpg, .gif, .png, .tif). Understanding the color, resolution, the physical structure, and size are the last components to creating your scanned image.

Dividing images into two broad categories will help you understand how to scan and save them. Think of your image as either a line drawing or photograph-like image. An example of a line drawing is a piece of clip art that is basically black and white with definite lines. Black-and-white cartoons might be another example. Just about every other kind of still image could be considered photograph-like. Even black-and-white images have shades of grey and therefore do have "color." Having some sort of perception of color will help you decide in which category to scan and save your image.

Image Types

- *Black and white.* 1-bit black and white, meaning the dots can be either black or white. Usually used for line drawings. You probably will have little occasion to use a black-and-white scan. Even if your image is a black-and-white photograph, there are shades of grey, and you will use either greyscale or color.

- *Greyscale.* 8-bit greyscale will give you 256 shades of grey. This is probably most useful for a black-and-white drawing or an engraving.

- *Color.* 8-bit and 24-bit color will give you 256-color and millions of colors, respectively. The 24-bit is closer to reflecting the real photograph but is, of course, a larger file size and will take up more storage space.

You must also consider the size and resolution of your image. Size is a bit more complicated in the digital world than in the printed world. Instead of thinking in inches and feet, you must think in pixels and dots per inch (dpi). Complex images need higher dpis because they have more detail to display. So if you have a line drawing, a simple image, scanning your image at 100 dpi is suitable. For a photograph, if your sole purpose is your website, scan your image at 100 dpi as the standard computer screen can handle only a resolution of 72 dpi. Higher dpis (400–600) are usually for archival images (.tif files) that are not meant to be viewed on a website but intended to act as master images from which other forms of that image can be created. As your dpi increases, so does your file size.

Organizing Still Images on Your Website

You can take several approaches to incorporating still images on your website, depending on its look. For example, you can integrate images into text. You can create thumbnails or small images that, when clicked, open the enlarged images in a separate window. Thumbnails are a good practice to save page space and loading time for your visitors. You can also have a separate section of images with browseable general subject headings. Because the structure of the Internet allows for nonlinear connections, in the form of hypertext, you can create new methods of associating ideas. As you are thinking of how to incorporate your images, always keep in mind your audience, your purpose for the website, and the fact that you want your visitor to be able to participate in that historical discussion, understand your analysis, and draw personal conclusions. While images are the easiest to incorporate into a website or a formal paper, the Internet also makes audio and video files readily available for your project.

Digital Video and Audio Files

The challenge in using digital video and audio files is delivering them to the desktop. Because of their size, having the entire file on your computer is usually impractical. Most digital video and audio files are streamed, that is, delivered to your desktop in small sections so that you can view or listen to the clip as it is being sent. To see or hear the files, you will need special software to decompress them.

Digital Video: Using Moving Images

While becoming more available on the Internet, digital historical moving pictures are still difficult to search for both online and in an archive. Doing your own digitizing of historical film is problematic as different speeds and sizes of film, not to mention the actual condition of the film itself, present problems. Doing the actual digitization requires archival assistance; this section will not discuss that process. However, some historical moving images, such as oral interviews, speeches, advertisements, music recordings, and early short movies, are available on the Internet and can be valuable for your research.

Searching on the Web

Finding digital moving images on the web is difficult because, like finding photos, deciding on search terminology is difficult. You will have to be creative about how you perform your keyword searches in the search engines below. In the advanced sections of most of the general search engines, you will be able to limit your search by file format. Motion picture file formats include .avi, .mov, .qt (*QuickTime* from Apple), and .rm (or sometimes .ram) (Real Video from *RealNetworks*). You can combine your search term with the word "history" or "historical," but often the descriptions will not include that word. Instead, they might say something like "New York City skyline, 1910." In some cases, you may just have to keep looking through your results until you find something useful. Collections of historical video exist but are usually copyright-protected and require fees to link their movies to your website. Read the terms of use on the websites carefully.

Selected Sites with Historical Video Collections

American Memory Motion Pictures, http://memory.loc.gov/ammem/browse/ListSome.php?format5 Motion1 Picture (accessed March 28, 2006). Films include early Thomas Edison silent shorts, 1950s advertisements, and reactions to the events of September 11.

Internet Archive Moving Image Archives, http://www.archive.org/details/movies (accessed March 26, 2006). Archive of freely available shorts, clips of movies, advertisements, etc.

Museum of the Moving Image, http://www.movingimage.us/ (accessed March 28, 2006). Online exhibits on themes such as presidential campaigns, 1952–1994.

Television News Archive (Vanderbilt University), http://tvnews.vanderbilt.edu/ (accessed March 26, 2006). Subscription service that indexes most of the nightly news broadcasts since the late 1960s.

British Movietone News, http://www.movietone.com/ (accessed March 26, 2006). Movie/television and newsreels. Site has become restrictive and requires registration to view any of the contents.

ITN Archive, http://www.itnarchive.com/ (accessed March 26, 2006). A wealth of footage that you can browse through if you register, which is free. However, there is a fee to actually use the footage. Includes such organizations as British Pathe, Fox News, Reuters, and ITN for much of the twentieth century.

Film Archives Online, http://www.filmarchivesonline.com/ (accessed March 26, 2006).Another site that you must register to use. Similar to the above.

Selected Video Search Engines

Singingfish, http://search.singingfish.com/.

State University of New York at Albany, http://library.albany.edu/internet/choose.html (accessed March 26, 2006). An excellent guide to all sorts of search engines. See the Multimedia section for others not listed here.

Audio, Music, and Speech Resources

No longer are scholars denied access to brittle cassette tapes or reel-to-reel tapes (a recording format even older than cassette tapes). Increasingly, speeches, interviews, and musical recordings are available though streaming audio on the Internet. As a researcher, you can now hear famous speeches given by dictators, such as Hitler, or presidents, such as John F. Kennedy, and can experience their charismatic vocal inflections. Likewise, musically you can hear the blues of Lead Belly (Huddie Leabetter, 1888–1949) recorded while he was in prison in the 1930s or famous recordings of pieces of classical music or examples of other cultures' music.

To analyze the content of speeches, the following criteria will be helpful. Many times you will have only the written text and, thus, will be limited to a critical analysis of the words. However, if you are able to obtain a copy that actually allows you to hear the delivery of the speech, be sure to incorporate that into your assessment.

Questions to Ask about Speeches

1. Who is the audience, and who else is the speaker trying to reach? Many times the individuals attending the speech are not the only audience. You many not know this or may have to do additional research.[23]

2. Do other versions of the speech exist? How do all the versions differ?[24]

3. How does the speaker have the authority to speak?[25]

4. How does the speaker's voice reflect the time in which he or she is speaking?[26]

5. What powers of persuasion does the speaker use? If you can listen to the speech, how does the speaker use his or her voice?

Analyzing music presents a more complicated task, especially if you do not understand the conventions, notations, and terminology of music. Still, music is integral to life and culture and can be a revealing piece of evidence in your research. Music can reflect or define an age, for example, ragtime, popular in the United States from the end of the nineteenth century to about 1918, couples black rhythms with European classical musical influences to evoke an era when American society was changing. Music can inspire nationalism, for example, Wagnerian opera in Nazi Germany, or define classes, for example, middle-class urbanites in 1950s Brazil rejected samba style music, which was based on folk traditions, for the bossa nova style but by the 1960s returned first to idealized traditional music and then to embrace protest songs against the military regime. Music can define social movements, for example, the civil rights movement in the United States, or incite spiritual commitment, for example, revival songs for tent meetings in nineteenth- and twentieth-century America.[27] For your analysis, it will help you to think of music in two categories, that which has been written down and that which is from an oral tradition and may have variations (although much of this music has been written down in order to preserve it). The former is often performed before groups in formal concerts, and the latter is often "common" people's music, such as folk music, jazz, lullabies, or songs performed by troubadours, and sung in casual company, often improvised. In the study of music, three categories of participants are involved: the composer, the performer, and the listener. So, as a researcher, you must consider not only the intent of the composer but also the interpretation of the performer(s) and the reception of the audience. In many cases, this both changes over time and place, in the case of the performer(s) and the listener, and is affected by the time in which the composition was written or created. With folk music, the composer is often undefinable, and many performers have changed the song over time, muddying your interpretation. Yet, each performance of a written piece of music is different as well. Use the following criteria to help you analyze the influence of a piece of music.

Questions to Ask About Music[28]

1. Is the work organized in some way and according to a recognized musical format (e.g., a sonata)?

2. Is the composition part of a series of compositions?

3. How does the composition relate to other compositions written around the same time? What is unique to this composition? What made this composition an example of its age? What does it say about fashion and convention?

4. How does the composition fit in with the composer's other works?

5. How does contemporary culture affect this composition? Can you see literature, art, and other forms of culture reflected in it?

6. How does the delivery of the composition affect its meaning? Was the piece meant to be performed in a concert hall? Sung in cotton fields? By troubadours in the manors of nobles? As a rally for protest? As part of a religious service?

7. Who would have heard this composition and how? Live, recorded? Was it a best seller in its time? To research the market of a composition, look at such magazines as *Cashbox* and *Billboard* as well as other popular magazines of the day and histories of music. See Chapter Six on primary sources for research techniques.

8. What was the composer's purpose in writing the composition? Was there a political purpose? Was the composition sponsored by a patron or by an organization such as a church? Was the composition written for a specific performer or a specific occasion?

9. How did the audience as well as critics respond? Look at concert reviews.

10. Are there other editions of the work? Especially with folk music that passes down melodies and lyrics, many variations by region and time period exist.

11. What is the message of the lyrics?

12. What emotions does the composition evoke?

13. If you are able, you may want to examine the meter, rhythm, melodic phrases, repetitions of phrases, and harmonies.

Searching for Audio Materials

A growing number of websites provide audio links to speeches, interviews, and historic recordings, although in some cases the links are to transcripts and sheet music, both of which can be valuable for your research. Many of the same search techniques for images apply for audio materials. If you are searching on the Internet in one of the search engines, use the topic, place, or person for a speech, the music genre, country, and/or words "historic music" or "sheet music" for recordings and "interviews" or "oral histories" for oral interviews. (See Chapter Six for a fuller discussion of oral history.) You may also find that your library has a collection of these types of materials. Use the directions in the search box below to search your library's catalog.

Below is a list of the most common file formats you will find on the Internet. Quality often depends on many factors, both the size of the file and the device over which the sound is played. For an explanation of sound on the Internet, see *Audio QuickStart: Common Formats* (http://www.devx.com/projectcool/Article/20112).

- *.aif.* Developed by Apple Computer and will work with most browsers.

- *.au.* Created by Sun Microsystems and compatible with most browsers.

- *.wav.* Developed by Microsoft and one of the most common formats supported by most browsers.

- *.mp3.* With the IPOD's popularity, this format is increasing in its prevalence, even for files of older audio material.

SEARCH TIPS (FOR A SEARCH ENGINE)

1. Use the topic, place, or person for a speech, the music genre, country, and/or words "historic music" or "sheet music" for recordings and "interviews" or "oral histories" for oral interviews.

SEARCH TIPS (FOR AN ONLINE CATALOG)

Note: these tips are independent of each other and not to be done step by step.

1. Do a keyword search and limit the results by words in subject speeches.
2. Do an author search with the name of the speaker. Look through the listing for a subheading "Oratory" or "Speeches, Addresses, etc.," for example, "Cicero, Marcus Tullius–Speeches, Addresses, etc."
3. Take special care in looking for music. Music is classified by the genre of music, (e.g., *jazz*) or by the type of song (e.g., *protest songs*). You will need to select your subject heading and then limit your results by the type of material, a sound recording or audio-visual, depending on how your library's catalog allows you to do such a limit. The same pattern follows for a particular composer. Use the composer's name as an author and do the same limit.

Websites with Audio (or Music/Sheet Music)

History Channel Speeches, http://www.historychannel.com/speeches/ (accessed March 26, 2006). Collection of excerpts of speeches from famous individuals in all areas of public life. Mostly mid-twentieth century to the present.

History and Politics Out Loud, http://www.hpol.org/ (accessed March 26, 2006). Significant political speeches, primarily from the 1960s and 1970s.

American Rhetoric, http://www.americanrhetoric.com/ (accessed March 26, 2006). Audio and video of selected famous American speeches.

Historical Voices, http://www.historicalvoices.org/ (accessed March 26, 2006). Links to other collections of speeches in the twentieth century.

American Memory, http://memory.loc.gov/ (accessed March 26, 2006). Click on the collections for sound recordings. Many folk music recordings and oral interviews are included in the list.

BBC Audio Interviews, http://www.bbc.co.uk/bbcfour/audiointerviews/ (accessed March 26, 2006). Late twentieth-century interviews with famous individuals.

Historic American Sheet Music 1850–1920, http://scriptorium.lib.duke.edu/sheetmusic/search.html (accessed March 26, 2006). Large searchable collection from Duke University. Only includes front of the sheet music, not the music itself. Part of the Scriptorium collections.

Virtual Gramophone: Canadian Historical Sound Recordings, http://www
.collectionscanada.ca/gramophone/ (accessed March 26, 2006). Early
Canadian music.

*Dismuke's Virtual Talking Machine: Vintage Phonograph Recordings,
1900–1939*, http://dismuke.org/ (accessed March 26, 2006). Digital
files from an individual's collection.

Maine Music Box Collection, http://mainemusicbox.library.umaine.edu/
(accessed March 26, 2006). Collections of sheet music, with some
audio, 1845–1997.

Smithsonian Folkways, http://www.folkways.si.edu/index.html (accessed
March 26, 2006). Index to Smithsonian recordings of folk music and
other recordings. See *Smithsonian Global Sound* below for online access.

Classical Music Library (Alexander Street Press), http://www
.alexanderstreetpress.com/products/clmu.htm (accessed March 26,
2006). Subscription database that provides access to authoritative versions of classical recordings.

Smithsonian Global Sound (Alexander Street Press), http://www
.alexanderstreetpress.com/products/glmu.htm (accessed March 26,
2006). Subscription database that provides historical tracks of folk,
country, African-American, world, and ethnic music.

Naxos Music Library, http://www.naxosmusiclibrary.com/ (accessed
March 26, 2006). Subscription database of classical, jazz, and world
music from major recording labels.

British Library Sound Archive, http://www.bl.uk/collections/sound-archive/
nsa.html (accessed March 26, 2006). By clicking on the Sound Archive
button, you will find a few pieces of music online. Mostly, however,
this is access to their collections through their catalog. Collections to
be digitized in the future are listed: (http://www.bl.uk/collections/
sound-archive/asrtencollections.html) (accessed March 26, 2006).

Digital Traditional Folksong Database, http://www.mudcat.org/, http://
sniff.numachi.com/~rickheit/dtrad/ (accessed March 26, 2006). An index created by the Mudcat Café, can be downloaded from their site or
an older version and made available at the second address.

Audio Search Engines and Directories

Fagan Finder, http://www.faganfinder.com/audio/.

Singingfish, http://search.singingfish.com/.

State University of New York at Albany (SUNY), http://library.albany.edu/
internet/choose.html. An excellent guide to all sorts of search engines.
See the Multimedia section of this guide for others not listed here.

Copyright

Copyright is a sticky and difficult issue. Just as you cannot take someone else's idea and claim it as your own, you cannot take an image and reprint it without the producer's permission. There are some basic rules you can follow. If you find that your situation becomes more complex, you will want to consult your library. If you are using an image in a paper that will be turned in to your professor, simply documenting your source and attributing its authorship, (i.e., the photographer and/or the source, such as the book, website, or archive) is sufficient. If you have created a website or written a master's thesis or doctoral dissertation, these are considered forms of publishing and you must obtain permission to use images just as you would for a book. Many sources of images, such as libraries, historical societies, and other websites, will allow you to include their images if you acknowledge them as the source, do not make money from your website or project, and use them for educational purposes as opposed to advertising something like a historic tour business. Look for instructions on the website. Usually, there is a link under the word "copyright." If you do not wish to reproduce the image, all you need to do is refer to it in your analysis and list the site as a source.

Manuscripts, oral histories you have collected, and photographs you have taken also have copyright issues. If you have taken a photograph or collected an oral history as part of your project, discuss the process with your professor. All oral history projects require release or consent forms from the individuals you have interviewed.[29] In the case of unpublished documents, such as letters, created after 1978, the general rule is that the author or the author's estate for the life of the author plus 70 years retains the copyright, unless renewed by the author's estate. Works published before 1923 are in the public domain and are copyright-free. However, you would have to digitize the original source, for instance, a photograph or document, and not download someone else's *copy* from a website. Copyright is complicated. When in doubt, assume that the item is copyrighted. Again, if you have any doubts, seek help at your library. A very detailed chart that clearly explains these rules is provided by Cornell University (http://www.copyright.cornell.edu/training/Hirtle_Public_Domain.htm).

FOR FURTHER READING

Baigrie, Brian S., ed. *Picturing Knowledge: Historical and Philosophical Problems Concerning the Use of Art in Science.* Toronto: University of Toronto Press, 1996.

Bellman, Jonathan. *A Short Guide to Writing about Music*. New York: Longman, 2000.

Berger, John. *Ways of Seeing*. London: British Broadcasting Corporation and Penguin, 1972.

Brett, Guy. *Through Our Own Eyes: Popular Art and Modern History*. Philadelphia: New Society Publishers, 1987.

Burke, Peter. *Eyewitnessing: The Uses of Images as Historical Evidence*. Ithaca, NY: Cornell University Press, 2001.

Care, Handling and Storage of Photographs. Library of Congress and International Federation of Library Associations and Institutions Core Programme Preservation and Conservation, http://www.loc.gov/preserv/care/photolea.html (accessed January 1, 2006).

Caring for Your Photographs. American Institute for Conservation of Historic and Artistic Works, http://aic.stanford.edu/library/online/brochures/photos.html (accessed January 1, 2006).

Dasilva, Fabio, Anthony Blasi, and David Dees. *The Sociology of Music*. Notre Dame, IN: University of Notre Dame Press, 1984.

Herbert, Trevor. *Music in Words: A Guide to Researching and Writing about Music*. London: Associated Board of the Royal Schools of Music, 2001.

Hogarth, Paul. *The Artist as Reporter*. New York: Reinhold Publishing, 1967.

Holliday, Peter James. *The Origins of Roman Historical Commemoration in the Visual*. New York: Cambridge University Press, 2002.

Langford, Martha. *Suspended Conversations: The Afterlife of Memory in Photographic Albums*. Montreal: McGill-Queen's University Press, 2001.

Levine, Robert M. *Images of History: Nineteenth and Early Twentieth Century Latin American Photographs as Documents*. Durham, NC: Duke University Press, 1989.

Nickell, Joe. *Camera Clues: A Handbook for Photographic Investigation*. Lexington: University Press of Kentucky, 2004.

O'Connor, John E., ed. *Image as Artifact: The Historical Analysis of Film and Television*. Malabar, FL: Robert E. Krieger Publishing, 1990.
    Section on movies as primary source evidence, documentary, news, and cultural artifact.

Ostrow, Stephen E. *Digitizing Historical Pictorial Collections for the Internet*. Washington, DC: Council on Library and Information Resources, 1998.
    Discussion on good practices for digitizing historical images.

Staley, David J. *Computers, Visualization, and History: How New Technology Will Transform Our Understanding of the Past*. Armonk, NY: M. E. Sharpe, 2003.

Stokstad, Marilyn. *Art History*. 2d ed. New York: Prentice Hall, 2002.

Trachtenberg, Alan. *Reading American Photographs: Images as History*. New York: Hill and Wang, 1989.

Tufte, Edward R. *The Visual Display of Quantitative Information*. 2d ed. CT: Graphics Press, 2001.
    Unique history of graphs and their use and development as a tool to summarize and create visual information.

UVA Electronic Text Center. *Image Scanning: a Basic Helpsheet*, http://etext.lib
.virginia.edu/services/helpsheets/scan/scanimage.html (accessed January 1, 2006).
Webmonkey: The Web Developer's Resource, http://webmonkey.wired.com/
webmonkey/ (accessed January 1, 2006).
Wingell, Richard J. *Writing about Music: An Introductory Guide*. 3d ed. Upper
Saddle River, NJ: Prentice Hall, 2002.
Zelizer, Barbie. *Remembering to Forget: Holocaust Memory through the Camera's
Eye*. Chicago: University of Chicago Press, 1998.

NOTES

1. Louise Schneider Adams, *Methodologies of Art* (New York:
HarperCollins/Icon Books, 1996), xv–xvi.
2. Peter Burke, *Eyewitnessing: The Uses of Images as Historical Evidence*
(Ithaca, NY: Cornell University Press, 2001), 9–10.
3. Motion Picture, Broadcasting, and Recorded Sound Division, Library of
Congress, "Theodore Roosevelt: His Life and Times on Film." *American
Memory*, http://memory.loc.gov/ammem/trfhtml/trfhome.html; American
Folklife Center, Library of Congress, *Voices from the Days of Slavery: Former
Slaves Tell Their Stories*, http://memory.loc.gov/ammem/vfshtml/vfshome.html
(both accessed January 1, 2006).
4. James West Davidson and Mark Hamilton Lytle, "Mirror with a Memory," in
After the Fact: The Art of Historical Detection (New York: Knopf, 1982), 216.
5. Barbie Zelizer, *Remembering to Forget: Holocaust Memory Through the
Camera's Eye* (Chicago: University of Chicago Press, 1998), 12–18.
6. Ibid., 16–48.
7. William A. Frassanito, *Gettysburg: A Journey in Time* (New York: Charles
Scribner's and Sons), 1975, 91–192, Library of Congress, "Does the Camera
Ever Lie? The Case of the Moved Body," *American Memory*, http://memory
.loc.gov/ammem/cwphtml/cwpcam/cwcam3.html (accessed January 1, 2006).
(See also the Learning Page on the *American Memory* website.) Other
examples of staged photographs during wartime include the raising of the flag
at Iwo Jima and the return of MacArthur to the Philippines.
8. Zelizer, *Remembering*, 7; Wendy Kozol, *Life's America: Family and Nation in
Postwar Photojournalism* (Philadelphia: Temple University Press, 1994).
9. Burke, *Eyewitnessing*, 85.
10. See Robert M. Levine, *Insights into American History: Photographs as
Documents* (Upper Saddle River, NJ; Pearson/Prentice Hall, 2004), 11; Frank
Goodyear, *Making Sense of Evidence: Scholars in Action:Analyze a
Daguerreotype*. History Matters, http://historymatters.gmu.edu/mse/sia/photo.htm
(accessed January 1, 2006); Elspeth H. Brown, "Appendix A: Reading the Visual
Record," in *Looking for America*. Ardis Cameron, ed. (Oxford: Blackwell

Publishing, 2005), 362–370; conversation with Lisa McLaughlin, Miami University Faculty, May 2004.

11. John Berger, *Ways of Seeing* (London: British Broadcasting Corporation and Penguin Books, 1972), 21, 25–26.

12. Ibid., 19.

13. Ibid., 7–8, 50.

14. Ibid., 90–94, Francis Haskell, *History and Its Images: Art and the Interpretation of the Past* (New Haven: Yale University Press, 1993), 1–25.

15. James Hall, *Illustrated Dictionary of Symbols in Eastern and Western Art* (New York: IconEditions, 1994). Use the subject heading in your library's catalog "Symbolism in Art" and look at the subdivisions by country and by type of reference source, encyclopedias and dictionaries.

16. Adams, *Methodologies*, 58–78.

17. Mark Roskill and David Carrier, *Truth and Falsehood in Visual Images*. (Amherst, MA: University of Amherst Press, 1983), 3.

18. Ibid., 1–28.

19. A nice discussion of this in the context of film and television can be found in John E. O'Connor, ed., *Image as Artifact: The Historical Analysis of Film and Television* (Malabar, FL: Robert E. Krieger Publishing, 1990), 6–7.

20. Technical Advisory Service for Images, *A Review of Image Search Engines*, http://www.tasi.ac.uk/resources/searchengines.html (accessed January 1, 2006).

21. Many of these issues are discussed at length in Stephen Ostrow, *Digitizing Historical Pictorial Collections for the Internet* (Washington, DC: Council on Library and Information Resources, 1998).

22. For excellent, succinct instructions, see UVA Electronic Text Center. *Image Scanning: a Basic Helpsheet*, http://etext.lib.virginia.edu/services/helpsheets/scan/scanimage.html and UVA Electronic Text Center, *Text Scanning a Basic Helpsheet*, http://etext.lib.virginia.edu/services/helpsheets/scan/scantext.html (both accessed January 1, 2006).

23. Carla Peterson, "Scholars in Action, Carla Peterson Analyzes Speeches," *History Matters*, http://historymatters.gmu.edu/mse/sia/peterson.htm (accessed January 1, 2006).

24. Ibid.

25. Ibid.

26. Ibid.

27. Fabio Dasilva, Anthony Blasi, and David Dees, *The Sociology of Music* (Notre Dame, IN: University of Notre Dame Press, 1984), 92–105.

28. The criteria listed here are a combination of those suggested in the following guides: Richard J. Wingell, *Writing about Music: An Introductory Guide*, 3d ed. (Upper Saddle River, NJ: Prentice Hall, 2002); Trevor Herbert, *Music in Words: A Guide to Researching and Writing about Music* (London: Associated Board of the Royal Schools of Music, 2001); Jonathan Bellman, *A Short Guide to Writing About Music* (New York: Longman, 2000); and Dasilva, Blasi, and Dees, *The Sociology of Music*, 150–156.

29. Some universities even require your projects to be approved by a group of people called something like the "Institutional Review Board for the Use of Human Subjects in Research." (IRB). Interpretations as to whether oral histories fall under "human subject" regulations are fuzzy. It is best to check with your university or college.

10

Presenting Your Research: Traditional Research Paper, *PowerPoint*, or Website?

WHAT YOU WILL LEARN IN THIS CHAPTER:

- the differences between a research paper, a website, and an oral presentation in presenting your research
- basics of writing a historical research paper
- basics of creating a *PowerPoint* presentation
- basics of designing a scholarly website

In the past, the only format for presenting your research was the research paper. While still the most popular choice, the Internet and presentation software such as *PowerPoint* offer additional ways to enhance your research presentation. These formats serve different purposes and should not be used interchangeably. While you would not confuse a *PowerPoint* presentation with a website or a research paper, sometimes it is tempting to take one format and transform it into another. Ultimately, your professor or teacher determines the requirements of your project. But when you do have a choice of format, you will need to use your chosen format effectively, according to its strengths, so that your research and argument will become clear to your audience.

A research paper directs your argument to a very focused conclusion. Heavily reliant on text, it clearly lays out your evidence for your audience to follow in a very linear manner. While you may have some illustrations, the focus is on the text, the narrative, and the argument. Papers are best for research topics that require the presentation of evidence with large amounts of footnotes and a directed analytical conclusion.

Websites allow for a different arrangement of text and graphics, greater freedom for the audience, as well as incorporation of material that the stricter, linear form of an essay makes more difficult. For instance, succinct textual analysis contained in a website can be linked to enhanced (enlarged, translated, etc.) primary source documents and images. Websites can be useful in presenting historical collections of materials, especially when you have a wealth of exemplary primary source materials that can be hyperlinked. Websites also allow for more in-depth research about individual historical artifacts. For instance, providing biographical information on individuals in a photograph can be a digression in a research paper but an enhancement to the quality of a website's evidence. While you will find papers posted on the Internet, good web scholarship and publishing is more than putting online a written paper with hyperlinks available or collecting and organizing primary sources. Web scholarship combines the analysis and discussion of a paper with the multimedia capabilities of the Internet to transcend the limitations of the written page. Use these capabilities to link textual evidence, documents, aural and visual evidence, photographs, and speeches and to draw the audience into interacting with that evidence. Perhaps instead of presenting your analysis, allow the visitors to make some of their own comparisons in an interactive question-and-answer session. For more on these issues, see the sections on designing your own webpage below.

Besides writing papers and creating websites, you might be asked to present your research orally to your fellow classmates, just as professors and academics present research findings at conferences. Using *PowerPoint*, you can produce and organize a series of slides for your audience to follow the key points of your verbal presentation. Just as a website should not be used in the same way as a traditional research paper, putting the complete text of a paper or a series of *PowerPoint* slides on the web is a misuse of that medium. Knowing how to use each medium for conveying research effectively will result in a stronger and more creative project, no matter which one your professor requires. Regardless of format, solid interpretation, synthesis, analysis, citation of sources, and discourse are contained in all good historical scholarship.

Creating a Research Paper

Writing Style

Writing a research paper is by far the most common method of presenting undergraduate research in the humanities. A research paper is most effective when you are presenting your argument in a linear fashion, have few images or other multimedia materials to link to the text, and are guiding the reader to your conclusion. Numerous guides, both printed and on the Internet, give detailed instruction on how to organize and construct a research paper. See, for example, Patrick Rael's *Reading, Writing, and Researching for History: A Guide for College Students* (http://academic.bowdoin.edu/WritingGuides/), especially its section on designing a research paper; William Kelleher Storey's *Writing History: A Guide for Students*, for its chapters on how to formulate a thesis, write text, and build sentences into an argument; and Mary Lynn Rampolla's *A Pocket Guide to Writing in History*, on writing a research paper. Each of these guides explains historical writing, and scholarly writing in general, in a different manner.[1] Rael's guide is excellent and online. At least one of the others should be in your library if you wish to consult them for more in-depth instruction beyond what is provided here. Remember, as noted in Chapter One, the *Chicago Manual of Style* is the authority on grammar and language for historians.

Chapter One also discussed creating a preliminary outline for your research, dividing your topic into related, manageable ideas to help you organize your thoughts. It would be surprising if, now as you are ready to compose, your original organization remained exactly the same framework you will use to write your paper. Before you begin to write, assess your intended argument, line up your evidence, and look at its logical flow with your intended interpretation. This will help you organize your sections and paragraphs as well as make sure you emphasize the most important parts of your argument.

You can choose to write your research paper in two basic styles common to history writers. William Kelleher Storey defines these two styles as follows:[2]

- *Analytical*. The analytical style makes a comparison around a concept or idea: for instance, examining how the discovery of moveable type and the printing press affected literacy among the gentry and less wealthy classes. The focus is on how the concept or ideas developed and influenced the participants (including individuals, nations, or institutions) and what led to a change in the environment (in this case, literacy).

- *Narrative*. The narrative style tells a story, what happened historically, often in chronological order. This usually centers on a person, place, event, or era. The topic can be as large as the history of the Roman Empire or something more manageable such as the Jesuits' attempts at converting the Guarani Indians in Paraguay to Christianity in the seventeenth and eighteenth centuries.

Narrative is the more common style. It is often used in political and intellectual history, while the analytical style is common in cultural and economic history, though it is not always so cut-and-dry.[3] No matter which style you decide to use, you will still have to present your argument logically, indicating to the reader why your evidence is significant and an important contribution to the scholarship already surrounding the topic.

Formulating an Argument

While you have already formulated your thesis and your argument with your professor, you must be cautious about how you carry out that argument. Indeed, you are supposed to present your educated opinion and analysis based on your evidence, but you should avoid deliberately incorporating your own personal biases and judgments into your research. In addition, true scholarship considers all opinions, including those critical and counter to your conclusion.[4] If you ignore other historians' works and primary source evidence that counter your conclusion, your argument is weakened. Good scholarship incorporates them and addresses how and why your argument differs.

It is all too easy to fall into fallacies and false conclusions. As you write, make sure that your argument makes logical sense. Do not make universal generalizations with such words as "all" or "every." Do use such words as "many," "most," and "some." Be careful about creating dichotomies in your thesis that leave no option for other choices. For example, Charles Mc-Dougald's title, *The Marcos File: Was He a Philippine Hero or Corrupt Tyrant?*, leaves little room for analyzing the complexities of Ferdinand Marcos' reign.[5] Be sure that your statistical data reflect your topic and that the data that you are presenting are really quantifiable and measurable. Watch for false data. Be careful about classifying individuals into groups and making broad statements about how those groups behave. For instance, not all African Americans, or nobility or Muslims or Russian soldiers in the Russian Revolution or any other group you may choose to categorize and characterize, necessarily behaved as a unified group or had similar characteristics. Be careful of extrapolating or ascribing the behavior or motivations of one individual to the whole group. Watch that your modern-day understanding of the world does not lead you to make assumptions about what individuals and societies knew in another time. This could lead to a misinterpretation of primary source materials. Finally, be careful not to overemphasize one piece of evidence over another. Rather, consider all of your evidence and its importance as a whole. Relying heavily on one piece of evidence could cause you to misinterpret its meaning. These problems of argument and many more are discussed in great detail and in complex philosophical terms in David Hackett Fischer's *Historians' Fallacies: Toward a Logic of Historical Thought*.[6]

Paper Construction

Once you have decided on a style and the divisions or outline of your paper, you need to think about the construction of tight paragraphs and the flow of your ideas. A typical eight- to 10-page paper begins with an introduction, outlining your argument and thesis, followed by a series of logical paragraphs that correspond to and support your introduction and ending with a conclusion that draws together the evidence, pointing out why the argument in the introduction is valid and credible. The introduction and conclusion need not be restricted to a single paragraph each, nor must they be written in order as you progress through the paper. You may begin with a vague, single-paragraph introduction with a fairly strong, single-sentence argument. By the time you have concluded the first draft, your introduction may be clearer to you and you will be able to return and lay out in an expanded introduction the purpose and thesis of your paper. Remember that you should write more than one draft of a paper. Scholarship is as much thinking, organizing, and presenting your collection of knowledge and evidence as it is the actual gathering of the sources. While you need a solid foundation of evidence, evidence alone will not "create" a quality paper. You need time to make connections. Write a first draft, put it away for a couple of days, and revise it after you have had some additional time to think about the connections you have made. Finally, let someone else read it (perhaps someone at a writing center on campus) and then revise it at least one more time. Your grade as well as your comprehension of the subject will reflect this process.

Ebb and Flow of Paragraphs

Connected together, your paragraphs fortify and build your argument. Below are some tips on creating effective paragraphs and sentences and on joining them together to create a flowing paper. These tips are fairly standard and not exclusively for historians; many can be applied to all scholarly writing. For a more detailed guide, consult Patrick Rael's *Reading, Writing, and Researching for History: A Guide for College Students* (http://academic.bowdoin.edu/WritingGuides/) and Mary Lynn Rampolla's *A Pocket Guide to Writing in History*.

- Begin each paragraph with a strong topic sentence, indicating what the paragraph is about. The rest of the paragraph should elaborate on this piece of your evidence with supporting details. Generally, stick with one idea per paragraph.
- Create transitions between paragraphs. Do not make your readers feel as if they are on a roller coaster as you switch between topic sentences.

Your paragraphs should be related because you are building an argument. Make your reader understand why all of your ideas connect. If you need to make an abrupt shift, consider a section heading.

- Write in the third person. Generally avoid using the pronoun "I." As the writer of the text, it is assumed that you are the source of the opinions and arguments that are not documented by footnotes. Remember that presenting others' ideas as your own is plagiarism.

- Do not use contractions.

- Avoid personal bias in your analysis. You have an argument, but becoming judgmental and letting your personal viewpoints color your assessment weakens your credibility.[7]

- Watch your verb tenses. Historians are permitted to use past tense since they are writing about the past, unlike most other scholarly disciplines. This can cause you to inadvertently shift between present and past tenses.[8]

These are only a few tips. Your professor or teacher will suggest others, as well as have more guidelines that he or she wishes you to follow. Writing well is important for conveying your ideas to your reader. Writing well means good sentence structure and formation, smooth flow of text, a tight argument that avoids common fallacies, and backing your research with primary and secondary sources. No matter how well you have performed your research by gathering sources, if your readers cannot understand the argument, your ideas will be lost. The same is true whether you are writing a research paper or presenting your research orally.

Oral Presentations and *PowerPoint*

Oral presentations require you to summarize your findings and evidence in succinct and outline form in a set time frame. Unlike a paper, which values narrative and prose style, an oral presentation consists of points of interest that reflect topics but not detailed analyses of those topics. Many use *Microsoft PowerPoint* software to illustrate to their audience the significant points of their research.[9] Organized effectively, it is a useful tool to *enhance* oral presentations. Effective *PowerPoint* presentations highlight the key points on slides to which you will verbally *add* information and analysis.[10] Used ineffectively, it can transform a learned presentation into an endless and uninteresting talk, and it can either dilute or totally destroy the flow of your argument and communication with your listeners.

Box 10.1 Historiographic Essays, Annotated Bibliographies, and Book Reviews

Writing an Historiographic Essay

Another type of paper your professor may ask you to write is a historiographic essay. Because history is based on arguments, the historiographic essay examines and compares other historians' arguments in opposition to each other. Whereas your research paper is built on both primary source evidence and other historians' interpretations, the historiographic essay concentrates only on the secondary works of historians. You will create in essay form a commentary that interweaves the titles and authors with their theories. Because this essay focuses on secondary works and their themes, your topic selection and your note taking will differ from the manner of a research paper. Your topic will of necessity be larger and less focused, for instance, the reign of Peter the Great of Russia (1672–1725). Your topic selection is not a thesis statement, but you will examine other historians' arguments about this given time. Some historians will look at the politics of Peter and his contemporaries, while others will look at society more holistically. Your essay may also be restricted to books and journal articles (and probably exclude websites) published between certain dates, perhaps the last 10 years. You will pick the best, most cohesive 20 or so titles (or a number specified by your professor or teacher) and discuss the works. Your conclusion will talk about the credibility of each argument. For a more detailed examination with excellent examples, see Chapter 4 of Anthony Brundage, *Going to the Sources: A Guide to Historical Research and Writing*, 3d ed. Wheeling, IL: Harlan Davidson, 2002.

Writing an Annotated Bibliography

A bibliography is a list of citations used in your research. An annotated bibliography provides information about those citations, usually a one- to two-sentence summary of the contents of the work in addition to the bibliographic information. A critical annotated bibliography provides a very short analysis of the work, highlighting in five to seven sentences how the work fits into the available literature and achieves its purpose. Critical annotated bibliographies are sometimes used in place of a paper so that students will find, examine, and contextualize resources but will not have to take the time to write an entire paper. In many ways, a critical annotated bibliography is a list of small book reviews (but will include journal articles in the same process). You will be asking the same questions as those for a book review, but you must be even more abbreviated in your writing. Your purpose is to give the reader a critical understanding of the sources you have selected. See *Annotated Bibliographies*, University of Wisconsin Writing Center (http://www.wisc.edu/writing/Handbook/AnnotatedBibliography.html) and *How to Write an Annotated Bibliography*, University of California, Santa Cruz (http://library.ucsc.edu/ref/howto/annotated.html).

Writing a Book Review

Writing a book review is more than just summarizing the content of a book. Remember that history is a discourse or discussion of research, so you must place your book in the context of the other literature on the topic. In fact, the content of a book review is more heavily an evaluation of the quality of the research and contextualization of the historian's argument than a summary of the content of the book. The length of your review is limited, so you must get to the point and focus on the main concerns both of the author and of your critique. Many of the considerations for a book review will mirror the questions you ask to evaluate sources listed in Chapter Five. However, in the case of actually writing a book review, you will elaborate more extensively on these questions and read your book with a different purpose in mind. The content of a book review should consider the following:

- What is the author's thesis and purpose?
- Has the author's background affected his or her analysis? What are his or her qualifications?
- Who is the audience, and does the author speak to that audience?
- A *brief* summary of the content.
- What does the author offer as evidence?
- How does the book fit into the existing research? Does it add anything of value, or is it a repetition of what has already been examined?
- What is missing from the author's analysis?
- Present your assessment of the successes and failures of the author's research.

You will write your review as an essay. Your professor or teacher will probably have a preferred format. If not, begin with the summary and organize your critique with specific examples of why the author is successful or unsuccessful. The *Book Review Writing Guide*, from the University of Alberta Faculty of Arts, Department of History and Classics, is a nice guide.

- *Book Review Writing Guide*, University of Alberta Faculty of Arts, Department of History and Classics (http://www.uofaweb.ualberta .ca/historyandclassics/bookreviewguide.cfm)
- *Write a Book Review with Rodman Philbrick* (http://teacher.scholastic .com/writewit/bookrev/)
- *Campus Writing Program, Indiana University Writing Tutorial Services: Writing Book Reviews* (http://www.indiana.edu/~wts/pamphlets/ book_reviews.shtml)
- *Writing in History 100: The History of Western Civilization*, George Mason University, Department of History and Art History (http://chnm.gmu .edu/courses/westernciv/writing/types_of_writing/book_reviews.html)

Remember that the purpose of a *PowerPoint* presentation is to provide an organizational framework for you, the speaker, to guide your audience through your research. It is not meant to contain all of the information you have gathered. Edward Tufte coined the term "phluff" in his diatribe against the misuses of *PowerPoint, The Cognitive Style of PowerPoint*.[11] Phluff, according to Tufte, is overpowering graphics and words that call more attention to the format of your presentation than to its content. So select a background that visually enhances but does not overshadow the data or text you wish to present. Animation and sound can also distract the audience from your message. Remember to keep the information at the center and not the bells and whistles of *PowerPoint*. Unable to control the pace of your lecture or the quantity of information presented, your audience can become bored, distracted, confused, and frustrated. Tufte warns, "Designer formats will not salvage weak content. . . . Audience boredom is usually a content failure not a decoration failure."[12] This is true not just for an oral presentation but for all methods of presenting your research.

Here are some "dos" and "don'ts" when creating an oral presentation using *PowerPoint*:[13]

- Provide a few statistics on a single slide. If you need to give your audience a chart or a significant quantity of facts or figures, provide them with a handout.
- Make bulleted lists simple in their organization and hierarchy. Complex lists and elaborate hierarchies visually confuse an audience and make it very difficult for them to make sense of the information presented. Complicated ideas should be verbally explained.

- Never read slides aloud verbatim. Let the audience read the material for themselves. In fact, seldom read anything to your audience that you display on the screen.

- Use the technology embedded in PowerPoint to enhance your presentation. Launching a webpage from a slide is useful to incorporate examples into your presentation. But just because *PowerPoint* has the capability of launching webpages from embedded links does not mean you can repackage your presentation into a website.

For an interesting illustration and parody of *PowerPoint* misused to its extreme, see Peter Norvig's *PowerPoint* presentation of Abraham Lincoln's Gettysburg Address (Fig. 10.1).[14] This is a prime example of how a *PowerPoint* slide cannot replace a good speech or adequately reflect its true content.

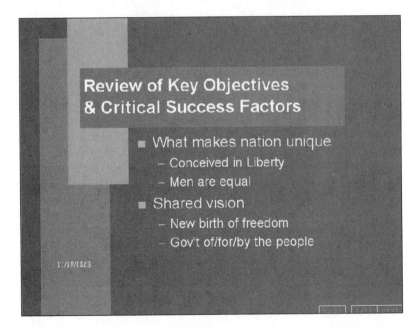

Figure 10.1. One of the slides from Peter Norvig's *PowerPoint* rendition of Abraham Lincoln's Gettysburg Address. This is both a silly and a serious example of a *PowerPoint* (.ppt) presentation. Seriously, Norvig in the persona of Lincoln has not attempted to put every word of the speech on this or the other series of slides illustrating the famous speech. On the silly side, a .ppt presentation cannot reflect the oratorical skill of Lincoln or convey the emotion of the speech for the speaker/orator or the thousands who have read and heard it spoken in the decades since 1863. ©*Peter Norvig, used with permission.*

Websites for Historical Research

Historical and Scholarly Websites: A Developing Frontier

A website can offer alternative methods of presentation for your research and argument that a paper and oral presentation cannot. Historians are just beginning to grapple with research that can be presented via the Internet. Much like the images of early photography, which mimicked painted portraits, many scholarly websites are text-heavy and appear to be either illustrated papers, nicely organized collections of primary sources, or websites with little or no analysis. These uses do have considerable value as they make scholarship and resources available to a wider audience as well as preserve historic resources, but they hardly use the special attributes of the web to its fullest. It may take years for historians to more fully imagine and use the web differently, just as it took photographers time to image new ways to take candid action shots, create landscape photographs, invent photojournalism, and treat photographs as an art form.

Common Categories of Historical Websites

Much academic web development has grown from theories designed for commercial use. Web designers are trying to sell a product or promote a company. What qualities might differentiate a website with historical qualities from other commercial and academic websites? Currently, many historical websites can be categorized as follows:

- *Website as a museum.* Either as a site for an existing, physical place or as a virtual museum, the website works as a single or series of exhibits, tying together artifacts, documents, memorabilia, etc. into a meaningful, interpretive structure. Generally, these sites speak to a wide level of visitors, from children to informed adults. While interpretive, they are seldom as rigorous as a site for an academic audience. Links can include learning modules for teachers and younger visitors, reading lists, and gift shops.
  - Examples:
    Alexander Palace Time Machine, http://www.alexanderpalace.org/palace/.
    Newseum, http://www.newseum.org/.
- *Website as a collection.* A group of related materials, usually providing full text, selected and arranged around a central theme. The act of collection often implies that someone selected what would be digitized and placed online. Sometimes interpretive essays and encyclopedia

articles may be included in the collection, but these articles do not attempt to synthesize the whole collection in the way a journal article, book, or even research paper would assess a complete set of primary source documents.

- Examples:
  Civil Rights Digital Archive in Mississippi, http://www.lib.usm
  .edu/~spcol/crda/.
  Making of America, http://www.hti.umich.edu/m/moagrp/.

- *Website as catalogs/bibliographies/web directories/databases.* These websites collect a list of print and online sources, primary, secondary, or both, on a broad subject. Sometimes a database is involved. Analysis is generally not provided, although links to sites might include a short evaluative abstract.
  - Examples:
    Internet History Sourcebooks, http://www.fordham.edu/halsall/.
    Diotma Materials for Study of Women in the Ancient World, http://
    www.stoa.org/diotima/.

- *Website as an analytic resource.* Few and far between, these sites attempt to thoughtfully integrate analysis, multimedia, and technology in a new form and allow visitors to draw their own interpretations. This is probably the type of website your professor or teacher would prefer that you create.
  - Examples:
    Valley of the Shadow Projects, http://valley.vcdh.virginia.edu/
    cwprojects.html.
    History Matters: Student Work on the Web, http://historymatters.gmu
    .edu/browse/studhist/.
    Some of the PBS history websites, http://www.pbs.org/history/.

In reality, many websites will combine these purposes, but thinking in these "historical terms" will help you with layout. If you imagine that you are doing a tour or creating an exhibit, think about how that arrangement would be different from one where you were trying to organize a collection of materials without any analysis. A collection may simply require arrangement by criteria such as chronology or geography, whatever makes it simpler to find the material. However, an exhibit requires analysis and context, so you will need to carefully consider that relationship depending on what discussion you want to have with viewers and how you wish to guide their experience. What is it that you want the viewer to understand most: time (chronology), place (geography), or people (an author, ethnic groups, etc.)?

Website Design: How to Begin

Today's culture promotes a multimedia approach that allows the viewer to construct his or her own means of understanding your analysis. The print newspaper *USA Today* provides a common example of how the hypertext format has invaded our lives even in resources that are not electronic. Information is presented in small paragraphs and short sections, while stories are much less linear in nature than they are in other newspapers. Additionally, the language of its headlines and the "navigation" between sections suggest a website motif.[15] Much of what is created for the Internet is still modeled on print formats, even though electronic resources have functions that allow them to transcend the confines of print. The integrated use of graphics and text with hyperlinks provides a multilayered set of arguments and evidence for a diverse audience. That audience, while reading and drawing conclusions, also participates in the process as individuals can make different decisions about which path of information to follow and in what order.[16]

The guidelines presented here will teach you how to lay out the kind of website that might be assigned as a project for one of your history courses. What you will not find here are instructions on how to write code in HTML, XHTML, XML, or any other version of markup language. There are a number of WYSIWYG ("what you see is what you get") programs that will allow you to build interesting websites very simply. Using them is like word processing, only you are creating a document that will be transferred to the web. Two highly recommended software programs are *Macromedia Dreamweaver* and *Microsoft Frontpage*.

While these two programs will perform the HTML coding, they will not design the layers and complexities of your site. Called "information architecture," the design and layout of the entire site is important for your visitors and your focus or argument. Architecture in this sense is not the programming of the website but, rather, how it is laid out, labeled, and organized, as well as how visitors will navigate through it. Just as a paper has an outline, so too a website has a framework. Right at the beginning is where your web project takes a different shape from a research paper. The quality of the content stays the same, but the new multilayered and multidimensional format will radically alter your method and style of presentation. Many of the recommendations about information architecture in this chapter are derived from several seminal books. For more in-depth information, see Patrick J. Lynch and Sarah Horton's *Web Style Guide*, Louis Rosenfeld and Peter Morville's *Information Architecture for the World Wide Web,* and Steve Krug's *Don't Make Me Think: A Common Sense Approach to Web Usability*.

These books were written for commercial website design, so while their principles are sound, you must adapt them for academic purposes. A very recent book by Daniel J. Cohen and Roy Rosenzweig, *Digital History: A Guide to Gathering, Preserving, and Presenting the Past on the Web*, takes many of these principles and applies them to historical web production.[17] To begin, think about your audience and your purpose and then adapt these design principles to the analytical properties of historical research and writing with the unique multimedia capabilities of the web.

Preplanning: The Major Considerations

As you begin to plan your website, both the main (or home) page and the subsequent (or under) pages, there are some important considerations to keep in mind:

- *Audience*. Think about who the visitors to your website might be. Certainly, your professor and your classmates, all of whom will probably have some knowledge of your topic, are part of the audience. Remember that the Internet is public and many individuals will use your site. When others find your webpage, who might they be, how will they use it, and what will they expect to find? Since you cannot satisfy everyone, be prepared to state your website's purpose and content clearly up front. You must think about how your audience will associate ideas and concepts and then decide how best to present various pages and levels of information. Be aware of some common assumptions about web audiences:
  - They are easily lost and need directions.[18]
  - Viewers will scan any section of a page to decide where to begin.
  - Readers read 25% slower online than in print.[19]
  - Web readers are more active in their reading.[20] More than just questioning your analysis, they will look for links that will supply concrete examples of your ideas.
  - Web users choose to read different types of materials on the web (generally, bits of information, such as encyclopedic facts) versus reading longer works in print.[21]
    - Your visitors also seek information in a variety of ways. Designing multiple access points to meet the needs of these kinds of users will help you plan your general layout. Seekers want to put in a single word and search for exactly what they need. Some easy search mechanism is useful for them. "Rummagers"

can deal with a bit of disorganization and will look through different areas of your website for what they want. "Classifiers" want categories and organization from which to select their topic. Frequent visitors desire a most recently added category.[22] Knowing which web visitors you desire to reach, how they will behave, and how you will accommodate them will help you to make decisions about the general layout of your website.

- *General layout.* Think about your layout in several ways, depending on the complexity and depth of your project. You should sketch out your ideas on a piece, or several pieces, of paper (Post-it® notes or index cards work well), thinking about the content of the top layer/page and the content of the subsequent, underneath layers/pages. Think about how the breadth and depth of your website relate. Is your site more cohesive, with more categories linked from the top/homepage and fewer linked beneath that page? Will your page seem more logical with fewer categories on the top/homepage but more associated with each category? If your site's navigation is poor, your visitors may not even be able to find their way backward. More about navigation design is below.

- *Site organization.* Having an organizational scheme will keep your website cohesive. Here are some common types that may be useful.[23]

  - *Alphabetical.* A listing of hyperlinks, in alphabetical order. An encyclopedia or a dictionary would use this kind of arrangement. For example, *Ecole Initiative*, http://www2.evansville.edu/ecoleweb/ (accessed March 29, 2006) (Fig. 10.2).

  - *Chronological.* By date. For example, *Timeline of Art History*, http://www.metmuseum.org/toah/splash.htm (accessed March 29, 2006) (Fig. 10.3).

  - *Geographical.* A listing by country, state, region of origin. For example, *Historic Cities*, http://historic-cities.huji.ac.il/ (accessed March 29, 2006) (Fig. 10.4).

  - *Topical.* By subject or some intellectual construct. This is a fairly common way to organize an academic website. For example, *The Labyrinth*, http://labyrinth.georgetown.edu/ (accessed March 29, 2006) (Fig. 10.5).

  - *Task.* By function or by software. For example, *American Memory*, http://memory.loc.gov/ammem/collections/finder.html (accessed March 29, 2006) (Fig. 10.6).

Figure 10.2. *Ecole Initiative, Ecole Glossary.* The encyclopedia or essay portion of this site lists its contents in simple alphabetical order. First, however, visitors select what type of information they desire, in this case an essay over an image. ©*Early Church OnLine Encyclopedia*, a service of the University of Evansville.

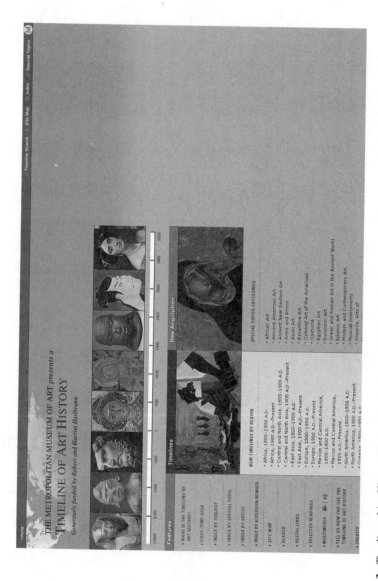

Figure 10.3. *Timeline of Art History, Metropolitan Museum of Art.* This site has a multiplicity of approaches, not only by date but also topical and geographical. Clicking on one of the timeline segments at the top of the screen takes you to a map that allows you to select a geographic region. After selecting a region, you are provided with a timeline of art history facts. ©*Metropolitan Museum of Art, used with permission.*

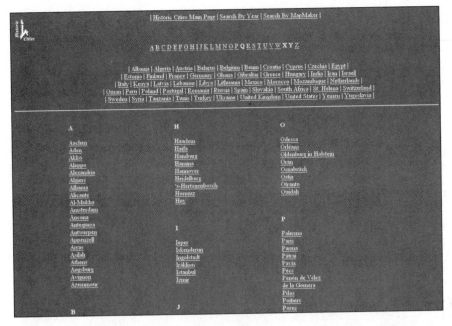

Figure 10.4. *Historic Cities* contains information about past and present cities. You can find a city name either by country or directly by city name. ©*Mitia Frumin and Historic Cities, used with permission.*

- *Audience.* Perhaps by reading level or scholarly level. For children, etc. For example, *Great Chicago Fire* on the *Web of Memory*, http://www.chicagohs.org/fire/intro/gcf-index.html (accessed March 29, 2006) (Fig. 10.7) and the education page from Monticello, http://www.monticello.org/education/index.html (accessed March 29, 2006) (Fig. 10.8).
- *Metaphor.* Using symbols, such as a house plan for navigation. For example, *Valley of the Shadow*, http://valley.vcdh.virginia.edu/choosepart.html (accessed March 29, 2006) (Fig. 10.9).

Most websites do not employ a singe organizational scheme. You will probably want to use multiple techniques to connect with the different ways your visitors will look for information, as well as the different modes in which your material is best organized, synthesized, and expressed.

- *Page layout.* Once you have a plan for the site, designing the single page will set the mood for the site. You must remember, though, that

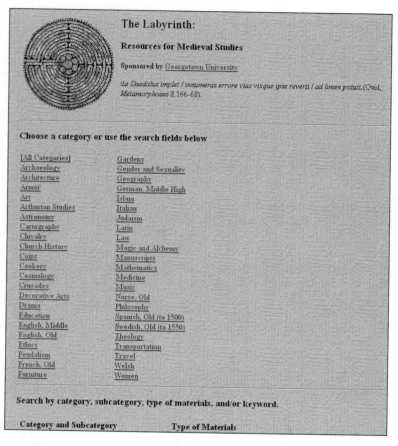

Figure 10.5. *The Labyrinth* is a large index of all types of materials on medieval studies. You have a choice of searching by categories or crossing fields, such as Cookery, with the type of material you want, such as primary texts or bibliographies. ©*Martin Irvine & Deborah Everhart used with permission.*

each page must not only link back to the homepage but also stand alone. Entry into your website may be via a search engine, which may not take the visitor directly to your first page. When organizing a single page, web designer Steve Krug suggests that you imagine dividing that page into zones or boxes. The more important the information is, the higher on the page and the more strategically positioned it should be.[24] Think of how a newspaper zones information into areas, boxes text, and enlarges and changes fonts. Information "above the fold" on a

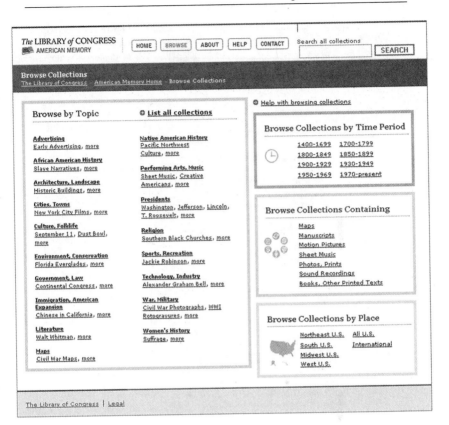

Figure 10.6. *American Memory* is a vast collection of primary sources relating to American history from the Library of Congress. You can search the collection in every way listed in this chapter. However, one unique way is by format in the box on the right side of the screen. If you wish to look at collections that offer maps, sound recordings, or motion pictures, for instance, you may look in only those collections.

newspaper and on the first screen of a webpage not only receives the most attention but also tells the visitor what is most important. Information below the first screen often does not get viewed.

Navigation

Navigation within a page and between pages can make or break your website. Consider where your buttons will be placed and the words used to convey their underlying content. You may have fantastic information that presents

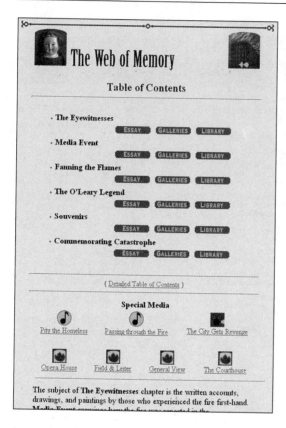

Figure 10.7. *The Great Chicago Fire* on the *Web of Memory* is written for a number of audiences. If a visitor wants just images, there is a gallery that supplies a museum exhibit and tour of the fire. The essay provides an explanation of the event, while the library provides primary source documents. *©1996 by the Chicago History Museum and the Trustees of Northwestern University.*

interesting discoveries and analogies but is unusable because your navigation is too cryptic. Once you decide on an overall organizational scheme, you need to decide how the information on your website interrelates. When writing a paper or a book, you create sections, paragraphs, and chapters. Through this flow and interconnectedness the text will contain sections of information. Connecting them with an argument is a challenge. When organizing your website, create general categories under which points, or "chunks," of evidence can be organized. Categories that are too specific or too general will confuse and distract your visitors. Make sure you speak to the level of audience you want to reach. Think about how visitors look for information and arrange it accordingly.[25]

- *Make your navigation "persistent and consistent."* Put the same buttons for navigation on every page and in the same spot, and use the same words. For example, if you have the categories shown in Figure 10.10,

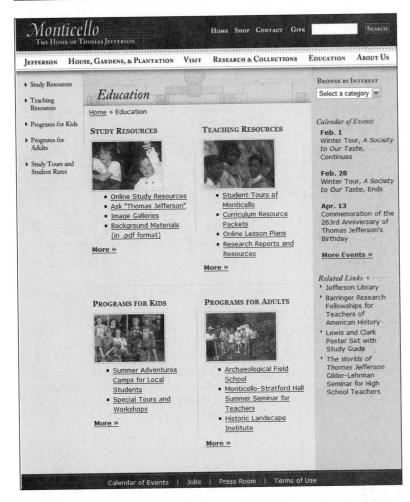

Figure 10.8. The site for Monticello, the home of Thomas Jefferson, has a section ti-tled "Education," as many historic museum websites do. *Reprinted with permission from the Thomas Jefferson Foundation/Monticello.*

place them either at the top, left side, or right side of the main screens and on *each* of your underlying pages. Your visitors will always know where to find these important navigational tools. Be sure the title of the content page matches the category title on your navigation bar. For ex-ample, a visitor should not click on the nineteenth century category and be brought to a page that is called "England in the Victorian Age." This

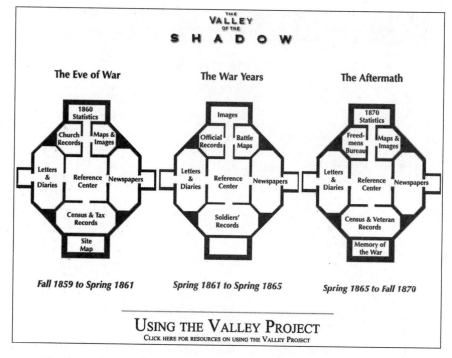

Figure 10.9. *The Valley of the Shadow* uses the navigation of a house plan to guide the visitor through its collection of primary sources. Note that it also divides the material by time/date. ©*Edward L. Ayes and William G. Thomas, Valley of the Shadow: Two Communities in the American Civil War. Used with permission.*

will momentarily confuse your visitors and perhaps even affect their understanding of your work. Not everyone may know that Victorian England was part of the nineteenth century.

- *Keep the quantity of buttons or links to an appropriate number.* Generally, humans remember ideas in groups of seven.[26] A large list of categories on your homepage will hopelessly confuse your visitor. Think of a better way to categorize your content into broader subjects and subcategories. Too many clicks to lead your visitor to the information simply cause frustration.

- *Make your clickable links, or hyperlinks, obvious.* Your hyperlinks, or links to other pages, and places on the page, should be obvious. They should either appear in a different color of text or be underlined. If the only way visitors know that a link to something else exists is to pass

| Home | 18th Century | 19th Century | 20th Century | Comments |

Figure 10.10. Example of a simple navigation bar.

the mouse over text, they will have no way to distinguish links from ordinary text.

- *Leave a "breadcrumb trail."* Your visitor must be able to find a way back through the page(s) from where she or he came. Not all browser back buttons will suffice. Perhaps your visitor wants to skip back several places or has forgotten where she or he is in your site. Provide a trail (e.g., "Women in Science France Chemists." so your visitor can click on any spot. If you decide not to leave a "breadcrumb trail," make sure the page is adequately titled so your visitor knows where she or he is.

- *Provide multiple means of navigation.* Previously in the chapter we discussed how different visitors use a website: through menus, as browsers, or as searchers. Accommodate many types of visitors and learners.

If your website becomes large and complex, you may want to add some additional navigational tools beyond the basic ones.

- *Sitemap.* A sitemap details, in textual form like a table of contents or an outline in a book, what is listed on each underlying page. A repeat visitor may not remember the path by which he or she found information. A sitemap allows visitors to retrace their steps.

- *Site index.* Similar to an index in the back of a book, a site index is an alphabetical list with hyperlinks to the page and place in the website where the idea is located.

What Every Good Website Must Have

Once you have established your navigation and layout, there are other content issues to address. Chapters Five and Seven describe how to evaluate sources. Just as sources must be evaluated for research, many of the same considerations are essential in website construction so that visitors can evaluate the information provided. Unclear or misleading content can lead your visitor to dismiss your evidence and website.

- *Biographical information about the author.* State who you are and your qualifications. It may be as simple as saying you are a history student and naming your school. Your audience will use this information to determine your information's credibility as well as your perspective.

- *Statement of purpose.* Understanding the intent of the site assists the visitor in placing it in the context of similar sites. False expectations about a site can cause visitors to be disappointed in its content and dismiss the evidence offered. Your statement of purpose can be as simple as stating that you identified a need for such a webpage and discussing your reasons for pursuing it.

- *Mail link to send questions.* Your visitors need to be able to contact you for everything from broken links to philosophical disagreements. Practically, you want to know when something on your page is not working. Remember, part of historical research is discussion. The Internet, unlike a research paper, makes this kind of discourse not only possible but also easy and immediate. If your technical skills allow, you might even think about including a forum for open discussion among your viewers through the use of a discussion board. Think about creating a blog through http://www.blogger.com. It provides the software for you to host a forum for ideas. Blogs have become influential in politics and academic debate. If you create a mail link, be prepared for spam.

- *Last updated date.* Currency of information for historians is not as critical a consideration as the latest medical discoveries for physicians. However, visitors want to know you maintain the links and the content on your site. Because the web is constantly changing, even if you have added no new material, tell your visitors when you last updated your site.

- *A title.* Display it on the front, usually top, of each page so that your visitors will know where they are and what they are looking at. Make sure there is a title in the title portion of the page. This is, in part, what the search engines use to index your site.

- *Metadata.* Metadata is the tag, or part of the coding in a webpage, that contains the words that describe the site and the data that search engines will use to index a site. Select terms that describe your site so visitors can find it. For instance, a website on Alcatraz Island might have the metadata or words "alcatraz," "native american occupation," "prison," "birdman," "capone."[27]

While navigation and structure (or information architecture) are crucial to your website, the text of a website is, of course, important. Even though the Internet is a visual, multimedia-driven medium, text is still an essential part of a website, especially for an academic one. However, writing for an Internet audience, even an academic audience, is very different from writing a formal paper.

Writing Text for the Web

Formal historical paper writing values text that flows, has connections and transitions between paragraphs, and draws the reader to a conclusion. For the web, you must change your style of presentation without sacrificing the critical analysis and discussion expected in a research project.[28] Large blocks of flowing text are visually distracting on a webpage. Most visitors scan the screen, catching blocks of text, or chunks, that are marked by headings and bullets. Create chunks of bulleted pieces of succinct text. Remember that, unlike a book or journal article, your website will not be read "from cover to cover." Do not try to force your visitor to read your website like a paper. The shifts of thought required of a research paper not only are unnecessary but can be difficult to process on screen. Text that goes on for more than four screens will not be read.[29] Make sure you stay with your topic and do not go off on a tangent; be succinct with your words and descriptions.

In *Hot Text*, Jonathan and Lisa Price, professional web developers and technical writers, offer the following six guidelines for writing website text:[30]

- *"Shorten text."* Do not repeat or summarize points as you would in a research paper. Be careful not to be so succinct as to make your ideas ambiguous. Use graphics to illustrate your ideas.

- *"Make text scanable."* Use headlines and subheadings with key words that reflect meaningful ideas to your audience. Make bulleted lists that highlight the text you want noticed.

- *Create useable links.* Let visitors know where they are on your site, when they are connecting to another site, and what might happen when they click on your link. For example, will they hear something from their computer when another website opens? Use links within sentences sparingly but appropriately.

- *"Build chunky paragraphs."* Create one-idea paragraphs with succinct topic sentences. Know when to write a paragraph and when to bullet ideas. Do not digress from the focus of your website.

- *"Reduce cognitive burdens."* Tell visitors what they need to know in the appropriate language. Do not use ambiguous phrases. Employ clear grammar, and write in the active voice. You should still use critical thinking and complex concepts; just avoid long paragraphs.

- *"Write meaningful menus."* Be precise about your navigational categories, but speak to your audience. Create a logical hierarchy of ideas that your visitors can follow.

Common Mistakes to Avoid on Websites

A few mistakes can lead your web endeavor astray. As you construct your website, keep the following in mind:

- *Too much text.* Duplicating what can be put in a printed text, such as a research paper, book, or journal article, can be deadly in a website. While a scholarly website can sustain a greater quantity of text than a commercial website, you should guard against an overabundance of text and too few multimedia elements. No one is inclined to sit at a computer screen for a long period of time and plow through dense text. Create a mix of text and graphics.

- *Too few graphics.* Integration of multimedia into your analysis is one of the main reasons for using a website in the first place. Be sure, however, that your website also incorporates insight, analysis, and an argument. There is no standard framework for including these more analytical components. This is where your creativity and scholarship converge.

- *Too many graphics or too fancy or complicated a layout.* If your page is too full of images and the latest technological innovations, it becomes hard to see your discussion, analysis, and research. Just because you can include all of this technology, does not mean you should. Technology should enhance your visitors' understanding of the information you present, not hinder their learning. Using animation in your graphics may be cute, but if it does not add to your interpretation, it will annoy some of your visitors and distract from the overall navigation. A webpage with too many graphics may take too long to load for some visitors. Remember, Internet visitors have extremely short attention spans, and they will leave your page before they get any information if your page does not load quickly.

- *Too hierarchical or too deep.* Do not make too many layers from the initial page. It will be difficult for visitors to find their way back and to change course. Your pages should always provide a good sense of where the visitor is in the site. Keep your navigation clean and consistent. Include in your navigation bar a one-click button back to the homepage.

- *Too little substance.* Remember that your research should add something to the existing body of known research, not just regurgitate known theories and facts. This, of course, should be true of a research paper or *PowerPoint* presentation as well.

- *"Scope creep."* Lynch and Horton in *Web Style Guide* coined this phrase for websites that add features and functions that are not central to the idea, diluting its focus.[31] It can be tempting to include information on a website because you enjoy the technology, for instance, creating a virtual tour or scanning in many primary documents. Make sure that the virtual tour enhances your argument and is not just for play and that the extra documents are focused on your topic and do not lead the visitor into some digression.

Case Study ▪ A Student-Constructed Website: Freedmen's Bureau

Now that you have the tools to construct a good website, it is time to look at another history student's website. Below you will find a discussion of one website that is rooted in historical scholarship and that follows many, but not all, of the practices discussed in this chapter. While it is not perfect, it has been selected because it exemplifies some of the principles discussed and because it was created by students and not a faculty member or a highly skilled web designer. For more examples of student projects, see the *History Matters* website and its section on class projects (http://historymatters .gmu.edu/browse/studhist/).

Case Study II: *Freedmen's Bureau*
Location: http://valley.vcdh.virginia.edu/HIUS403/freedmen/bureau.html
Student Creators: Peter Brownfeld, Ji Sun Hwang, Dominique Picou, and Alessandro Santarelli
Class/Affiliations: HIUS 403: Digital History and the American Civil War, Valley of the Shadow Project (http://valley.vcdh.virginia.edu/projects/projects .html).

This website combines academic research with logical, easy-to-use navigation. While its audience is definitely academic and the site would probably not appeal to the general public, it still follows the basic principles of web design.

The main page (see Fig. 10.11) cleverly uses graphics to create the equivalent of chapters or sections. These sections will be echoed in the navigation bar on each of the subsequent underlying webpages. On the top of the page, next to the title, is the introduction, just as in a paper or journal

Newspapers Archive

𝔅𝔲𝔯𝔢𝔞𝔲 𝔬𝔣 𝔅𝔢𝔣𝔲𝔤𝔢𝔢𝔰, 𝔉𝔯𝔢𝔢𝔡𝔪𝔢𝔫 𝔞𝔫𝔡 𝔄𝔟𝔞𝔫𝔡𝔬𝔫𝔢𝔡 𝔏𝔞𝔫𝔡𝔰,
OFFICE 4TH DIVISION, 9TH SUB-DISTRICT, VIRGINIA.

Introduction

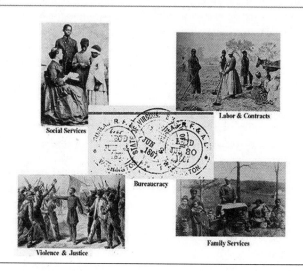

Social Services   Labor & Contracts   Bureaucracy   Violence & Justice   Family Services

Figure 10.11. Front navigation page from Bureau of Refugees, Freedmen and Abandoned Lands. ©*Valley of the Shadow Student Projects, used by permission Edward L. Ayes and William G. Thomas III, Valley of the Shadow: Two Communities in the American Civil War.*

article. In this introductory section, we find the purpose of the project, something about the authors, the definition of the Freedmen's Bureau, and a separate works cited page, as well as a list of primary sources, complete with some full-text links. So if you wished to examine the footnotes or the evidence, you could do so, just as if you were browsing the notes of a paper or article.

Selecting one of the underlying categories (Fig. 10.12), you can see how the layout appears on each of these pages. Each page has a central image, a top navigation bar, with categories written in clear language that remains consistent and matches the homepage categories. When appropriate, the image is clearly defined as a link and takes the visitor to a list of images that provide information about each. Footnotes in the text are linked to the bibliography.

| Bureau Office | Social Services | Violence & Justice | Family Services | Labor & Contracts | Bureaucracy | Newspapers |

Labor & Contracts

The Freedmen's Bureau in Staunton was deeply involved in labor issues arising in both the black and white communities. Contract disputes were frequently brought to the Bureau's attention for settlement, and Bureau agents also played a role in helping the freedmen negotiate labor contracts with their former masters. Claimants of both races also turned to the Bureau for aid in filing claims against the United States government to collect on contracts made by military officers for property commandeered or destroyed during the war.

Despite the sizable flow of paperwork resulting from the Bureau's involvement in labor and contract issues, it is difficult to ascertain the degree of success that the Bureau acheived in furthering the cause of the freedmen. Much of the correspondence that survives is written by white citizens, from which a picture of the freedmen emerges that is less than flattering. Also, while the Bureau did play some role in aiding the freedmen to negotiate fair contracts with their former masters, more often it was called in after the fact, to referee disputes arising from unclear contracts, or more often, from contracts that clearly took advantage of black laborers.

The Freedmen's Bureau also operated as an employment agency, fielding requests for labor from white employers across a wide area.

* Claims against the government
  received by the Bureau generally came to a dead end, as they did not fall within its jurisdiction.

10.12. Sub page on Labor and Contracts from Bureau of Refugees, Freedmen and Abandoned Lands. ©*Valley of the Shadow Student Projects, used by permission Edward L. Ayes and William G. Thomas III, Valley of the Shadow: Two Communities in the American Civil War.*

The content or text is chunked into manageable but somewhat analytical paragraphs. Below are bulleted lists of "points" of discussion in each section. Each page, however, does not flow like a paper or a journal article. Some of the sections seem more like reporting than analysis. Your webpage could profit from being more analytical.

Overall, this is a highly successful website. Given more time, the creators might have been able to add more primary source materials and graphics. However, not knowing what parameters their professor set, it is hard to be too critical. Take a look at the other student projects within the

Valley of the Shadow (http://valley.vcdh.virginia.edu/projects/projects.html). They all combine scholarship and the capabilities of the Internet in very imaginative ways.

FOR FURTHER READING

Cohen, Daniel J., and Roy Rosenzweig. *Digital History: A Guide to Gathering, Preserving, and Presenting the Past on the Web.* Philadelphia: University of Pennsylvania Press, 2006, http://chnm.gmu.edu/digitalhistory/.

Hammerich, Irene, and Claire Harrison. *Developing Online Content: The Principles of Writing and Editing for the Web.* New York: John Wiley & Sons, 2002.
This text is especially useful for creating text for a more academic website, instead of a commercial one. It pays a great deal of attention to how to focus and tightly write your text, just as you would for a research paper. Excellent source.

Holmes, Merlyn. *Web Usability and Navigation: A Beginner's Guide.* Berkeley: McGraw-Hill/Osborne, 2002.
This source discusses page layout and provides lots of examples of usability tests. This will help you with navigation issues rather than text development.

Jakob, Nielsen. *useit.com*, http://www.useit.com/ (accessed January 1, 2006).
Website dedicated to usable information technology. See especially his *Alertbox* columns.

Krug, Steve. *Don't Make Me Think!: A Common Sense Approach to Web Usability.* Indianapolis: New Riders Publishing, 2000.
Sensible, positive approach to organizing a website. One of the best books to read. Includes chapters on how to evaluate the usability of your own website.

Lynch, Patrick J., and Sarah Horton. *Web Style Guide*, 2d ed. New Haven: Yale University Press, 2001, (http://www.webstyleguide.com/index.html.
Aimed at scientists, this is an excellent guide to website construction. Particularly useful for inclusion of images.

Price, Jonathan, and Lisa Price. *Hot Text: Web Writing that Works.* Indianapolis: New Riders Publishers, 2002.
Step-by-step guide to designing, writing, and placing text. Excellent tips on how to refine and target your audience.

Reiss, Eric L. *Practical Information Architecture: A Hands-on Approach to Structuring Successful Websites.* New York: Addison Wesley, 2000.
Alternative guide to the others listed here.

Rosenfeld, Louis, and Peter Morville. *Information Architecture for the World Wide Web.* 2d ed. Sebastopol, CA: O'Reilly & Associates, 2002.
The best, most comprehensive source for information architecture. Readable. This is the place to begin!

Veen, Jeffrey. *The Art and Science of Web Design.* Indianapolis: New Riders, 2001.
More technical than most guides in terms of the mechanics of creating websites.
Integrates the technical with information architecture issues.

Webmonkey, http://www.webmonkey.com (accessed January 1, 2006).
Website with tips on design and programming tips.

Williams, Robin. *The Non-Designers Design Book.* 3d ed. Berkeley: Peachpit
Press, 2006.
Graphic and visual discussion of page layout, whether for the web or for a more
traditional paper layout. Discusses such issues as font choices, sizes of fonts
and graphics, and image vs. text placement on a page.

NOTES

1. Patrick Rael, *Reading, Writing, and Researching for History: A Guide for
   College Students* (Brunswick, ME: Bowdoin College, 2004), http://academic
   .bowdoin.edu/WritingGuides/ (accessed January 1, 2006); William Kelleher
   Storey, *Writing History: A Guide for Students,* 2d ed. New York: Oxford
   University Press, 2004; Mary Lynn Rampolla, *A Pocket Guide to Writing in
   History*, 4th ed. Boston: Bedford/St. Martins, 2004.
2. Storey, *Writing History*, 61–65, 81–86.
3. Ibid., 81.
4. Storey has a nice discussion of including counterarguments on pages 76–78.
5. Charles C. McDougald, *The Marcos File: Was He a Philippine Hero or
   corrupt Tyrant?* (San Francisco: San Francisco Publishers, 1987).
6. David Hackett Fischer, *Historians' Fallacies: Toward a Logic of Historical
   Thought* (New York: Harper and Row, 1970).
7. Storey, *Writing History*, 74.
8. Ibid., 88.
9. For an open source alternative to *PowerPoint*, see *S5: A Simple Standards
   Based Slide Show System.* It is based on XHTML, CSS, and JavaScript,
   although as a user you do not need to know anything about these coding
   languages. See http://www.meyerweb.com/eric/tools/s5 (accessed January 1,
   2006).
10. Jamie McKenzie, "Scoring Power Points," *From Now On: The Educational
    Technology Journal*, 10 (Sept. 2000), http://www.fno.org/sept00/powerpoints
    .html (accessed January 1, 2006); Trevor Shaw, "Dodging the Bullets: The
    Danger of Reductionism in PowerPoint Presentations," *Multimedia Schools*, 10
    (Nov. 2003): 46 (*Academic Search Premier Database, EBSCO*, htpp://
    search.epnet.com/login.aspx?direct-true&db5 aph&an-11355901 (accessed
    January 5, 2006).
11. Edward R. Tufte, *The Cognitive Style of Power Point.* (Cheshire, CT: Graphics
    Press, 2003).

12. *Ibid.*, 24.
13. *Ibid.*, 22–25.
14. Peter Norvig, *The Gettysburg PowerPoint Presentation*, http://www.norvig.com/ Gettysburg/ (accessed January 1, 2006).
15. Jay David Bolter, *Writing Space: Computers, Hypertext, and the Remediation of Print*, 2d ed. (Mahwah, NJ: Lawrence Erlbaum Associates, 2001), 51.
16. *Ibid.*, 68.
17. Patrick J. Lynch, and Sarah Horton, *Web Style Guide*, 2d ed. (New Haven: Yale University Press, 2002; also on the web, http://www.webstyleguide.com/ index.html); Louis Rosenfeld and Peter Morville, *Information Architecture for the World Wide Web*, 2d ed. (Sebastopol, CA: O'Reilly, 2002); Steve Krug, *Don't Make Me Think: A Common Sense Approach to Web Usability* (Indianapolis: New Riders, 2000); Daniel J. Cohen and Roy Rosenzweig. *Digital History: A Guide to Gathering, Preserving, and Presenting the Past on the Web* (Philadelphia: University of Pennsylvania Press, 2006).
18. Michael Gold, *Best Practices for Your Website. Making Your Website Work for Your User*, Steve Kantola, prod. Mill Valley. Kantola Productions, Stanford Video, 2003, videocassette, 46 min.
19. Jakob Nielsen, *Designing Web Usability: The Practice of Simplicity.* (Indianapolis: New Riders, 2000), 106.
20. Jonathan Price and Lisa Price, *Hot Text: Web Writing that Works.* (Indianapolis: New Riders, 2002), xiii.
21. Judy Gregory, "Writing for the Web Versus Writing for Print: Are They Really so Different?" *Technical Communication* 51 (May 2004): 278.
22. Gold, *Best Practices.*
23. Rosenfeld and Morville, *Information Architecture,* 56–64.
24. Krug, *Don't Make Me Think,* 31–39.
25. These navigation rules, common to most websites, are a summary of information presented by both Krug and Rosenfeld and Morville.
26. Ibid.
27. Metadata taken from the National Park Service website for Alcatraz Island, http://www.nps.gov/alcatraz/ (accessed January 1, 2006).
28. Many ideas and suggestions in this section come from Lynch and Horton's *Web Style Guide*, Chapter 6: Editorial Style. (http://webstyleguide.com/style/index .html) See also Constance Hale, ed. *Wired Style: Principles of English Usage in the Digital Age.* (San Francisco: HardWired, 1996); Price and Price, *Hot Text*; Gregory, "Writing for the Web," 276–285.
29. Lynch and Horton, "Page Design," in *Web Style Guide* (accessed January 1, 2006).
30. Price and Price, *Hot Text,* 84–269.
31. Lynch and Horton, "Process," in *Web Style Guide*, 2.

Index

Ancient history: categories of sources, 124; definition of as primary source, 122–26; selected bibliography of sources, 125–26

Annals, 126

Annual reviews, 63

Archaeology, as source of primary evidence, 124

Archives: definition of, 98; directories of, 112–13; selected indexes to collections, 111–12

Argument: formulating and phrasing of, 9–10, 209, 212–13; perspectives in, 88–91; in website, 226, 232

Artifacts and relics, as primary source, 122–28

Artwork: evaluation of, 182–83; selected bibliographies of collections, 186–89; use in history research, 181–83. *See also* Images; Media

Atlases: definition of, 160; list of 166–68. *See also* Maps

Audience, characteristics for website, 219

Audio: digital file formats, 198; on the Internet, 195; as primary source, 95; search strategies, 198–99; selected bibliography of sources, 199–200; speeches, evaluation of, 196

Bias. *See* Perspective

Bibliographies: annotated bibliographies, writing, 210 (box 10.1); creating footnotes or endnotes (*see* Documentation); for finding primary sources, 128–29; on the Internet, 138; selected bibliography of, 28; using print bibliographies as a reference source, 27–29

Biography, 30–32; selected biographical sources, 32–34; using biographical sources, 30–32

Blogs, 140, 151–52

Books (monographs): as primary source, 100–103; definition and history of, 44–45, 99; history of, 44; other sources of, 58–59; as primary source, search strategy, 131; as primary source, selected bibliography of, 102–3; using for historical research, 45–48

Book reviews: as a reference source, 38–39; selected bibliographies of, 30; writing, 211–12 (box 10.1)

Boolean logic, 70–71; diagram, 70; in Internet searching, 144

Business records: in ancient history, 123–25; in medieval European history, 126–28; as primary source, 118; search strategies, 132; selected bibliography of directories, 119

Cartography. *See* Maps

Center for History and the New Media, 12, 139, 145 (fig.7.1)

Charters, 126

Chronicles, 126

Chronologies: selected bibliography of, 34–35; using, 34

Citations. *See* Documentation

Commentary periodicals, 67–68; selected bibliography of, 68

Coordinates. *See* Maps, components

Copyright, 201; of images, 184

Deep web, 147–48; directories of websites, 149